JAMES LEASOR

Who Killed Sir Harry Oakes?

Published by
James Leasor Publishing, a division of Woodstock leasor Limited
81 Dovercourt Road, London SE22 8UW

www.jamesleasor.com

First published 1983
This edition published 2016

AT SEVEN O'CLOCK on the morning of Thursday, July 8, 1943, in the fourth year of the Second World War, Sir Harry Oakes, the richest baronet in the British Empire, was found dead in bed at Westbourne, his house overlooking the ocean near Nassau.

Harry Oakes, by his own efforts and perseverance, had created a fortune estimated at $300 million. In a colony where a labourer's daily wage was $1.00, his income was around $40,000 a day, tax free. More than this, he was unique among the world's wealthiest men because he had not inherited his fortune nor made it by exploiting any other person, company, or country. Instead, after devoting many years to a concentrated search for gold, he had discovered his own gold mine, Lake Shore, at Kirkland Lake, the largest gold mine in Canada, the second most important in the world.

Harry Oakes was a man of considerable sensitivity and erudition, which, for reasons of his own, he carefully cloaked beneath a gruff, often crude manner. Now, at sixty-nine, he lay dead; brutally and viciously murdered. Whoever had killed him had also deliberately humiliated his corpse in a horrifying way. The body had been drenched with petrol and then set alight, along with his bed and mosquito net, bedroom rugs and curtains, and the staircase leading up to his room. An electric fan had been placed on the floor near his bed, apparently to fan the flames.

The left side of Sir Harry's pyjamas was almost completely burned away and his face blackened by soot. Fearful heat blisters had erupted on his neck, his chest and groin, on his left knee and his right foot.

Someone had ripped open his pillow and scattered the feathers over him. These stuck to his blackened flesh, fluttering faintly and grotesquely in the morning breeze, like the wings of singed and feeding moths. Seemingly, the murderer had hoped to burn the corpse and the house in a gigantic funeral pyre so that crime would never be suspected. It would then be assumed that Sir Harry, a millionaire philanthropist, as likely to give a thousand-dollar bill to a stranger as to order him roughly off his land, had been burned to death in a tragic accident while he slept.

Whoever killed him needed this conclusion to conceal evidence that could point to a totally different way of dying. The left side of Harry

Oakes's head was marked by four triangular indentations, each less than half an inch across, set about two inches apart in the form of a square.

Blood had flowed from these wounds, which cracked his skull and presumably caused his death, but although Oakes was discovered lying on his back in bed, the blood had flowed the other way, up towards his nose and face. So, clearly, he had not been hit while he lay on his back — or even where he lay. Only the chance freak of erratic July weather allowed this to be discovered: a heavy rain storm with a very high wind had sprung up and quenched the flames.

The wounds, resembling the claw marks of some giant bird, the burning of the body, its coating with feathers, gave rise to theories of voodoo and obeah, African cults that generations, descended from slaves, still followed in secret. Was this a ritual murder? Certainly, more than one person appeared to be involved, for the walls of the bedroom were smudged with handprints. A half-burned ornate Chinese screen near the bed was splattered with blood and other fingerprints, and its lacquer blistered by heat. Sand and mud and footprints on the stairs showed that several people had used them during that night.

Sir Harry Oakes had no obvious enemies. During his nine years in Nassau, he took Bahamian citizenship — and one of his first charitable acts had been to give £5,000 to the Governor to help the unemployed. Apart from land projects, on which he employed fifteen hundred men to cut roads through his ten-thousand-acre estate on the island and to build two airfields to help the Allied war effort, he gave three Spitfires to the RAF, which flew in the Battle of Britain, and he provided work directly and indirectly to scores of other black Bahamians who would otherwise have been unemployed.

He bought the British Colonial Hotel and started a training school for local coloured staff. He imported a bus from England to take his workers to and from their shanty homes in Grant's Town, the poor area in the centre of the island, and financed a free milk service for their children.

New Providence is surrounded by seven hundred other islands, some larger and some smaller, known as the Out Islands. Since medical care on them was primitive or non-existent, Oakes organised seaplanes and light aircraft to bring patients to Nassau. He also offered to pay half the cost of building a new hospital in Nassau, if the government would come up with the other half. They could not raise the money, so Oakes built a new wing on the existing Bahamas General Hospital.

Some young Bahamians liked polo but could not afford to buy ponies. Oakes imported polo ponies from England for them and all the necessary equipment — and then laid out a first-class polo field.

He had imaginative schemes and ideas to help others to help themselves, like bringing Italian craftsmen to Nassau, on his wife's suggestion, to teach

locals to make cameo necklaces and earrings from conch shells — the conch being the Bahamas' most common shell-fish. He planted thousands of citrus plants, coconut palms, and acres of strawberries, imported sheep to help improve the local breeds, bought a huge old house and converted it to a boarding school for children evacuated from London during the air raids.

Etienne Dupuch, the editor and publisher of the local evening newspaper, *The Tribune,* voiced the opinion many held when he wrote:

By contrast with the activities of so many wealthy people in the community, Sir Harry's investments were not made with any regard to his personal future. They were made with the sole idea of helping others, and his death is a great loss to the community, and a great loss to anyone who had the privilege and pleasure of knowing him.

Who would wish — or need — to kill such a generous man?

On this particular night, Sir Harry's five children, three sons and two daughters, were in Canada or the United States. His Australian wife, Eunice, was waiting in their home, The Willows, in Bar Harbor, Maine, for Sir Harry to join her on Friday. His exit papers, necessary in wartime, were already stamped, and his ticket booked for the afternoon Pan Am flight to Miami, after a game of golf with the Duke of Windsor, the Governor of the Bahamas.

Sir Harry's local manager had left Nassau and was on a fishing trip to Abaco, about seventy miles north of New Providence. His Bahamian lawyer was on holiday on Harbour Island to the north-east.

Oakes did not lock the outer doors of his house after dark, but he employed two watchmen to patrol the grounds and to keep an eye on his sheep. Although neither of these watchmen was near Westbourne on this particular night, and his three indoor servants had gone home, Sir Harry was not entirely alone. The Honourable Harold Christie, a forty-seven-year-old bachelor and Nassau's most successful real estate agent, who counted Oakes as his best friend — as well as his best customer — was sleeping in the next bedroom, separated from Sir Harry's by a small ante-room and bathroom. Christie's title came with membership of the Governor's Executive Council. Mosquitoes and the storm briefly disturbed his slumber, but the death of his friend did not. He neither heard nor saw anything unusual. At seven o'clock in the morning, Christie opened the doors onto the verandah and walked along to Oakes's bedroom. This was the third night he had stayed at Westbourne, although he had his own house in Nassau, only a couple of miles away. Whenever he slept at Westbourne, the two men usually breakfasted together in the open air.

"Hi, Harry," he called in greeting, and pushed open the doors to his friend's room. Then he saw the body.

Christie ran downstairs and telephoned to his brother Frank to fetch a doctor. He was so distraught that he forgot to say where he was. Frank contacted the police, and by the process of eliminating other houses where Christie sometimes spent a night, set off with them for Westbourne. Hardly had Christie replaced the receiver, when it rang. Etienne Dupuch was on the line. He had an appointment with Oakes that morning and was ringing early to confirm it. Sir Harry had recently imported fifteen hundred sheep from Cuba,- with the intention of breeding more to help with the wartime meat shortage. Unfortunately, the first batch was infected with screw-worm, and Dupuch and a reporter from the rival *Nassau Guardian* had arranged to interview Sir Harry on the subject.

"He's dead!" cried Christie hysterically. "He's dead!"

"Who?" asked Dupuch.

"Sir Harry. He's been shot!"

"Shot? Are you serious?"

"Of course I'm serious. I've just discovered him. He's dead."

"This is a very big news story, Mr. Christie, and I'm a journalist," replied Dupuch. "I propose to cable it around the world. You *are* certain?"

"I'm positive."

Christie rang off and stood by the front door, still in his pyjamas, waiting for the doctor to arrive.

Not only were the circumstances of Sir Harry's death mystifying, but the search for his murderer proved equally bizarre. The Duke of Windsor announced immediately that he would cancel all other appointments to take what he called "a personal hand" in the investigations. His first action was to use his prerogative as Governor to forbid any information about the death to be published. This came too late to stop the brief cabled message that Dupuch had already sent to newspapers and news agencies in Britain and the United States, but it effectively prevented any further reports of the murder from leaving the island for forty-eight hours. As an editorial writer in *The Tribune* complained later:

What the official mind has never been able to grasp is the fact that this country has daily contact with the U.S. and while officials may censor legitimate press releases they cannot censor the mouths of people who go across to Miami and who most often carry garbled and damaging tales which are naturally believed by the American Press because of the suspicions aroused by censorship.

Everyone by now knows about the way Sir Harry met his death, but local newspaper correspondents will not be allowed to tell a straight, factual story, nor can anything be published in the local Press, but the news will be carried by word of mouth. And the tales that will be told will be largely incorrect and a reflection on the Colony...

Next, the Duke decided that the Bahamas' own Criminal Investigation Department, under experienced British officers, should not be allowed to investigate this particular crime. Instead, he telephoned to the Chief of Police in Miami and asked him to allow two policemen — whose names he gave — to fly south to Nassau to handle enquiries into what he delicately described as "the death of a prominent citizen." Murder and Sir Harry Oakes were not mentioned.

These two officers, Captain James Barker and Captain Edward Melchen, described in the *New York Times* as "a personal friend of the Duke," possessed peculiar qualifications for their task. Barker was forty years old. He had begun his police career as an ambulance driver, became a motorcycle patrolman, then a clerk in the Bureau of Criminal Identification. He lost this job through insubordination and was returned to uniformed duty, but later became Superintendent of the Bureau.

Melchen was ten years older and had spent many years as a clerk in various police departments, until he was appointed chief of the Homicide Bureau in Miami. For the previous ten years he had been assigned to guard visiting dignitaries and diplomats.

Now described as fingerprint experts of the highest calibre, with several hundred successful cases behind them, they arrived in Nassau that afternoon — but without the basic specialist equipment required to photograph any fingerprints they might find.

They immediately announced that they would postpone the search for prints until the following morning; the atmosphere was too humid for dusting powder to have a proper effect. Neither officer appeared to have any idea what weapon the murderer had used to kill Sir Harry, and no search was made for it. Footprints which showed clearly that several men had walked *upstairs,* wearing muddy and sandy boots, they claimed led *downstairs.*

Because of Sir Harry's wealth and social position, numbers of acquaintances and sightseers arrived at the house as news of his death spread around the island. The two Miami detectives readily allowed them to see the room where he had died. No effort was made to prevent these ghoulish visitors from touching objects in the house and so putting their own fingerprints on doors and windows.

From time to time, the Duke of Windsor telephoned to ask impatiently what progress they were making. On Friday afternoon he drove over to Westbourne to discuss what was happening. After this visit, Captain Barker announced (to his colleague's surprise) that they were now in a position to make an arrest.

The British Police Commissioner, Colonel R. A. Erskine Lindop, and his colleagues had been forced to wait idly in the grounds under the Duke's strict orders not to take any part whatever in the investigations. His policemen were now informed that they could scrub the walls of Sir Harry's bedroom to remove hand- and fingerprints, because, as one of them explained, these prints "did not match those of the accused."

This was thirty-three-year-old Alfred de Marigny, born in Mauritius, holder of an ancient French title, and married for little over a year to Sir Harry's nineteen-year-old daughter, Nancy.

So, at half-past seven on Friday evening, barely thirty-six hours after Harold Christie had discovered Sir Harry's body, Marigny was charged, cautioned, and incarcerated in the tiny and verminous number 2 cell in the basement of the Nassau jail.

In a statement he gave voluntarily, Marigny declared that he had not spoken to Sir Harry Oakes since March 30, and that the last time he had been inside Westbourne was two years earlier.

"It is a ridiculous charge," he said.

1

The Long and the Short of It

APART FROM BEING related to Nancy Oakes, all that Sir Harry Oakes and Count Marie Alfred Fouquereaux de Marigny really had in common were their masculinity, titles — one British and bought, the other French and inherited — and the experience of having been medical students, Oakes in the United States and Marigny in London.

But where Oakes was within months of his seventieth birthday, cleanshaven, and five feet, six inches tall, Marigny was thirty-three and bearded and stood six feet five in his socks. Oakes was heavily built, old-fashioned in his ways, puritanical in his tastes. "Get it, whatever it costs," he would command gruffly if he wanted something; only later would he haggle over the price.

His son-in-law early in life had discovered its many pleasures. He did not greatly mind who picked up the bill — or how much it was for — as long as everyone enjoyed himself before the kissing had to stop.

Sir Harry was born in Sangerville, Maine. He became a Canadian for personal reasons, then a Bahamian, for Bahamians could be ennobled, and once he had made his fortune, he believed that a title would bring him the respect and social acceptance to which he felt his money entitled him. Bahamians also paid a lot less in taxes; in fact, virtually nothing. And when Sir Harry's personal annual tax bill in Canada grew to around $3 million, the alternative was undeniably attractive. So Oakes became a Bahamian citizen, gave £50,000 to St. George's Hospital in London, and in July, 1939, was created a baronet, taking the motto *Per Ardua* — "Through hardship."

Marigny was born to his title on the island of Mauritius, five hundred miles east of Madagascar in the Indian Ocean. Mauritius was originally French, but when it became British, after the Napoleonic Wars, no attempt was made to change the titles or rights of the islanders, so Marigny still held his inherited family title of Count. When he arrived in Nassau shortly before the war, however, he specifically asked that this not be used. He had no wish to capitalise on an inherited distinction earned by a forebear. Like Napoleon, Marigny was content to be his own ancestor.

The family backgrounds and upbringing of the two men were as dissimilar as their individual attitudes and appearance.

Harry Oakes's mother had been active in the temperance movement and in her local church. Marigny's mother had left her husband and eloped with another man when her son was only three, and her husband refused to allow her name ever again to be mentioned in his house.

Oakes's father had trained as a lawyer, but, because of indifferent health, he preferred to work outdoors as a land surveyor. Money was tight, and what he had, he earned. Marigny's father was a Fouquereaux — Marigny was his mother's maiden name — and he had inherited sugar plantations, along with the aristocratic family background.

Harry Oakes had a brother and three sisters. He attended Bowdoin College and then Syracuse University Medical School in the United States.

Freddie Marigny was an only child, and since he provided a constant reminder to his father of his wife's infidelity, the boy was packed off to board at the school of the Freres de St. Joseph when he was only four. His father never visited him at school. While other boys had parents to applaud at prize-givings and sports days, Marigny was on his own. Nor did his father ever give him a present directly on his birthday or at Christmas; any presents were delivered by servants.

Their relationship was totally lacking in warmth or love. As a result, Marigny became introverted, insecure, lonely. When he left school, he studied scientific methods of sugar cultivation at the Royal College of Mauritius, with the intention of working eventually on the family plantations.

Harry Oakes abandoned his medical studies after two years, when he discovered that doctors were relatively poorly paid. Above all else, he wanted to be rich. Even so, he was sufficiently his mother's son not to wish to become rich at anyone else's expense. Newspapers at that time were publishing regular reports about the Klondike Gold Rush, and the prospect of digging wealth from the earth, the basic source of all the world's riches, strongly appealed to him. He decided that, instead of qualifying as a doctor, he would become a gold prospector.

Such was the closeness of the Oakes family that no one thought this ambition unusual or unrealistic, or criticised him for it. Instead, they all helped him. His mother pledged her savings to buy equipment. His brother, Louis, promised him $75 every month from his own small salary until he struck lucky. His sister Gertrude, starting her first job as a bank stenographer in Washington, promised him as much as she could spare for as long as he needed the money.

Marigny never experienced this closeness, or indeed any feeling whatever of belonging to a family, and when he was in his teens an incident occurred that made him decide to leave home precipitately. He was playing tennis with a slightly older but infinitely more sophisticated friend, Georges de Visdelou-Guimbeau, who had a taste for the life of ease and plenty that he felt should accompany his French title of Marquis. A middle-aged couple on the next court congratulated them on their shots. Georges introduced himself, and when Marigny gave his name, the woman's face became so pale that he thought she would faint.

"I am your mother," she explained quietly.

That night, Freddie confronted his father with the situation. Why had he not even been told that his mother had returned to Mauritius?

"Because as far as I am concerned, she died the day she left me," his father replied shortly.

"You've always thought of me as a Marigny," replied his son bitterly, "because that's her name and I'm her son. You've quite wrongly blamed her behaviour on me. I've had enough of this treatment. I've decided to leave home, and I will also leave behind me your name, Fouquereaux. From now on, I will be a Marigny."

That night he packed his few belongings, and in the morning left for Paris with Georges. He never saw his father again.

Marigny, having recently inherited a small legacy, could afford this gesture of independence. Harry Oakes, at the same age, was about to inherit years of almost unbelievable hardship, laced with frequent danger and constant disappointment. He almost froze to death in Alaska, and in order to eat, worked as a medical orderly helping frostbite cases. He narrowly escaped sunstroke in Death Valley. One night there, he crawled wearily into a cave to sleep — and woke up next morning to find he had shared it with a nest of rattlesnakes.

He heard rumours of gold strikes in Central Africa and found nothing. He worked his passage to Australia as a deckhand, went on to the Pacific islands, back to New Zealand, took a job briefly as a government surveyor, earned some money on a farm, then moved on to California to continue his life's work: the search for gold. Never did he lose faith in his destiny. One day he would discover the big vein; one day he would be rich, and all previous miseries and privations would be forgotten. One day ...

But where should he try next? Finally, the choice seemed to be between the Yukon, where he had started prospecting years earlier, and Ontario, where gold had been found more recently in small quantities. Harry Oakes hated going back; to him this smacked of retreat. His urge was always to go on, so he chose Ontario and lodged in the mining town of Swastika.

He took a room in a boarding house run by a middle-aged woman, Roza Brown, who had come to Canada as a child from Budapest with her parents. She shrewdly held most prospectors in contempt.

They used their muscles more than their brains and did not approach the quest scientifically. When they could not dig up gold quickly where others had found it, they speedily lost interest and moved on, instead of studying all the surrounding terrain and rock formations in case they concealed more gold. Roza Brown took a liking to Oakes, for he always listened to what she had to say about the sites of possible seams. On her advice, he travelled to Kirkland Lake, where rocks, lava, and the sand on river beds seemed promising.

Others had already laid claim to the area, but while looking through files in the local mines office, Oakes discovered that a number of claims were to fall vacant within hours, simply through default. The prospectors concerned had not maintained them for the basic legal forty days' work a year. Maybe they had lost heart or lacked money. The reasons were unimportant. What Oakes considered very important was the realisation that if he could raise cash, he could buy their options. But who would stake him for such a venture? Every prospector had his own theory about where gold could be found. But if they were all correct, then why weren't they all rich? What made Oakes's theory so different — or more reliable?

The proprietor of the local hardware store, Jimmy Doige, had already refused to let him have even a pair of trousers on credit. It proved pointless to ask him for a loan; but in the back of his shop, Oakes saw four men he had not seen for several years, the Tough brothers. They worked as lumberjacks or in construction gangs for six months of each year to finance their search for gold during the other six. He explained his theory and made them an offer. If they would put up the necessary money, he would show them exactly where the claims were, and they could split the proceeds.

They shook hands on this arrangement and that same night set off through fifty degrees of frost to stake their claims. The cold was so intense that Harry Oakes wore five pairs of trousers. Breath froze in their nostrils. Skin on their faces cracked and bled, and lips split, as they hammered iron marking stakes into freezing rocks.

This Tough-Oakes mine did produce gold, but in small quantities. The partners quarrelled, and Oakes sold out his share to finance another venture nearer the lake, finally *under* the lake, where no one had previously attempted to dig.

No one believed he would ever find gold there. The local newspaper refused to accept his advertisements for finance; the object seemed far too speculative. Brokers would not sell shares in his project; private investors laughed at him. Charlie Chow, a Chinese immigrant who ran a rooming house in Kirkland Lake, agreed to accept shares instead of cash for money that Oakes owed him, and Harry's mother readily gave him all her remaining savings. So, short of backing but high in hope, Oakes sank his mine at Kirkland Lake.

He struck gold almost immediately, and suddenly he no longer needed to tout his shares: financiers came to him begging to be allowed to buy into his mine. For a start, Oakes sold them half a million shares at 35 US cents each. Within two years, each share was worth nearly $70 — and he kept the majority for himself. Kirkland Lake proved to be the greatest gold mine in Canada, and the second most productive in the world.

Afterwards, all manner of different accounts spread about his good fortune. One of them held that a conductor had thrown him off a train because he had no ticket. Where he landed on the ground became the site of his great strike. Later, Oakes sought out the conductor and gave him a pension. Alternatively a Chinese down-and-out, who did not care for material success, told him to dig — and he found gold.

Oakes never contradicted these stories. Why should be bother? What mattered was that, at forty-seven, after nearly a generation of struggle and gruelling, lonely labour, he was a multi-millionaire. Now he suddenly faced the one question he had never anticipated in all the hungry years as a prospector. What was he going to do with all this money? How was he going to use it?

Freddie Marigny never had any such doubts, for Georges Visdelou's love of pleasure soon infected him. Money was for spending, for enjoying; but first, it had to be acquired. In Paris, Marigny discovered he possessed two assets that could lead to wealth: he was extraordinarily handsome and unusually attractive to women. He had the indefinable yet irresistible appeal that all men seek and so few possess.

Georges moved on to London, where he felt his title would count for more than in Paris. A second, equally unexpected, inheritance of £5,000 enabled Marigny to follow him. The excuse he gave to the older woman who was then his closest companion was that he wanted to use this legacy to pay his fees at a medical school; he wished to qualify as a doctor.

He had no real idea why he chose medicine. Perhaps it was because Georges claimed to be a student of anthropology, or perhaps he just wanted to end an affair with an excuse that would cause his partner the least pain.

He joined Georges, who was already distributing visiting cards that described him as "The Marquis de Visdelou-Guimbeau."

"I'm sick of titles," Marigny told him. "I want to make my own way."

Georges shrugged. "In England," he replied, "you'll find that society loves two things — a title and a good address. The rest is up to us."

Georges found the widow of a diplomat living in Chesham Place. She agreed to rent them a room, and this provided a good address. She also provided another, unexpected bonus, for she received invitations to parties and balls from her late husband's friends, but invariably declined them, because she did not wish to go alone. Now her two handsome lodgers became her escorts, and these invitations led to others. Within months, Freddie de Marigny abandoned his medical studies and, like Georges, devoted himself to the pursuit of pleasure.

At the rate he spent, his legacy soon dwindled, and finally he could not afford even the small rent that the widow charged them. They moved out, and he and Georges were reduced to sleeping on the floor of a friend's office. Marigny's last remaining financial asset was a stamp collection that his grandmother had given him. This he sold to buy a ticket back to Mauritius, returning like the prodigal son, but to a different welcome.

His father refused to see him. His grandmother had died meanwhile and left him a third legacy, and on an impulse he took a boat to Reunion, a French island in the Indian Ocean, about 440 miles south-west of Mauritius, to decide his future. He was in his twenties, totally untrained for any career, and his greatest assets — perhaps his only ones — were good looks and charm.

The inhabitants of Reunion farmed the land but did not fish the ocean, because high cliffs and variable winds made navigation extremely dangerous for the small boats that were all they could afford. The challenge and the size of a potential income from fishing here on a commercial scale appealed to Marigny: like Oakes, he was sure he could succeed where others had failed.

He returned to Mauritius, bought a pirogue, a strongly built boat of teak with shallow hull and wide beam, and sailed back to Reunion to establish a fishing business. This prospered, and soon he bought a second pirogue, then a third, and his business became so profitable that he could afford to go to London for the wedding of Georges Visdelou. Georges's marriage made Marigny feel unexpectedly restless. Perhaps he should also settle down?

Viewed from London, the capital of the British Empire, life in Reunion seemed dull and uneventful and on a very minor scale. He decided he would stay in London and make his career in the City. An older friend advised him never to work for anyone else full time, only for himself, since he could pay himself far more than any employer. Through the help of a cousin he now joined a stockbroking firm on a small salary and the promise of half commission on all business he could bring in.

Marigny possessed the rare gift of making friends easily: one was an international financier, Jaime Weinstein, based in Paris. Weinstein one day advised Marigny to put all the money he could borrow or beg into lead and zinc. Marigny took his advice. Within weeks, every pound he had invested was worth fifty. Suddenly, he was rich.

Harry Oakes, who was infinitely richer, had also made certain decisions. He built himself a chateau near Kirkland Lake, took up golf, and constructed his own course. Since he repeatedly hit the ball into one particular bunker, he had the bunker bulldozed away. When his mother died, he took off on a rather aimless world cruise, expense no object, and yet with no real destination in sight. For the first time in his life he had time to kill, and was not sure he enjoyed its death.

His ship docked at Sydney, and here he met a twenty-four-year-old stenographer in a local bank. Eunice MacIntyre was the antithesis of Harry Oakes: half his age, gentle, and calm where he was mercurial, even volcanic. She was then about to sail to England, stopping on the way in Mozambique to visit a sister, whose husband was, like Marigny, a Mauritian. Oakes volunteered to accompany her. They became engaged and returned to Sydney to marry — exactly twenty years and one week before he was murdered.

Now the wealth of Harry Oakes took on a new purpose and meaning. He endowed a skating rink for local children at Kirkland Lake and bought an even larger house at a cost of half a million dollars. He rebuilt parts of it in the style of a Tudor castle, and to add authenticity, he used panelling imported from Hampton Court. The view was marred by some factory buildings, so he bought the factory and moved the buildings.

But being an American living in Canada had one grave drawback. It meant that Eunice Oakes was technically a stateless person, for she was in the anomalous position of having forfeited her Australian passport when she married Oakes, but could not become an American citizen because he was not living in the States. To change this unsatisfactory situation, Harry Oakes became a Canadian.

Now began a time of immense philanthropy. He gave huge sums to his old school and to charities generally. He donated and built the Oakes Garden Theatre, a superb amphitheatre near Niagara Falls, provided parks for local councils, and land where surveyors wished to run new roads.

He loved trees and personally financed a huge scheme to help the unemployed by planting thousands of trees in the Ontario Valley.

He himself lived splendidly, with a house in Palm Beach for the winter, a town house in London, an estate in Sussex. With a pleasant wife and a young family, he seemed set to become the archetypal millionaire, crotchety outside, warm-hearted within, enjoying his money, yet making sure that it also bought happiness for others. But Harry Oakes was actually a rather more complex character.

Now that he was rich, he could indulge any whim, and he prided himself on never forgetting a good turn — or a bad one. His family, who had backed him so loyally, were rewarded with prodigal generosity.

Oakes also paid what he considered to be a debt to Jimmy Doige — by forbidding any of his employees to shop at Doige's general store. This edict cost Jimmy Doige so much trade that he had to sell up and leave. As soon as he did so, Oakes relented and had a secretary send him a cheque for $10,000.

Whereas Harry Oakes waited until he was rich before he married, Marigny, delighted by the unexpectedly generous return on his relatively modest investment, celebrated this good fortune by marrying a French girl, Lucie-Alice, whom he called Lucette. He did not know her very well. They had met only briefly on his visits to Paris to see Weinstein — and almost immediately after the wedding both realised how little they shared in common. Lucie-Alice was pretty but seemed to have no real interest in creating a home for him. His enthusiasms were not hers, and their relationship rapidly deteriorated. In an effort to improve it — and always believing rather naively that any change must be for the good — Marigny decided to leave Europe and join his cousin in New York, who was now working for Fahnestock and Company, stockbrokers. Here, in a new job, in a new world, might they not also make a new and happier start?

To Marigny's surprise, Lucie-Alice was unenthusiastic at this prospect.

"I won't go to New York unless Georges comes too," she announced.

"Georges?" asked Marigny in surprise. Georges Visdelou had visited them several times in Paris, and they had stayed with him in London, but Marigny did not think that his wife either liked him or even wholly approved of him. Now, he learned the truth.

"I'm in love with him," she explained. "Georges will come with us and get a divorce in America, and so will 1.1 want to marry Georges."

After his initial shock — for this was the first time any woman had told him that she preferred another man to him — Marigny felt almost relieved. This would be a painless way out of an increasingly tedious union. All three remained friends and travelled to New York together aboard *Normandie*. Marigny was reading Noel Coward's play *Design for Living*, about three people in much the same predicament, and found the parallel entertaining.

A fellow passenger was Ernest Hemingway. They met while clay-pigeon shooting, and both were so much better shots than any other passenger that they became friends. When they reached New York, Hemingway introduced Marigny to his lawyer, who arranged a speedy and amicable divorce in Miami.

Marigny, single again, now applied himself energetically to his job, selling stock. He was good at it. He had charm and enthusiasm, and he took the trouble to learn the business. Soon he met Ruth

Fahnestock, whose cousin was senior partner in the firm. Ruth was married and had a daughter of six. She declared herself to be unhappy with her investments, and sought Marigny's advice about reinvesting her money. It then became clear that she was also unhappy with her husband. Marigny soon realised that Ruth had been thoroughly spoiled as a child, and he was wary of any emotional attachment, because she appeared to be mentally unstable.

"I'm going to divorce my husband," she told him bluntly one day.

"Why?"

"Because I love you — and you love me."

Marigny was horrified. Friendship was one thing; marriage something else entirely. And who ever had mentioned love? He begged her to think again. Ruth refused to consider her decision. If he would not agree to marry her as soon as she was divorced, she would kill herself. Finally, weakly, reluctantly, and with many inward misgivings, Marigny did marry her. Was it because he was flattered — or alarmed — by her threat to commit suicide? Or did her wealth help to sway him?

They left for an extended honeymoon in Paris and London, returning to the United States by way of Tobago and the Bahamas. These islands took their name from the Spanish *bajamar,* meaning a shallow sea, which early explorers found treacherous because of the sharp spears of coral that could so easily rip open their ships' hulls. Something about the casual, easy-going atmosphere of the Bahamas, scattered across 100,000 square miles of sunlit sea, held a special appeal for Marigny. Here, the New World had begun when Columbus landed on the island he called San Salvador. Marigny thought that perhaps a new era might also start for his wife and for him in these surroundings.

With this hope they bought land in Eleuthera and built a house at Governor's Harbour. The name Eleuthera came from the Greek word for freedom, and was chosen by the original settlers, who had sailed from Bermuda in 1647 to found a community with total religious freedom. They did not succeed in their dream, any more than the Marignys found the contentment and happiness they sought. They moved into their new house shortly before the Second World War, but Marigny still had to admit, that, as far as he was concerned, their marriage was a grave mistake.

Ruth also knew that it was a misalliance, but unlike Lucie-Alice, she was reluctant to consider divorce. She felt it would be humiliating to explain to friends in New York that her second marriage had failed like her first, and not in seven years, but in barely as many months.

When Ruth moved south to the Bahamas, she brought her wealth with her, and she inherited more money on the death of her father. Because she was now married to a British subject, with Britain at war she found herself governed by the stringent British Exchange Control Regulations. She could not move her own money from the colony to the United States, even to meet genuine debts. She was therefore in the uneasy position of being wealthy in the Bahamas, but far less so in her own country. This unhappy situation, Freddie Marigny explained to her, could be altered at once through an ingenious scheme he now proposed.

"If we go through what I would call a divorce of convenience," he told her seriously, "you can then transfer any amount of money to New York, because you'd no longer be legally married to a British subject. You would have reverted to your original American nationality. Then, after the war, when all these absurd regulations are rescinded, we can remarry. Maybe before then, if the regulations end."

"You're on the level?" his wife asked him, wanting to be convinced. To a wealthy woman, the thought of losing her money can be even worse than the prospect of losing her looks.

"Of course," Marigny assured her. "This is really the one simple and obvious solution to your problem. You can, of course, stay on in our house here, and for business purposes we'll rent something in Nassau."

He carefully said "we," not "I," and Ruth, after more tears and talks, agreed to this unusual but apparently convenient arrangement. But as with many arrangements reached between people of differing tastes and aims, each expected to receive different benefits. Ruth wanted to be able to move her money, and her husband wanted his freedom.

He took a house in Nassau and rented part of it to his old friend Georges de Visdelou, who turned up unexpectedly, out of money and out of luck. Georges explained that his marriage was not going well, either. His wife was pregnant but wished her child to be born in England. He had tried to join the army, but was rejected on medical grounds. Lucie-Alice had also left him, and when he heard rumours that Marigny had married an heiress in the Bahamas, he decided to emigrate and see what life might hold for him in Nassau.

Harry Oakes had arrived in Nassau several years before Marigny, because he too wanted to be free, not from his wife, but from the predatory Canadian income tax. He had subscribed heavily to the Liberal Party there, apparently on the understanding that after the general election, which they seemed set to win, he would become a member of the Canadian Senate, roughly equivalent to the House of Lords. But in politics as in horse-racing, the favourite does not always win, and the new Conservative government taxed him heavily, and not only on his gifts of parks and land: they even introduced a new tax on gold mines. The news that he was now liable for $3 million in personal taxes brought on all the symptoms of a seizure. He was confined to bed for weeks, and in order to convalesce, moved to Palm Beach.

Here he met Harold Christie, a real estate agent from Nassau, who told him enthusiastically what the Bahamas had to offer a very rich man. First, a climate unmatched anywhere in the world, so delightful that Columbus, their first European visitor, had called them "the isles of June." Secondly, a benefit even greater than this: no income taxes, no inheritance taxes; in fact, no taxes of any sort.

This was the answer to Harry Oakes's problem. All symptoms of ill health vanished when he sold out and moved with his wife and family to Nassau.

Christie, seeing that Oakes had an interest in land — for, after all, the earth had yielded up its treasure for him — soon sold him six times as much property as he sold anyone else in his distinguished and energetic career.

Oakes, who had spent years digging for gold with pick and shovel, now found a new and agreeable challenge. Within months, he had become the colony's greatest benefactor and largest employer. He drove a tractor or bulldozer through swamps and forests to reclaim land and build the airfield that would soon bear his name, Oakes Field. He drained marshes and planted hundreds of young trees that one day would cast welcome shade on his project. Other men had attempted to grow sisal, pineapples, oranges on parts of this land before him and had failed for many reasons: poor soil, competition from growers in Florida and California, sheer bad management. But other men had also failed to find gold, and hard-luck stories neither influenced him nor deflected him. He felt he had found his destiny at last, and as far as he ever could be, he seemed content.

Harry Oakes and the man who was to become his son-in-law had, in fact, found the same two basic attractions in Nassau: money and a challenge. Oakes liked Nassau because here he could keep money; Marigny, because here he could make it. And within days of arriving in Nassau in his new status as a single man, Marigny bought a plot of land near the beach, drew up designs for two apartment houses, built them — and then sold both houses as going concerns. With the profit, he bought a bankrupt grocery shop and all its stock for $5,000. Then he hired local youths to deliver groceries to hotels, restaurants, and private houses on motorcycles. Soon this business was flourishing, and again Marigny sold out. For Marigny, as for Oakes, the challenge was always more important than the victory, the journey ever more enjoyable than arrival.

With the capital Marigny had now acquired, he bought more land and began chicken-farming on a large scale. With so many troops and evacuees from Britain, and with American construction crews, the demand for broilers and eggs soon outstripped his capacity. Harold Christie sold him a second, larger plot, to which he moved his business. There was one technical hitch, however: he did not have official permission for the transfer of ownership. A local lawyer, Godfrey Higgs, a yachting friend, was working on this for him, and everyone assured him that permission was only a formality. In any case, Marigny could afford to wait. He was making $20,000 a year clear profit from his farm — and this was only the beginning.

Until Harry Oakes moved to Nassau, he and his family had travelled the world from one home or fashionable resort to another, with the children going to local schools. Now that they had settled, they went to schools in Canada and the United States, and sometimes returned to Nassau for the school holidays. On one of these, Harry Oakes's eldest daughter, Nancy, met Freddie de Marigny; she was seventeen years old, red-haired, and not simply pretty, but beautiful.

Nancy knew of Marigny's reputation as a twice-married playboy — everyone knew that in Nassau — and was attracted to him before they even spoke, either because of his past or in spite of it.

She took time off from school to see him race his yacht off Long Island, for the challenge of yachting also appealed to Marigny. His experience in the Indian Ocean, around Reunion, proved invaluable, and soon he was one of the most successful members of the Nassau Yacht Club. When he had won every race off Nassau, he became equally successful in Cuba, New Orleans, and even in California, towing his boat across the States behind his Lincoln.

Ruth — they were still married then — used to complain that he spent too little time with her and too much time with his Star Class yacht.

"I can't be married to you *and her*" Marigny had replied. "She's not a wife. She's just a concubine." So *Concubine* became the name of his yacht, a choice that appeared to shock some middle-aged members of the more august Royal Nassau Sailing Club, to which Harry Oakes belonged, and which added to the general allure that surrounded Marigny.

During the war, the most popular meeting place for younger people in Nassau was the Prince George Hotel, between Bay Street and the sea. Here, British servicemen off duty, rich young wives who had come with their children to the Bahamas to escape from air raids in Britain, and the wealthier young white locals, would meet for drinks and dinner and dancing. It was inevitable, therefore, that eventually Marigny would meet Nancy Oakes here. A mutual friend introduced them, and, making conversation, Nancy asked Marigny whether he would be coming to a charity ball later that week at her father's British Colonial Hotel.

Marigny was due to fly back to Governor's Harbour before then, but the aircraft developed engine trouble, and unexpectedly he had an extra night in Nassau. Having nothing better to do, he decided to join another party going to the British Colonial ball. This decision was to change his life completely and have incalculable consequences, for he danced with Nancy Oakes.

The dance led to other meetings, to trips in his Gar Wood speedboat, and moonlight picnics. As Marigny grew to know Nancy better, he decided, with surprise, that she was unhappy. It appeared that her family had so much money, and owned so many houses, that they rarely seemed to be in the same place together. They did not even seem to be particularly close to each other. Her parents were generous enough, but in a formal, stilted way. A present would never be spontaneous; it might be a block of stock certificates accompanied by a lawyer's letter. She felt stifled by so much wealth and so little understanding of human relationships, human needs, especially the basic wish of every woman to be loved and appreciated. She knew that she wanted a life of her own — but what life could she choose?

Freddie Marigny chose for her. He asked her to marry him. He had no qualms about proposing, because he felt that at last he had found the girl for whom unconsciously he must have been searching all his adult life. He was so certain of his own feelings that he did not consider what Ruth's feelings might be when she learned he wished to marry a girl almost half his age. After all, he was legally divorced. The fact that he had a private oral arrangement with Ruth did not concern him. Technically, he was free to marry, and that was all that mattered.

So Nancy went back to the States to start a new school term, engaged. Marigny flew up to see her several times. They were married in the Bronx two days after Nancy's eighteenth birthday. Nancy called her parents with the news. Her mother was very shocked and hurt. Her father telephoned her from Nassau.

"How much money do you need?" he asked her drily.

"None," she replied firmly. "I'm being well looked after."

Lady Oakes was disappointed that her eldest daughter had not told her about her intentions, but she decided to put the best face on it that she could, and invited them both to join the rest of the family at their summer home in Bar Harbor.

Harry Oakes also went out of his way to be friendly; he even offered Marigny a job. Marigny declined, with thanks, for he remembered the advice he had been given in England: always be your own boss. Oakes then suggested that he take over a stretch of his land on New Providence known locally as the Jones property. Again, Marigny said, No. He felt that it would be better to keep family and business relations apart. Also, this land was sixteen miles out of Nassau, and he wished to concentrate his activities there.

Oakes was sorry, but he seemed to understand. He gave his new son-in-law a cheque for $5,000 as a Christmas present, and promised him finance for any deal he might have in mind.

Marigny, in fact, possessed a certain fascination for Harry Oakes: he was handsome, independent, debonair, and he knew how to enjoy himself, something that Oakes had taken years to learn. When Oakes looked at Marigny, it was almost as though he saw himself as he might have been, as perhaps he wished he was: handsome, attractive to women, his way still to make, no illusions left to lose.

Now Sir Harry Oakes was dead, and Alfred de Marigny was in jail, charged with his murder.

2

"Did You Kill Sir Harry Oakes?"

BAY STREET, the widest and most important thoroughfare in Nassau, stretched from the British Colonial Hotel in the west to the Yacht Club and beyond in the east. Along it, close as pearls on a string, shops and bars lined each side. Tiled canopies above the pavements shielded walkers and customers from the unwelcome distractions of sun or rain. The pillars that supported these canopies had originally been useful as hitching posts for horses and gave a quaint, almost Wild West atmosphere to the street. Now, black Bahamian chauffeurs, wearing starched white duck uniforms, waited patiently at the wheels of Buicks and Chryslers while their white employers shopped or gossiped.

The floors above the shops were given over to offices, many with a score or more of names of registered companies painted in gold letters on their solid black doors. Everyone of note in Nassau's business or professional life — merchants, agents, lawyers, accountants — aimed to have an office, or at least an address here, because Bay Street was synonymous with money: where it could most easily be made — and even more easily spent.

Alleys and narrow openings between the buildings led to less salubrious dwellings behind the pretty pastel-coloured fronts that faced the street. Here the smell of sewage was strong, and black crabs scuttled on dry claws across uneven paving slabs. Some found the contrast between the facade and what lay behind symbolic, since not a few of Nassau's fortunes and more notable families had dubious foundations that only time could sanctify and gild with honour.

At the far and eastern end of Bay Street, within sight and smell of the harbour, behind the statue of Queen Victoria and the Assembly building with its Palladian front of white pillars, pink-washed walls, and green shutters, a huge silk cotton tree cast welcome shade over an open square.

This tree stood virtually in the administrative centre of the capital. On one side was the Post Office; on another, Fire Brigade headquarters and the Central Police Station — green wooden verandah, white shutters, Victorian police lamp with blue glass. Next to this stood the Supreme Court, another Palladian building, but smaller than the Assembly House. Under the tree every day that the court was in session, litigants, lawyers, witnesses, and policemen in their white duck jackets and solar topis, dark blue trousers and highly polished black boots, waited until their cases came up, rehearsing statements, discussing the relative merits of this course of defence or that.

The morning of the day Sir Harry Oakes died was also the first day of the Quarterly Criminal Session for the Supreme Court, but, despite this, very few people waited in the square. The Chief Justice of the Bahamas, Sir Oscar Daly, commented with some satisfaction that the whole calendar contained only three cases for trial. Sir Oscar was sixty-three and had been appointed Chief Justice four years earlier. He was a member of the Irish Bar, and for many years had been in private practice in Kenya. He still belonged to two Kenyan clubs — the Mombasa and the Nairobi — and in Nassau belonged to the exclusive Country Club, next door to Westbourne.

Within days, a fourth case was announced, which would become the most controversial in island history. Despite news of Allied landings in Sicily and Italy, the extraordinary elements in this murder case assured it of instant, world-wide publicity. A millionaire was murdered after midnight at the height of a storm on a tropical island governed by the former King of England. His thrice-married son-in-law, whom he was known to dislike, had immediately been arrested and charged with the crime, but his wife, the millionaire's nineteen-year-old daughter, stood loyally by her husband. As *Time* magazine commented: "It remained to be seen whether all this would be capped with a conviction and a noose."

Many American newspapers ran daily verbatim reports of the trial. The *New York Journal American^* for example, devoted four whole pages to the case *every day* — as many pages as wartime paper-rationing allowed British newspapers. Daily, reporters cabled thousands of words from Nassau — 18,750, a quarter of the length of this book — when Marigny, asked bluntly by his counsel, "Did you kill Sir Harry Oakes?" replied vehemently: *"No, sir."*

All hotels and boarding houses in Nassau were packed, every bar filled with visitors, who sensed that this trial would be a spectacle in the old Roman sense. Bets totalling thousands of pounds and dollars were made on various permutations: *Did* he do it? If so, *why* did he do it? Or is the whole trial just a cover to shield someone else, perhaps much richer or infinitely more important? If so, who?

Everyone had an answer, and a theory, but most seemed united in a fierce and irrational dislike of the accused, whom only a few had ever met.

Local feeling ran so strongly against Marigny that it was feared a crowd might rush the Central Police Station, drag him from his cell, and lynch him. The Colonial Secretary, Leslie Heape, a civil servant who advised the Duke of Windsor on local matters, ordered the Fire Brigade to stand by with hoses, ready to swamp the first to riot.

The Duke approved this move, for, with mounting unease, he remembered violent disturbances during the previous summer when Bahamian labourers, employed at four shillings a day on government contracts to enlarge the airfield for its use by bombers being ferried from United States factories to Britain and North Africa, had rampaged wildly through Nassau's streets. The catalyst for this fury was their sudden discovery that they were working alongside white Americans who were being paid nearly twenty times as much.

In their rage, the rioters overturned cars, broke windows, set fire to every building that would burn. They smashed open liquor stores and drank them dry on their way to raid the offices of rich merchants in Bay Street. Many of Nassau's best-known citizens hurriedly barricaded themselves in upstairs rooms, fearing for their lives. Others fled in terror to the houses of friends in the countryside or along the coast; anywhere the mob could not come to seek them out. The rioters were armed with sharpened machetes, used for clearing jungle undergrowth around the airfield. No one cared — or dared — to argue with them as they systematically pillaged shop after shop.

The looting was quelled when a company of British troops, bayonets fixed, were rushed into town from their quarters in Fort Montagu Hotel, on the east of the island. They were stationed in Nassau not for this purpose, but as a bodyguard to the Duke of Windsor, who feared a German attempt to kidnap him by U-boat. He would then — according to this theory — be exchanged for Germany's Deputy Führer, Rudolf Hess, incarcerated in Britain since 1941, after his mysterious flight to Scotland. Apart from his distaste for the indignity of being captured, the Duke had a pathological, almost hysterical dislike of submerging in a submarine; his wife was equally vehement in her distaste for flying.

This riot had caused hundreds of thousands of dollars of damage, but worse than this huge financial loss was the dreadful blow to public confidence, meaning white confidence. For generations,

Bahamian blacks had apparently accepted a subservience based in part on their background as the descendants of freed slaves. The whites were largely descended from British settlers in North America, who, still loyal to the British Crown after the War of Independence, left the United States and moved south to the Bahamas, bringing slaves or other coloured retainers with them. Here the two groups re-established themselves in much the same relationship.

Now, for the first time since the eighteenth century, this outward acceptance of master and servant had been violently questioned. Troops had restored order quickly, but nothing would ever be quite as it had been, although on the Duke's promise that labourers would now be paid five shillings a day and given a daily free meal, they had sullenly returned to work. They all kept their loot — and their pride — and, having erupted once, their anger and resentment could easily do so again. Indeed, some said their leaders were only seeking an excuse, which Marigny's arrest could very easily and conveniently provide.

Many white Bahamians who had never met Marigny simply disliked what they had heard about him. He seemed flashy, a bit of a dago, a lounge lizard, they said; too smooth and too handsome, by far. Perhaps Marigny had passed them in his new Lincoln or had physically towered above them in a shop. Possibly some had seen him, head and shoulders above other men, at a private party in the Prince George Hotel or at the British Colonial, on the beach or in the Yacht Club, usually with a pretty woman at his side. He was the kind of man other men envied and many women wanted; both sexes therefore had the best of reasons to denigrate him behind his back.

Another reason for white envy was his prosperity, for Freddie Marigny never seemed short of money. He ran his chicken farm on mass-production lines — and who ever heard of such a thing? Yet, amazingly, the farm prospered, which made it all the more irritating. Why should he succeed when others had failed? One answer was that, although Marigny played hard and long, he could also work just as hard when he had to. Not many people of any colour in Nassau were prepared to do the same.

Perhaps New Providence was itself partly to blame. While other Caribbean islands were green and luxuriant, it was rocky, stony, barren. The earth was thin and could not sustain crops. It was tempting to make a living by easier means. When Marigny saw the inertia that hung over the colony like sunlit fog, he declared that the locals suffered from what he called "the pirate mentality." Few families in the Bahamas had grown rich through their own sustained efforts. Many were indeed descended from pirates, because Nassau had been home port for Captain Morgan, Blackbeard, and the Caribbean's two women pirate captains, Anne Bonney and Mary Read — along with at least fourteen hundred others.

As many more were descended from wreckers, who deliberately lured cargo ships onto the rocks and then pillaged them. As late as the 1850's, nearly half of all able-bodied men in the Bahamas held what they quaintly called "wrecking licences." The 302 ships they operated were officially described as "salvage vessels"; wrecking was their trade. The American Civil War put an end to this by offering far greater rewards for running the Confederate blockade.

Abraham Lincoln optimistically declared a four-thousand-mile sea blockade from Cape Henry in Virginia, around Florida, and west to the borders of Mexico. This was impossible to patrol, especially when people in the South still needed food and other supplies and were willing to pay for them. Nassau was about 560 miles from the port of Charleston and 640 from Wilmington. Steamers full of goods from Britain transferred their cargoes in Nassau Harbour to locally built blockade runners. On the return journey, they brought back crates of cotton for the Lancashire mills, making a big profit from both trips.

A hundred dollars' worth of cotton fetched the equivalent of $1,000 in England; $10 worth of medicine bought in Nassau was worth $400 in the Southern states. The captain of an average runner would make £1,000 for the round trip, and his backers fifty times as much. Years of slump followed this unprecedented boom — and then Prohibition in the United States brought back riches from "running" on an even more prodigal scale.

In Nassau, effort was often lacking. The climate corroded enterprise and effort; people wanted wealth without work — and Marigny was willing to work.

Another reason for his unpopularity among the whites was that he was not Bahamian. He was a Mauritian, and he looked and sounded foreign, with his tall body, his Mephistophelean beard, his French accent. Also, he had a dark complexion, and treated blacks not as inferiors but as equals; and this in a colony where white shop assistants were not always willing to serve black customers. The Bahamians he employed on his chicken farm, and the servants in the house he shared with Georges de Visdelou in Victoria Avenue, liked him. The rest now viewed him with doubt and reserve, for if he was not guilty beyond all possible doubt, then why had these two American detectives, brought in specially by the Governor, arrested him so quickly? His guilt thus agreed on, the next question centred on his motive.

Why had Marigny chosen to kill the one man who had done more to help underprivileged islanders than everyone else put together? Might not this be part of a sinister white man's plot to kill Sir Harry in case others were tempted to follow his good and generous example? Perhaps Marigny was the instrument of such men of power, who by this murder had decided to demonstrate to the blacks that they would never reach equality with whites.

Sir Harry Oakes was a familiar figure to everyone in Nassau. Whatever the temperature, he would walk along Bay Street, hands deep in his breeches' pockets, wearing high boots and a jacket, hat jammed on his head, whistling tunelessly, nodding a greeting here, grunting a good morning there. All he needed was an axe and a sieve and a billy-can and he could have been a gold miner, setting out for another day's prospecting. This was the image he seemed to cultivate; perhaps it was partly true.

With his death, hopes for more benefactions, steady employment, a brighter future, had diminished. Through the sullen crowds milling outside the police station, the jail, and the Magistrates' Court, rumours and counter-rumours flared like a forest fire against an ominously increasing swell of anger. Soon the risk to Marigny was considered so great that he was taken to a jail some miles outside Nassau. This move was a blow to his confidence, and he soon received several more in sharp succession.

On his arrival at the jail, he was given a thorough medical examination by Dr. Ulrich Oberwarth, the prison doctor, a pre-war refugee from the Nazis who had been allowed to settle in Nassau. Dr. Oberwarth, who was also attached to the General Hospital and who knew Marigny slightly, reported that the accused was in good physical shape and, as far as he could see, bore no marks of any burns. Within hours of making this report, Dr. Oberwarth was summarily dismissed from his post as prison doctor. He had served satisfactorily in that post for many years and thus he demanded a reason — but none was given him. As a refugee, Dr. Oberwarth felt — or was made to feel — that it would be unwise to pursue the matter.

Nancy Marigny was in Bennington, Vermont, at a ballet school, when her husband cabled her with the news that her father had died, but not how he died. She had recently undergone an operation on her mouth, and the doctors had advised her to get away from humid Nassau during the summer. She had always liked ballet and decided to put her enforced trip to its best use.

Immediately on receiving the cable, she went to see her mother at the family home in Bar Harbor, and here she learned that her father had been murdered and that two American detectives were now in charge of the case. She discovered the home telephone number of Captain Barker, in Miami, and rang him to ask for more details. Barker was evasive. He could not discuss such delicate matters on the telephone, but he could say that in his view there was no doubt whatever about the murderer's identity: it was her husband.

Barker said that he would be at the funeral in Bar Harbor, however, and they could talk afterwards. He had returned to Miami from Nassau with photographic plates he had taken of Sir Harry's body and his bedroom. He wanted to develop these and print enlargements in a laboratory he had used in other cases, because, he said, Nassau had no proper facilities for such work.

In Nassau, meanwhile, Sir Harry's corpse had been embalmed and was to be flown to Bar Harbor for the funeral, but after the plane had taken off, Nassau police received a telephone call from Captain Barker. Most unfortunately, light had somehow spoiled the plates in his camera, and all pictures of Sir Harry's fingerprints and handprints on the walls of his room had been ruined.

The duty police officer in Nassau immediately sent an urgent radio message to the pilot, who then turned back to Nassau. A waiting ambulance took Sir Harry's body to the General Hospital, where the cerements were removed and his fingerprints re-photographed. The baronet's body was then taken off again for burial. But by that time, all chance of comparing his handprints with the prints on the walls had gone, for the walls had been scrubbed clean.

At the funeral in Maine, a friend of the Oakes family, the Reverend Gordon Chilson Reardon, gave the address, in which he reminded the mourners that Oakes had possessed "the greatest asset a man can possess — his mother's confidence," a reference to the fact that she had willingly given him all her savings to help him in his search for gold. Barker and Melchen attended the funeral and returned afterwards to Lady Oakes's house to enlarge on their interpretation of the case. Sir Harry's murderer, they now told his widow and daughter, had gone into the garage of Westbourne late at night and carefully selected a long wooden stake from a pile left there for repairing a fence. He then climbed the outside stairs to Sir Harry's bedroom and clubbed the old man about his head. The murderer, seeing a tin of Fly-ded, an insecticide with an inflammable base, had decided to conceal the crime by fire. He poured or sprayed this liquid over the bed and over Sir Harry while he was still alive but stunned, and set the bed alight. The fierce rush of heat from the flames had revived Sir Harry, and although in agony from his wounds and burns, he bravely attempted to fight off his attacker.

During the struggle, a Chinese screen, which Sir Harry kept beside the bed, must have been knocked over. The murderer picked this up and placed it across the window to conceal the flames from any passers-by. A detailed examination of the screen clearly showed Marigny's fingerprints — probably left when he moved it.

Lady Oakes, at this point in the story, was so distraught that she became almost hysterical, and Nancy asked the two policemen not to say any more in front of her. Nancy then took them into another room, where they continued.

"Your father was burning alive," Barker told her bluntly. "But finally the flames and his attacker — *your husband* — killed him."

The account, given quietly and gravely by two senior police officers, of course made an indelible impression on Sir Harry's widow and daughter. Nancy returned at once to Nassau and repeated the officers' account to her husband, in jail.

Until then, Marigny felt that he had been arrested mistakenly and would soon be freed, no doubt with suitable apologies, once the police realised their mistake. The charge, he thought, was so ridiculous as to be laughable. Now he recognised the gravity of his situation. His wife, nevertheless, remained loyal and, despite all Barker and Melchen had told her, was convinced of his innocence. Lady Oakes, however, had never liked Marigny as a son-in-law, and her earlier feelings about his unsuitability now seemed to her sensationally vindicated.

Marigny might survive the enmity and resentment of blacks and whites alike, but if his mother-in-law appeared hostile to him in court, her feelings would weigh very strongly against him with any jury. He had, in addition, a curious sense of being judged in advance, as though the trial would simply be a ritual affair, with the ultimate verdict already beyond dispute.

As though to underline official certainty of Marigny's guilt, even before his trial, the Duke of Windsor sent his aide-de-camp to offer condolences to Lady Oakes when she returned to Nassau from Bar Harbor. The ADC also informed her that, in the Duke's private opinion, there was no doubt that her son-in-law had murdered her husband.

In his cell, Marigny recalled a strange feeling of unease he had experienced at Westbourne when the Duke of Windsor had arrived to see Captain Barker on the day after Sir Harry died. Everyone had stood up respectfully as the former King walked up the stairs. The two men were closeted together for half an hour in a bedroom, and then the Duke had come downstairs alone.

As he went out to his car, he looked at Marigny in a cool, appraising way. Something in his glance had made Marigny instantly feel uneasy and in great personal danger. Later that afternoon, be believed this must have been a premonition, for he was formally charged with the murder of Sir Harry Oakes.

The feeling of being trapped now returned with even greater intensity. He knew that a very strong case was being built against him. With this knowledge came an even more disturbing realisation: that he was being deliberately set up as the murderer, perhaps because he had no powerful friends to protect him. He was more French than English, an interloper from the other side of the world, a stranger in a closely knit community, and thus expendable.

Innocent as he knew himself to be, he now accepted that he needed the best lawyer he could find. He sent an urgent message by a policeman to Alfred Adderley, a black Bahamian barrister who had read law at Cambridge and returned to practise in the Bahamas.

Adderley was a giant of a man who exuded the easy, infectious confidence of great size. He was the best barrister in Nassau, with a magnificent court record; he had never lost any murder case in which he had appeared, either as a prosecutor or defender.

Freddie Marigny thought that if he could persuade Adderley to take his case, no matter who was against him, he would have nothing to fear. But, to his surprise, he was informed brusquely by the police that Adderley had already been briefed to appear for the Crown against him.

Both men recognised the irony in this choice. Before Sir Harry Oakes could be elected to the House of Assembly in 1938, an existing member had to resign. The choice fell on Alfred Adderley, who withdrew with good grace. Now Adderley was to prosecute Marigny on the charge of murdering Sir Harry.

The prison superintendent was a naval officer, Captain R. M. Millar. Captain Millar might not personally approve of Marigny's life style, but he was a fair man and did not care for the prejudice he saw building up against the prisoner. In his book, a man was innocent until he was proved guilty.

"You probably know that the whole of Nassau seems to be against you?" he remarked bluntly to Marigny.

"I have that feeling," Marigny agreed.

"The courtroom will be packed, not only with spectators, but with hatred and disapproval. I want you to give yourself the best chance you can. Be dignified. Be calm. Don't show your own feelings. Conduct yourself, not only like a man, but like an *innocent* man."

Marigny, who earlier had jocularly advised press photographers, when pointing their cameras at him, "Make it a good one," took the captain's advice. He decided to shave off his beard, because he knew that many people were prejudiced against bearded men. For too long he had been a playboy; worse, he had appeared to be a playboy. Now, the game was over. But before he could shave, he needed permission from the Attorney General. This was not given. The Crown also knew of the prejudice against men with beards.

Marigny's second choice for a barrister to defend him was Godfrey Higgs, a fellow member of the Nassau Yacht Club, but although they had known each other for several years, and Higgs had acted for Marigny over the matter of his farm licence, Marigny believed that Higgs was not entirely certain of his innocence and therefore not enthusiastic about appearing for him.

"Godfrey," he said desperately, "I did *not* kill Sir Harry. I give you my word on that. I want you to give me *your* word that if you ever think I did, or that I had anything whatever to do with it, then you'll withdraw."

Godfrey Higgs nodded. They shook hands on this arrangement.

With Attorney General Eric Hallinan and Mr. Adderley appearing for the Crown, Godfrey Higgs selected a young and eloquent barrister, Ernest Callender, as his junior. In a small community like Nassau, members of every profession and trade knew each other well. Alfred Adderley and Godfrey Higgs had appeared on opposite sides in several previous cases; the best-remembered was one in which Mr. Adderley represented Pepsi-Cola in an action and Mr. Higgs took the stand for Coca-Cola.

The preliminary hearing in the Magistrates' Court began within days of Marigny's arrest. As he entered the court, he passed Adderley in a corridor.

"You may not have wanted to defend me," he said bitterly, "but at least you could have given me an answer to my request."

"What do you mean?" Adderley asked him.

"As soon as I was arrested, I sent a message to you through the police, asking you to act for me."

"I never received any message," Adderley replied in amazement. "No one ever said anything about your wanting me to defend you."

Once more, Marigny felt fingers of fear tighten around his heart.

Captain Barker gave a summary of the evidence against Marigny. Mr. Christie described finding Sir Harry's body, and various other witnesses described their involvement. Usually, in such a hearing, the Defence does not cross-examine, but allows the Prosecution to state its case. But such was Marigny's growing concern about his chances that he instructed Godfrey Higgs to cross-examine from the start. At the end of the hearing, Marigny was remanded in custody until October, when he was to appear in the Supreme Court.

The most damning evidence had been given by Captain Barker, who testified that he found Marigny's fingerprints on the Chinese screen in Sir Harry Oakes's bedroom at lunch-time on the day of his arrival. Marigny, he said, had not subsequently entered the room until three or four o'clock that afternoon. Two Bahamian policemen on duty at Westbourne that day corroborated this. The inference was obvious and unarguable: Marigny *must* have left his prints on the screen during the previous night.

Afterwards, Godfrey Higgs reminded Marigny of their arrangement. How could he possibly explain how his fingerprints came to be on the screen?

"Quite easily," Marigny replied. "I agree I was in the room — *but in the morning.* Not in the afternoon. As soon as I heard that Sir Harry had been killed, I drove over to Westbourne and went upstairs, before Melchen and Barker had even arrived in Nassau."

"How can you prove that?"

"Colonel Erskine Lindop, the Commissioner of Police, was with me. He can vouch I was there at that time."

"I hope he can."

Barely a week before Marigny was due to appear in the Supreme Court, he understood the hidden significance of his counsel's guarded answer, for it was suddenly announced that Colonel Erskine Lindop had been unexpectedly posted away from the Bahamas, to become Assistant Commissioner of Police in Trinidad, and he would leave immediately. This effectively denied Marigny the corroboration he desperately needed. Without it, he could hang, for in the thirteen weeks before the trial he had experienced other examples of orchestrated hostility against him.

Police took his driver, Curtis Thompson, to a local police station and advised him to admit that he had driven Marigny to Westbourne on the night of the murder. Thompson refused. He had not driven Marigny anywhere on that night. Two policemen beat him up systematically in an attempt to make him change his mind. He still refused.

"You'll be out of a job when your boss is hanged, as he will be," one of the policemen warned him. The inference was clear: the police — or those who controlled them — could make life difficult for him.

Marigny's friends who agreed to testify in his defence were also visited by the police. Were they not standing by him simply because Marigny had offered them money to do so? Did they realise all the consequences? Did they wish to consort with a murderer?

Several of them thought that, in view of the strong feelings against the accused, it would be wise to have the venue of the trial moved to some more neutral setting, perhaps Bermuda, Jamaica, or even Canada. They were right, but the expense would be prohibitive, and Marigny had very little money behind him.

Nancy Marigny, torn three ways between loyalty to her mother, her husband, and the memory of her father, now also realised — and feared — the full extent of the campaign against the man she had married. To provide money for his defence, she sold out her shares in Kirkland Lake and cashed savings bonds to pay Godfrey Higgs's fee of

$2,500. Marigny sold his sailing boat, *Concubine,* to Mrs. Higgs for $125, and a black Bahamian, Roland T. Symonette, who had made (and kept) a fortune during Prohibition, bought his properties and land on Eleuthera at a knock-down price.

Nancy Marigny also helped her husband in another way. She had recently read a series of articles in *The New Yorker* about the skill of an American private detective, Raymond C. Schindler, for whose unorthodox methods remarkable results were claimed. She contacted Schindler and asked him to fly to Nassau and conduct an impartial investigation. Schindler agreed, for a fee of $300 a day and expenses.

Schindler was in his late fifties, and had begun his career as an insurance agent working on commission. When his total earnings for the first year amounted to exactly $18 (on a policy sold to a shopkeeper in Alliance, Ohio), he sought other, more lucrative, employment. He drifted briefly into gold-mining and out again when he failed to make a quick fortune. Then he answered an advertisement and became a researcher for the grand-sounding G. Franklin McMacken Historical Society of San Francisco.

There, he was instructed to discover how much damage a recent earthquake had caused to buildings before the subsequent fire destroyed them. A little basic research showed Schindler that the society was not the learned body he had imagined, but simply a cover for a private investigator, hired by insurance underwriters to prove that, although there had indeed been a serious fire, the real damage to San Francisco was caused by the earthquake. For damage through such an Act of God, as specified in their policies, the insurers would not be liable.

In the event, this ingenious ploy failed to convince the court, so Schindler's employer disappeared abruptly, and Schindler founded his own detective agency, employing his fellow researchers as his staff.

The case that had most impressed Nancy Marigny concerned an American Negro, one Black Diamond, indicted for murder. Black Diamond had a criminal record, was a stranger to the area, and had been seen near the scene of the crime. While he was in jail, these three facts put him in danger of being lynched by the crowd. She felt that his situation had some remarkable parallels with her husband's predicament.

A wealthy liberal believed Black Diamond was innocent and hired Schindler to prove it. Schindler discovered that seven other people had also been in the neighbourhood at the time of the murder, and quickly eliminated six. The seventh, a German florist, had no police record whatever, but Schindler sensed something odd about this man, who kept a large dog chained in a kennel outside his house. Remembering *The Hound of the Baskervilles,* Schindler threw some pebbles at this dog every night to make it howl and bark. After ten nights, the owner was so upset that he left his house and his job. Convinced that this was the act of a guilty man, who somehow felt the murder had unhinged his dog's mind, Schindler followed him. He became the florist's acquaintance, then his confidant — and the man finally admitted his guilt.

On several cases, Schindler had used what was called a spymograph, invented by a German professor, which recorded changes in a suspect's blood pressure under questioning. If a suspect replied untruthfully, the needle would fluctuate wildly. If the question did not alarm him, and he replied honestly, the needle maintained a regular pattern.

Schindler realised that he might discover evidence of Marigny's guilt, so he stipulated that if this occurred, he could bow out and pass any such evidence to the police. Nancy Marigny was so convinced of her husband's innocence that she immediately agreed to this condition.

Schindler brought with him to Nassau Professor Leonarde Keeler, who had pioneered the Police Crime Laboratory at Northwestern University in Evanston, Illinois. Keeler was an expert on fingerprints and had devised his own lie-detecting machine, an improvement on the German professor's device, for in addition to noting changes in the suspect's blood pressure, it also monitored his respiration rate, pulse, and the electrical conductivity of his skin while he was under questioning.

Schindler had to wait in Nassau for nearly a week before he was allowed into Westbourne. There, he found two policemen still methodically scrubbing the landing walls outside Sir Harry's bedroom. Their orders, they told him, were to remove all fingerprints and handprints they could find. He begged them to desist. They were destroying evidence that could be crucial. They refused; they had their orders.

"But whose prints are those?" Schindler asked them.

"They're not those of the accused person, sir," replied one policeman seriously. "They will therefore only confuse the evidence."

Inside Sir Harry's bedroom, Schindler discovered that Barker and Melchen, after their short delay, had swamped other fingerprints with dusting powder. In the humidity of July, this had completely destroyed them.

The two watchmen on duty on the night of the murder could not be found. No one appeared to know their names, let alone their addresses. They were apparently not on any permanent staff. Like the fingerprints, they had disappeared, and in an island of labourers paid in cash by the day or by the hour, Schindler realised, they never would be discovered.

Although Sir Harry Oakes did not lock the doors of his house, he often slept with an automatic pistol by his bed. This had disappeared, and no one could remember precisely when it had last been seen. Fingerprints were still visible on a Thermos flask and a glass on the bedside table, but whose were they? Damp had affected them to such a degree that they were no longer identifiable.

Now Schindler understood the full significance of the damage to the photographic plates in Miami. If there was no record of Sir Harry's fingerprints, then they could never be compared to any others in the room. But Barker had telephoned too soon, and now there was a second set of photographs, so all other prints on the walls of Sir Harry's room had to be removed before they could be checked and matched against his.

Who, Schindler wondered, would have the authority to destroy evidence on which a man's life could depend?

Captain Barker was in charge of the investigation, but not of the local police, and in any case, he would not discuss the matter with Schindler. Local police officers also declined to assist him in any way.

On the way back to his hotel, Schindler felt that he was being followed. Was he — or was this simply part of the strange, oppressive feeling that had gripped him since his arrival, as though a weight of guilt and concealment hung over the island? Someone — maybe more than one person — was desperately covering up either for himself or others. But who was it — and what secret had he to hide?

Once back in his room, Schindler decided to put his suspicions to the test and discover whether his telephone was also being tapped. He picked up the receiver, looked through the thin telephone directory —

there were relatively few subscribers on New Providence — picked out a number with a pencil point, and asked the operator to connect him.

When the subscriber answered, Schindler did not even introduce himself but said hurriedly, "I'll see you, as agreed, outside Fort Charlotte. On the approach road. In exactly half an hour."

He rang off before the bewildered person could ask who he was or what this strange message meant. He then rang two other strangers, after picking their numbers at random, and gave them the same instructions. Then he took a taxi out beyond Fort Charlotte, an eighteenth-century fortress, named after the Prince of Wales's daughter and built by Lord Dunmore, Governor of Virginia before the American Revolution and Governor of the Bahamas afterwards. Schindler walked carefully towards the fort, taking advantage of all cover. When he came in sight of the approach road, he saw what he had expected: two police cars were waiting. So his telephone *was* tapped. But on whose orders — and why?

He walked back to his taxi, wondering who was being shielded so totally. It seemed to him that Marigny had been chosen as a scapegoat because he had no one except his wife to stand up for him. Also, Marigny's past was cloudy, his morals arguable, his life style an affront to the puritanical and the envious. Circumstantial case against him could be made to appear very strong. If he was found guilty, as seemed likely, he would be hanged, and with his death, the case would be closed forever.

Who on the island was in a position so desperate and so powerful that he — or she or they — would be willing to organise what was virtually the ritual legalised murder of an innocent victim, simply to protect himself or themselves?

3

In Which Two Witnesses Appear Uneasy

FOR SEVERAL HOURS before sunrise on Monday, October 18, black Bahamians packed the square outside the courthouse. They had not come to listen to the trial. As the servants of rich white Bahamians, they were there to claim seats in the public gallery for their employers.

Other servants also brought cane chairs, camp stools, even wooden chairs, to cram into any space they could find. So great was the crush in the court that two people would gladly share a single chair. Fearful that they might lose their place during lunch adjournments, many brought sandwiches and bottles of soda water, and stayed in court throughout each day, for the corridors outside were crowded with others eager to seize any empty seats.

At half-past ten, with police standing shoulder to shoulder in the square to hold back the crowds, the Court Crier struck the floor with his staff and shouted, "Court!"

Sir Oscar Daly entered in his robes, slowly ascended the dais, and stood facing the bar.

The Crier then addressed the court: "Oyez! Oyez! Oyez! All manner of persons having anything to do before His Majesty's Supreme Court in the Bahama Islands, draw near and give your attendance and you will be heard. God Save the King!"

The Crier and Counsel bowed towards the Bench as the judge took his seat. The case of Rex *versus* Marie Alfred Fouquereaux de Marigny was about to begin.

"Marie Alfred Fouquereaux de Marigny, you are charged with murder under Section 335 of the Penal Code, Chapter 60, particulars of the offence being that during the night of the seventh and eighth July, 1943, at New Providence, you did murder Sir Harry Oakes, Baronet. Are you guilty or not guilty?"

"Not guilty."

The Court Crier lifted up a small box and shook it. Inside were thirty-six wooden balls, each painted with a number. He put his hand through a hole in the box, lifted out one ball, and announced its number. The Court Registrar glanced at a list of numbers against names and read the name to the Crier, who shouted it to the court. The jury was being selected.

Sometimes Counsel for the Crown or the Defence called, "Challenge!" when a name was announced. The man being challenged was banned from the jury.

Finally, twelve men were chosen: a sponge merchant, an insurance agent, a grocery clerk, and the owner of a grocery store, three accountants, a baker, two general merchants, a liquor dealer, and the manager of a factory that made blocks of ice.

Four aspects of the case, but not to be mentioned during the trial, provoked almost as much discussion and argument outside the court as whether Marigny was guilty or innocent.

First, why had the Duke and Duchess of Windsor, who had arrived back in Nassau from eight weeks' vacation in the United States only a few days before Sir Harry's murder, discovered it necessary to return to the States yet again for a stay of indefinite length?

The second point of discussion was that many witnesses who would testify had not actually been in Nassau at the time of the murder. Lady Eunice Oakes was at Bar Harbor. Walter Foskett, Sir Harry's American lawyer for the past thirteen years and a close friend, was in Palm Beach. His Bahamian lawyer, Kenneth Solomon, was on Abaco. Newell Kelly, the manager of his estates, whose wife, Madeline, would give damning evidence against Marigny, was on a fishing trip to Harbour Island. Dr. Sayad, a consultant at the hospital where Nancy Marigny had earlier undergone her operation, and who claimed that Marigny had told him he would "crack Sir Harry's head," was in his consulting rooms in Palm Beach. And Nancy Marigny, who would give evidence for her husband, was at a ballet school in Vermont.

Rumours persisted that a strange motor launch had tied up at the quay in Nassau on the evening of Sir Harry's death, but was not there on the following morning. A watchman employed at a property at Lyford Cay said he had noticed a motor launch, of much the same size, lying off-shore. He claimed that several men had landed from this vessel and were driven to Nassau in a car that had waited for them. Others thought that men had been seen driving from the launch in Nassau Harbour. Were these two different boats or one? Whose version — if either — was correct? And had this launch and these men anything whatever to do with the murder?

An attempt was made to interview the night watchman, but this proved impossible: he was found drowned. Was this an accident, or another thread in the shroud of silence with which someone — or some people — felt it imperative to cover his own activities or secrets?

Sir Harry Oakes was said to have kept gold bars and coins in his house. A number of people in Nassau quoted this as fact, and declared that they had actually seen this gold (which seemed unlikely). They also said that Sir Harry had frequently expressed his dislike and distrust of paper money, which could lose its value overnight, which seemed much more likely.

Since medical evidence showed that blood had flowed from wounds in his temple towards his forehead, he must have been hit when leaning forward. Was it not possible that a thief had entered his house, knowing that the doors were never locked, and had seen Sir Harry kneeling on the floor above an open chest of ingots or coins — and killed him for his treasure?

This theory gained greater circulation after the publication of Sir Harry's will. Application for probate was made a week before the trial opened, and proved to be a puzzle. The will covered five pages and gave his personal fortune as £3,671,724 13s. 5d., which did not include the value of shares or his houses. Lady Oakes would receive £50,000 and a third of the entire estate, in cash or otherwise, which would be held in trust.

The remaining two-thirds would be divided equally among the five children, who would not come into full possession of their shares until they were thirty years old. In the meantime, each would receive an annual income of $12,000, about £2,500.

While more than £3.5 million was a very large sum of money, it was still only a fraction of other previously published — and never contradicted — estimates of Sir Harry's wealth, which had varied between $200 million and $300 million. The most conservative Nassau estimate of his private fortune was between £10 million and £20 million, so what had happened to the missing millions? Had they ever existed, or had they somehow disappeared?

Alfred Adderley, in his opening speech, listed the main points that the Crown would make against the accused.

First, there was what he called "the compelling motive of hatred, humiliation, and gain." To this was added Marigny's "desperate financial position." Marigny had also been alone "outside the gates of Westbourne on this night of all nights."

When Marigny returned home afterwards he had slept badly, and paid what Adderley called "a significant visit" to the police station at a very early hour. He was also concerned about moving gasoline from his house. Sir Harry's body had been burned by some liquid with a petroleum base, and Marigny's explanation for scorched hairs on his hands, face, and head was "unconvincing."

Marigny was also unable to produce the shirt and tie he had worn on that night; his fingerprints had been found in Sir Harry's bedroom; he had expressed hatred for his father-in-law and referred to him callously after his death.

Lastly, Marigny had asked a police officer whether a conviction in a murder case could result if the police did not discover the murder weapon, and whether anyone could be convicted on circumstantial evidence alone.

Before the witnesses stepped forward to tell what they knew about these episodes — or what they claimed to know, which was not always the same thing — the jury were taken out to Westbourne to see for themselves the site of the murder. All had passed by the house many times, but never before had they actually been inside. They peered shyly around the richly furnished rooms, trying to imagine Sir Harry here, wondering what it would be like to be as wealthy as he had been.

Mabel Ellis, a housemaid, one of three inside staff employed at West-bourne, described how she had prepared Sir Harry's bedroom on the day before he died. She laid out his pyjamas on his bed, tucked the mosquito net beneath the mattress, then sprayed the room with an insecticide against mosquitoes. She left a fan on the floor near the door that led to the north balcony, facing the sea. The fan was not plugged in and was not at the foot of the bed, where it was found, switched on and working, on the morning after Sir Harry's murder.

Guest rooms at Westbourne were always kept prepared, and she was not always told in advance whether a visitor would be staying for the night. She had not known that Mr. Christie would be staying the night at Westbourne. On the morning of that day, July 7, she served breakfast on the north porch to Sir Harry and Mr. Christie. Both were dressed, and Mr. Christie's car was parked at the entrance to Westbourne, where he usually left it.

Mr. Christie, described as "the Honourable Harold George Christie, real estate agent and member of the Governor's Executive Council," was now called. He explained that he had known Marigny since about a week after Marigny's arrival in Nassau before the war, and recalled that Marigny had told him several months earlier that he wanted a piece of land which Sir Harry refused to let him have.

"The piece of land was at Westward Villas in the Cable Beach section. He stated that he and Sir Harry were not on friendly terms. I think perhaps there were a number of reasons. One reason was that he wanted the land and couldn't get it. I think another reason was that Sir Harry felt Marigny hadn't treated his former wife with due consideration, and Marigny was annoyed because Sir Harry would not listen to his side of the question ... He told me that Sir Harry had not treated him fairly and had been unduly severe."

Harold Christie also said that Sir Harry had owned land on the west of the island, the Jones property. This plot, around seven acres in area, was next to another thousand acres that Sir Harry also owned. Together, both plots were worth about £30,000. Oakes had offered all this to his son-in-law, but Marigny had refused it.

Christie explained that in the past he had stayed with Sir Harry ("one of my closest friends") in Bar Harbor, in Palm Beach, in Mexico, and at Sir Harry's home in England. Now he described how they had passed the last evening of Sir Harry's life.

"I spent more than half my time with Sir Harry in the first week of July," he said. "I slept at Westbourne on the fourth, the sixth, and the seventh. I left Westbourne alone to go to an Executive Council meeting on the morning of the seventh. Sir Harry joined me at my office about four, and we went to the Security Office in the Royal Victoria Hotel, because he was leaving on the ninth to join Lady Oakes at Bar Harbor. We drove to Westbourne in Sir Harry's car, after stopping at my house to collect a pair of tennis shoes."

At Westbourne they played tennis with two girls — his niece Sally Sawyer, and Miss MacMahon, a friend of hers — and afterwards walked from the courts to Westbourne to have drinks upstairs on a verandah overlooking the ocean.

Mr. Charles Hubbard, an Englishman who had retired to Nassau and was a neighbour of Sir Harry's, and Mrs. Dulcibelle Henneage, an evacuee from England, joined them at Sir Harry's invitation.

"Miss Sawyer and Miss MacMahon left before dusk, between seven and seven-thirty. Mr. Hubbard offered to take us out to dine in the Prince George Hotel, but Sir Harry invited us to stay for dinner."

Christie meanwhile took a shower and changed his clothes, but he said that Sir Harry remained in his tennis clothes until he went to bed.

"We finished dinner between nine-thirty and nine-forty-five and played Chinese chequers in the living room until about eleven o'clock, when Mr. Hubbard and Mrs. Heneage left."

The two men accompanied them to Mr. Hubbard's car.

"My car was at my office, because I went to Westbourne in Sir Harry's car. Before we finished dinner I telephoned my chauffeur and told him to bring the car to Westbourne. I did not see the car that night. If it had been at the main south entrance, I would have seen it.

"After Mr. Hubbard and Mrs. Henneage left, Sir Harry and I walked back to the house and went directly to Sir Harry's room. We talked for a short while. Then Sir Harry put on his pyjamas, got into bed, and started to read a newspaper.

"I borrowed a pair of reading glasses and a magazine and went to my room between eleven-fifteen and eleven-thirty. I read for half an hour or three-quarters of an hour after going to bed. After reading, I went to sleep and was awakened by mosquitoes. I got out of bed, killed a few mosquitoes, and went back to sleep. Later, I was awakened by a heavy rain storm. I do not think I got out of bed on that occasion. I do not know what time it was, but I was awake for about ten minutes.

"I next woke after daybreak. I went to the north porch, where Sir Harry and I usually had breakfast. Sir Harry wasn't there, so I went to the screen door of Sir Harry's room and called, 'Hi, Harry.'

"There was no reply, so I opened the door and went in. I noticed that the mosquito net had disappeared and the wooden frame was charred. I rushed to the bed and saw Sir Harry lying diagonally across it, his head about a foot from the south side. I was greatly shocked, naturally, because we were so friendly. I can hardly describe the feeling.

"I lifted up his head, shook him, and poured some water from a Thermos bottle, on a table between the two beds, into his mouth, and held his head up so that he would not choke. I wet a towel and wiped his face. I believe the towel came from my bathroom. Sir Harry's body was warm, and I felt there was still hope. It was approximately seven o'clock. I moved a pillow from the other bed and put it under his head.

"I rushed on to the north porch and shouted for help. The servants' quarters were below the western end of the porch. I went back to the room and shouted for the watchmen from the northern window. I went downstairs, but I cannot remember going outside.

"The first person I succeeded in contacting was Mrs. Madeline Kelly, who lived in the Country Club grounds. I called her on the telephone, and then my brother, Frank Christie. Then I rang the Commissioner of Police, but he was not at home. His wife, Mrs. Lindop, came to the telephone. I went upstairs, shook Sir Harry, wet a towel again, and wiped his face once more.

"The mattress was burned and there were burn spots on the carpets. There was no fire, but there was a little smoke. I went through the whole eastern end of the building, but there was no sign of fire. I went through all the rooms, including my own, and into the hallway, and saw burn marks on the staircase.

"An electric fan was at the north-eastern corner of the bed. It was on the floor and was in motion. I believe I called Mr. Hubbard after Mrs. Kelly arrived.

"Dr. Quackenbush [a local doctor] arrived shortly after Mrs. Kelly. I was still wearing a mottled-brown pair of Sir Harry's pyjamas. I did not change into my clothes until nine or nine-thirty. Sir Harry and I planned to go on a tour of Sir Harry's sheep farm with Mr. Moss of *The Guardian* and Mr. Dupuch of *The Tribune* that morning. My driver was probably the only person apart from Mr. Hubbard and Mrs. Henneage who knew I was spending the night with Sir Harry."

Nearly everyone in the court knew Mr. Christie, either socially or professionally. He was descended from Loyalists who had left America after the War of Independence to start new lives for themselves in the Bahamas, and his family was one of the oldest in Nassau. His office in Bay Street was remarkable, because anybody seemed able to visit him in it at almost any time, not only on business matters, but with personal problems about which they sought his advice, which was always freely given. He was a kindly man, sometimes vague in his manner, more, it sometimes seemed, a dreamer or a visionary than a businessman. For the past eight years he had been one of Cat Island's two representatives in the House of Assembly, and, with Sir Harry Oakes, was one of the best-known men in Nassau and also one of the most generous.

In any natural disaster, such as hurricane or drought, he would not wait to go through what were called "official channels" to give aid to his constituents. He helped them at once, drawing out as much as £2,000 from his own bank account and taking it personally to Cat Island. He would leave money with the head man in each settlement to distribute as he thought best among those in need.

If they were short of food, he shipped in more — and charged it to an importing company he owned. He had started an inter-island air service some years earlier, and sometimes, if paying passengers were few, he would fill the aircraft with Cat Islanders living on New Providence and fly them home and back for a free day trip.

On one visit to the island, so many people had asked him the time that he made enquiries and learned they could not afford to buy even the simplest clock. He thereupon bought a job lot of eight hundred alarm clocks and gave them all to constituents as Christmas presents.

Christie, like Sir Harry, was careless of his appearance. He usually wore a creased jacket, unpressed trousers, and seemed to be without any inhibitions or vanities; he was a very agreeable companion, with the gift of putting everyone at ease, because he was so easy-going himself. People who could not visit his office to seek advice felt free to call at his home, often before he was even dressed in the morning. Christie did not object; what were affectionately called "Harold's breakfast receptions" were well known. His usual wear for such early appointments was a pair of pyjama trousers. Sometimes, if he had forgotten an appointment elsewhere, he might jump out of bed, as the locals would say, "blood naked," and continue to give advice while he dressed.

But now in the witness box there was a different Harold Christie, no longer relaxed, genial, and generous, but obviously very ill at ease. He sweated profusely, although the court was not unduly warm, and kept dabbing his forehead with a handkerchief. As Godfrey Higgs rose to cross-examine him, a dark stain of sweat spread across the back of Christie's white linen jacket, and as he answered Counsel's questions, he gripped the rail of the box until his knuckles showed white as bone, and he shifted his weight uneasily from one foot to the other. He had the appearance of a man who was not simply nervous — as indeed anyone might be, giving evidence in a murder trial, when one friend has been killed and another charged with killing him — but terrified. Of what? Or of whom? Or could the memory of discovering Sir Harry murdered be so fearful that even to recall it caused him such anguish?

Godfrey Higgs began conversationally, for barristers are like actors, with solicitors providing their scripts. The good ones realise instinctively how to make the most effective use of their lines. Godfrey Higgs was one of the best.

"You know Mabel Ellis, Sir Harry's housemaid?" he asked casually, with the air of one remarking on a matter of no importance.

HAROLD CHRISTIE: Yes.

Godfrey Higgs: You know that she says that you always left your car outside Westbourne when you came there. Is that correct?

HAROLD CHRISTIE: No, I did not always leave my car outside the main

entrance.

GODFREY HIGGS: Did you leave your car there on Tuesday night?

HAROLD CHRISTIE: On the northern end of the tennis court, a little east of Westbourne, nearer to Westbourne than to the Country Club.

GODFREY HIGGS: You know that Mabel Ellis says that on Tuesday night, July sixth, you left your car immediately outside the entrance to the southern court?

HAROLD CHRISTIE: Mabel Ellis is incorrect. It was to the east of the main entrance. The courts are about three hundred feet away.

Godfrey Higgs: You know that Mabel Ellis says that on Tuesday morning you drove up to town with Sir Harry Oakes?

HAROLD CHRISTIE: I do not remember that. I am sure that I went alone and went to the Executive Council. If Mabel Ellis says that I went with Sir Harry in his car, she is saying what is not true. I am positive of this because I was in a hurry; I had to be there at ten o'clock.

While Higgs paused deliberately to glance around the courtroom, then adjusted his wig and twisted his head slightly in a gesture that would imply either that he accepted or rejected these statements, Christie wiped his forehead again. His handkerchief, perfectly laundered, was now a sodden linen ball.

Higgs continued. "Do you remember if you got there on time?" he asked. HAROLD CHRISTIE: I believe so. It meets at ten o'clock. To the best of my recollection, it met at ten o'clock that day.

GODFREY HIGGS: And yet you say you left Westbourne between nine-fifteen and nine-thirty?

HAROLD CHRISTIE: I said I did not remember exactly. I remember that I was in a hurry because I was late.

GODFREY HIGGS: If you did not have a watch, how did you know what time it was?

HAROLD CHRISTIE: I may have seen a clock some time before.

GODFREY HIGGS: Do you think your recollection is better than Mabel Ellis's?

HAROLD CHRISTIE: I could not say that.

GODFREY HIGGS: Have you a good memory sometimes? HAROLD CHRISTIE: Sometimes.

Higgs now returned to a statement Marigny had made in the preliminary hearing: that he had invited Christie to join the impromptu dinner party he had given at his home on the evening of his father-in-law's death. Christie, he said then, had declined, because he was dining with Harry Oakes and staying the night at Westbourne.

GODFREY HIGGS: Would you say that the accused was lying if he said you told him that you were staying with Sir Harry Oakes that night?

HAROLD CHRISTIE: Yes.

GODFREY HIGGS: Why are you so positive of these two facts?

HAROLD CHRISTIE: I should hate to do an injustice to the accused, but I did not tell him that. I did not know myself that I was going to dine with Sir Harry.

GODFREY HIGGS: When did Sir Harry invite you to dine that night?

HAROLD CHRISTIE: About eight o'clock.

GODFREY HIGGS: When did Sir Harry invite you to sleep there?

HAROLD CHRISTIE: He did not invite me. I had slept there on Sunday and Tuesday night.

GODFREY HIGGS: When did you decide to sleep there?

HAROLD CHRISTIE: After dinner. There was nothing that I had to do in town, and I had an appointment in the morning.

GODFREY HIGGS: I put it to you that you had planned to stay at Westbourne on Wednesday night.

HAROLD CHRISTIE: Had we dined at the Prince George, I probably would have slept at home.

GODFREY HIGGS: Why did you want your car?

HAROLD CHRISTIE: I always want my car with me and have it brought to me. I particularly wanted it that night, because I was going on a trip the next morning.

GODFREY HIGGS: So it was during dinner that you decided to stay at Westbourne?

HAROLD CHRISTIE: Yes.

GODFREY HIGGS: Did you instruct your man Gibson to leave your car at the Country Club?

HAROLD CHRISTIE: I did.

GODFREY HIGGS: Why?

HAROLD CHRISTIE: Because I wanted to conserve my gasoline, and if it had been brought over to Westbourne, there was a good chance of my car being used.

GODFREY HIGGS: Why? When was there a good chance of it being used?

HAROLD CHRISTIE: There were guests at Westbourne, and there were suggestions of going to the Prince George, or possibly some other place.

GODFREY HIGGS: Was it not the suggestion that dinner be had at the Prince George?

HAROLD CHRISTIE: We could have gone afterwards.

GODFREY HIGGS: Wasn't Mr. Hubbard's car there, as well as two of Sir Harry's?

HAROLD CHRISTIE: Yes.

GODFREY HIGGS: Why were you then fearful that your car would have been used?

HAROLD CHRISTIE: In the circumstances, there would have been every possibility of my car being used if it had been there.

GODFREY HIGGS: Is that your best reason?

HAROLD CHRISTIE: Yes. I was going on a trip the next day and might not have had enough gasoline to use the next day. Gasoline is rationed.

GODFREY HIGGS: Did you know how much gasoline you had in your car?

HAROLD CHRISTIE: No.

GODFREY HIGGS: If you did not know, you were not in a position to say whether you would have had enough for the next day in any event?

HAROLD CHRISTIE: That is correct.

GODFREY HIGGS: Did only you and Gibson know your car was there?

HAROLD CHRISTIE: Gibson, his wife, and another boy knew it was there.

GODFREY HIGGS: No one at Westbourne knew your car was there?

HAROLD CHRISTIE: Not that I know of.

At the preliminary hearing, Christie had given a third reason for leaving his car near the Country Club. He had said that this was "the logical place" to leave it. Higgs now returned to this past statement.

GODFREY HIGGS: What do you mean that the Country Club is the logical place to leave the car?

HAROLD CHRISTIE: It was the logical place to leave it because there was a watchman there, and none at Westbourne.

GODFREY HIGGS: Then you left it there for security?

HAROLD CHRISTIE: I did not think of that at the time.

GODFREY HIGGS: Why are you so especially careful to say you did not want to use the car that night?

HAROLD CHRISTIE: I said I wanted to conserve my gasoline, and if my car was brought to Westbourne, there was a possibility that it might be used.

Obviously, Harold Christie could leave his car wherever he liked outside Westbourne, provided, of course, that his host did not object. But to many in the court, the reasons he gave for having it parked out of sight seemed insubstantial. Gasoline was rationed, but not that strictly; and in any case, extra petrol was always easy to obtain, if illegally, off the ration.

The excuse that the car would be more secure if hidden was ridiculous. There was virtually no theft in Nassau. If there had been, Sir Harry Oakes, and others like him, with large houses containing expensive furniture and ornaments, would never have left doors unlocked day and night.

His explanation that it was "logical" to leave his car concealed only provoked another question: logical for what reason? Could it be that since his car — a station wagon — was well known, he wanted no one to see it outside Westbourne, but needed it because he had to drive somewhere during the night? Could this journey have been so important to him and so essential that he had kept it secret; that he had appeared willing to perjure himself by insisting, however unconvincingly, that he had never left Westbourne?

Why was Christie so eager for privacy — and what could have been the object of the journey he denied making? Those who asked such questions privately received a blunt reply from Mr. Christie's friends: Harold Christie is not on trial; Alfred de Marigny is.

Godfrey Higgs now proceeded to Christie's recollections of what had happened on the morning of July 8, when he discovered the body.

GODFREY HIGGS: You know that Mabel Ellis, the housemaid at Westbourne, says that usually you and Sir Harry were dressed before you had breakfast?

HAROLD CHRISTIE: If we were going out early, we dressed. If not, we probably would not.

GODFREY HIGGS: Why did you not dress for breakfast on Thursday morning?

HAROLD CHRISTIE: After I had discovered the body?

GODFREY HIGGS: Before you discovered it. Were you going out after breakfast?

Christie did not answer immediately. Between several previous questions and answers he had paused for several seconds, but now he stood staring at Counsel as though mesmerised and bereft of the power to speak.

One chronicler in the court timed the delay in his reply. For thirty-seven seconds after this question, Harold Christie stayed silent, biting his lip, glancing desperately around the courtroom.

Finally he said, "Sir Harry rose at daybreak, and he usually could be found looking out over the water."

GODFREY HIGGS: But you were planning to go out that morning?

Christie nodded like a man in a daze or a dream. "Yes," he agreed dully. "At ten-thirty."

Godfrey Higgs now reminded Christie of evidence given by Charles Hubbard at the preliminary hearing, in which he said he had specifically noted lights burning at Westbourne when he drove past at half-past eleven on the previous evening.

Christie said that the lights were out — except possibly for one left on in the downstairs porch. He could not be certain. Perhaps Hubbard had seen this light when he drove past, or the light in his own bedroom, for he was still reading. He seemed flustered, like a tiring swimmer when the tide is on the turn.

He explained once more how he had twice been woken during the night, once by mosquitoes and then by the storm.

GODFREY HIGGS: Were they the only two occasions when you woke that night?

HAROLD CHRISTIE: They were the only two occasions I woke that night.

GODFREY HIGGS: Did you leave Westbourne *any* time that night?

HAROLD CHRISTIE: I did not leave Westbourne any time during the night of July seventh, or until the next night of July eighth.

GODFREY HIGGS: Do you know Captain Sears, Superintendent of Police?

HAROLD CHRISTIE: I do.

GODFREY HIGGS: You are friendly with him?

HAROLD CHRISTIE: I am not friendly or unfriendly. I see very little of him.

GODFREY HIGGS: Have you known him since boyhood?

HAROLD CHRISTIE: Yes.

GODFREY HIGGS: He has no ill-will against you that you know of?

HAROLD CHRISTIE: No.

GODFREY HIGGS: If Captain Sears were to say that he had seen you in town the night of July seventh, what would you say?

HAROLD CHRISTIE: I would say that Captain Sears is very seriously mistaken and should be more careful in his observations.

GODFREY HIGGS: I put it to you that Captain Sears saw you at about midnight in a station wagon in George Street.

HAROLD CHRISTIE: Was he certain?

GODFREY HIGGS: I put it to you.

HAROLD CHRISTIE: Captain Sears was mistaken. I did not leave Westbourne after retiring to my room that night until the next night, and any statement to the effect that I was in town is a very grave mistake.

GODFREY HIGGS: Would you say that Captain Sears was a reputable person?

"I would say so," Christie agreed. "Nevertheless, reputable people can be mistaken."

The Defence later produced Captain Edward DeWitt Sears, Superintendent of the Bahamas Police Force, in charge of its uniformed branch, including the traffic department, to give his recollections of that night.

Sears had served in the army during the First World War, and still kept his rank. He had been a sponge merchant for some time, and when this trade slackened, had joined the police force. He was a close friend of Frank Christie and had known Harold, the younger brother, since he was a boy at the local grammar school.

"I was on duty at the Central Police Station on the night of Wednesday, July seventh," Captain Sears explained. "A few minutes before midnight I left the Central Station and drove down Bay Street into George Street. As I entered George Street, I saw a station wagon come from Marlborough Street into George Street.

"I passed the station wagon opposite the old site of the Island Bookshop and saw the Honourable H. G. Christie in the wagon. Mr Christie was sitting in the front seat of the wagon, but someone else was driving. Mr. Christie was being driven in the direction of Bay Street, and I was going away from Bay Street."

The Attorney General cross-examined him, but Sears would not be shaken from his story. He had seen Christie that night, just as he described; he had not made a mistake. Afterwards, he had asked colleagues to try to check on the station wagon, for since he had not seen its number, he could not say who owned it.

Dr. Hugh Arnley Quackenbush, a local medical practitioner with Canadian qualifications, now testified that at approximately seven-thirty on the morning of July 8 he received a telephone call from Mrs. Kelly. He immediately drove to Westbourne, arriving there at seven-forty. Mrs. Kelly and Mr. Christie were in the hall, Mr. Christie still wearing his pyjamas. Dr. Quackenbush went upstairs at once and examined the body of Sir Harry, which was badly burned. Sir Harry had a perforating wound in front of his left ear large enough to admit the tip of the doctor's left index finger. He could feel that the skull had been fractured there.

In his opinion, Sir Harry had been dead for two and a half to five hours, but it was very difficult to fix a time, because both the body and the bed had been burned. While examining the body, he noticed that a small part of the mattress, about the size of his fingernail, was still glowing and smouldering.

"I subconsciously reached for a glass sitting on a night table between the two beds and put out the fire."

He also noticed marks on the walls that seemed to be handprints or fingerprints. In his opinion, they were not bloodstains. He saw an electric fan on the floor in such a position that it was blowing across Sir Harry's bed, but the flow of air from it had not blown away the feathers that covered part of the body.

The doctor noted blisters on Sir Harry's neck, the upper part of the chest, his left shin, the toes of his right foot, and his right hand. He assumed that the blisters had occurred before death, because blistering depends upon the circulation of the blood; if blood stops circulating, the body will not blister. The greater part of the burns, however, had occurred after death.

Dr. Quackenbush, cross-examined by Mr. Higgs, admitted that blood had stopped flowing by the time he arrived, but since blood had run from the wounds towards the top of the head, "this would indicate that the body was face down, or it had been moved, because blood naturally would not flow uphill."

Later that day, Dr. Laurence Whilley Fitzmaurice, Acting Chief Medical Officer of the Bahamas, who held Canadian and American medical qualifications, performed a post-mortem examination on the body at the Bahamas General Hospital.

He also described Sir Harry's burns, and noted the wound on his head, "in the front of the upper part of the left ear, about .8 by .5 inches in size. There was a second one, approximately two inches above the first, about .7 by .3 inches in size."

Behind the upper lobe of Sir Harry's left ear was a third wound, approximately .7 by .5 inches deep, and a fourth about one and a half inches above the third, .7 by .2 inches in size. These wounds were "somewhat triangular in shape," with the apex in each case pointing towards the front of Sir Harry's head.

In his opinion, death was caused by shock, by haemorrhaging around the brain, and fracturing of the skull. The wounds had been inflicted "by a heavy blunt instrument with a well-defined edge."

The stomach contained four ounces of thick, dark, viscid liquid. Part of the stomach contents were sent to the laboratory for examination, but he admitted, "I did not examine the viscous substance I found in the stomach." It had not given off any particular odour. He calculated that death had occurred four to six hours after the completion of Sir Harry's last meal.

Mrs. Effie Dulcibelle Henneage testified that she and her two children had had lunch with Mr. Charles Hubbard at his house on Cable Beach near Westbourne on July 7.

After lunch, the children returned with their nurse to the house Mrs. Henneage rented in East Bay Street. At about six o'clock that evening, Mr. Christie telephoned and, on behalf of Sir Harry, invited Mr. Hubbard and her to Westbourne. They drank Tom Collinses and then saw some palm trees that Sir Harry had recently planted between his house and the beach. They stayed for dinner and afterwards played Chinese chequers. Mr. Hubbard took her home in his car at about eleven o'clock that night.

Mr. Charles Heman Hubbard corroborated this, and added that after he finally returned home, it would have been about eleven-forty-five P.M. when he turned off his light. He had passed Westbourne on the way home — which would have been around eleven-thirty. He noticed that lights were still on downstairs. He could not say whether there were any burning upstairs.

During the early part of the evening, Sir Harry had seemed to be in good health and spirits.

Mrs. Madeline Gale Kelly, the wife of Mr. Newell Kelly, who managed Sir Harry's Nassau properties, described how the telephone woke her on the morning of July 8. Harold Christie was calling. She immediately telephoned to Dr. Quackenbush, then dressed and went across to Westbourne. . She returned to her cottage in the grounds and was there later in the morning, when Alfred de Marigny and John Anderson, manager and director of the Bahamas Trust Company Limited, which dealt with some of Sir Harry's business interests, came to see her. She spoke to them from the porch. Marigny said, "This is terrible, terrible." He leaned against the side of the porch and placed his hands on his stomach. "I think I'm going to be ill," he said. "I think I'm going to be ill." The two men came into Mrs. Kelly's cottage, and Mr. Anderson went to her bedroom to use the telephone. Marigny followed her into the living room and asked for a glass of water. His manner struck Mrs. Kelly as being "very theatrical," and in order to get away from him, she followed Mr. Anderson into the bedroom. Marigny joined them and once more said that he thought he was going to be ill.

"I told him to get a hold of himself," said Mrs. Kelly shortly.

Mrs. Dorothy Clarke, the wife of an RAF officer, said that she had met Marigny for the first time in the Prince George Hotel on Tuesday evening. He asked her and a friend, Mrs. Jean Ainsley, whose husband was also in the RAF, to come to dinner at his house on the following evening.

Afterwards, he drove her and Mrs. Ainsley to the cottage she and her husband rented beyond Westbourne. This was at about one o'clock the following morning. She did not notice any lights burning when she passed Westbourne.

Constable Wendell Lamond Parker, of the Bahamas Police Force, said that he was on duty early on the morning of July 8, at the Central Police Station. Mr. Marigny came into the station at about seven-thirty and spoke to him. Marigny explained that he had come to notify the police that he had recently converted a car into a truck and wanted to know whether it would be necessary for the police to inspect it.

The constable was surprised to see him, because callers did not usually arrive before nine o'clock. He was struck by Marigny's appearance.

"He appeared distressed, his eyes were wild, and his lips protruding," he said.

Mr. Thomas Lavelle, who ran the Victoria Guest House in Victoria Avenue, opposite Marigny's house, had made a statement before the trial, because he was leaving for the United States to undergo a serious operation and so could not be present. He claimed that he was walking with an electrician who had come to mend an element in a heater when he saw Marigny and Sir Harry Oakes standing by a car in front of Marigny's house. From the front room of his guest house he had heard Sir Harry tell Marigny: "You had better not write any more letters to my wife. You are a sex maniac."

Sir Harry then called, "Sydney!"

This was the name of his elder son, who inherited the baronetcy. A young man came out of Marigny's house, climbed into the car with Sir Harry, and they both drove off towards Bay Street.

Mr. John Herbert Anderson, of the Bahamas Trust Company Limited, said that Marigny had asked him to help in achieving a compromise with his former wife, Ruth. She was claiming about $125,000 from him.

On the afternoon after Sir Harry Oakes's murder, Marigny invited Anderson to lunch at his house. Then they drove back to Westbourne and arrived as Sir Harry's body was being carried out. On the way, Marigny mentioned that he had several drums of gasoline in his garage, and asked how best they could be moved. Gasoline was rationed, and clearly this had been bought on the black market. Anderson suggested that he hire a truck. He also recalled that several weeks before Sir Harry's death, Marigny had told him that Sir Harry was drinking heavily and was "likely to drink himself to death."

Anderson testified that a financial statement made only the previous month would show that Marigny had received a total of £25,000 from his former wife in the past two years. He also said that, in his opinion, Marigny was hard up. He had sold properties in West Street, Nassau, and on Cable Beach to raise money.

The manager of the Nassau branch of the Current and Savings Departments of the Royal Bank of Canada, said that on the night Harry Oakes died, Marigny had an overdraft of £57. 8s. 9d. Earlier, there had been transfers in and out of the account; £7,708.2s. 6d. to Georges de Visdelou, a credit from Nancy Marigny of £4,000 to her husband, then £3,500 back to her from Marigny.

Lieutenant John Campbell Douglas, the Assistant Superintendent of the Bahamas Police Force, said that he had been instructed by his superiors to keep the accused under observation. He travelled with Marigny in Marigny's car from his house to Westbourne. On the way, Marigny spoke of the strained relations between himself and Sir Harry as a result of gossip about his former wife, Ruth. Marigny said, "That guy, Sir Harry, the old bastard, should have been killed anyhow."

When they reached Westbourne, they had walked along the beach together, discussing the case, before going into the house. Marigny asked whether a man could be convicted in a British court for murder if the murder weapon was not found.

Douglas had replied that he thought he could, but added, "Don't worry about it, Freddie."

Marigny then asked whether a man could be convicted on circumstantial evidence alone.

"Yes, I think so," Douglas had replied.

Bit by bit, like bricks in a prison wall, evidence against Marigny seemed to grow with every witness.

Captain Melchen climbed into the witness box to deliver what the Prosecution believed would be the *coup de grace*. He was short and stout and puffy-faced. He wore spectacles, which he kept adjusting on the bridge of his nose as he talked. First, he explained that he was Chief of the Homicide Bureau of the Miami Police Department, a title that sounded formidably efficient in the little colonial court. Then he described how the Duke of Windsor had personally telephoned to Miami police headquarters to ask that he and a colleague conduct the investigation: not any two detectives, but these two. This gave immense weight and prestige to both officers. In all history, had any other American policemen ever been requested by a former King of England to solve a crime on British colonial territory?

Melchen said that he brought with him to Nassau two microscopes, a Speed Graphic camera, and a fingerprint outfit containing dusting powder, a camel-hair brush, Scotch tape, rubber patches of the type used to mend tyre punctures, a small pair of scissors, and a magnifying glass.

He declared that a chemical with a petrol base had been used in Sir Harry's bedroom to start the fire. A few hours before Marigny was arrested, he had told Melchen how Sir Harry hated him and how he in turn hated his father-in-law, whom he had called "a stupid old fool." In Melchen's view, Marigny resented Sir Harry's wealth: he and his wife had spurned a gift of $10,000 from Lady Oakes because he thought that it would look like "a gift to a poor relative or an orphan child."

Then Melchen's testimony became rather more obscure. Under Godfrey Higgs's careful questioning, the initial impression of self-assurance and importance and efficiency began suddenly to crumble.

Melchen said that marks on the walls of Sir Harry's bedroom *appeared* to be fingerprints, but he had not actually examined them. He had left this to Captain Barker. Similarly, only Barker had examined the Thermos flask and drinking glass on the bedside table.

When Sir Harry's body had to be removed, the Chinese screen was folded and placed against a wall, and then put outside. Captain Barker wrote an "O" on the screen to indicate the outside of one end panel, and "Handle with care" because he wished to preserve the fingerprints it carried. Barker then lifted these fingerprints on to a transparent Scotch tape and photographed them.

Melchen and Barker went together to Marigny's house, and both were surprised that Marigny could not find any shirt in the house that resembled the shirt he had worn on the night of the seventh.

Now Melchen admitted to the court that not until July 19 or 20 — ten or eleven days after Marigny was arrested — was he told that Marigny's fingerprint — singular, not plural — had definitely been found on the screen, although several days previously Captain Barker had assured Lady Oakes and Mrs. Marigny in Bar Harbor that his prints — plural — had been positively identified.

At the preliminary hearing, Melchen had described how he took Marigny upstairs to Sir Harry's bedroom for questioning between three and four o'clock in the afternoon. The time had been corroborated on oath by two Bahamian policemen. Melchen was now informed, however, that Lieutenant Douglas's diary for that day showed that Marigny had driven him away from Westbourne between one-thirty P.M. and two o'clock, and therefore the accused could not possibly have been in the house between three and four o'clock.

"When I fixed the time of going upstairs between three and four," Melchen explained lamely, "it was not my intention to prove the accused was riot upstairs before the fingerprint was left. It was just a mistake."

Ernest Callender: "What a mistake! What a coincidence that you *and* two constables should make the *same* mistake!"

Melchen agreed that he and Captain Barker had visited Lady Oakes after her husband's funeral, but he did not agree that they had explained how Sir Harry had been murdered.

ERNEST CALLENDER: What did Barker say to Lady Oakes and Mrs. Marigny?

CAPTAIN MELCHEN: Barker told them about fingerprints or a fingerprint of the accused having been found on the screen.

ERNEST CALLENDER: To whom did Barker say this?

CAPTAIN MELCHEN: I believe to Lady Oakes and the accused's wife.

ERNEST CALLENDER: What was the date of the funeral?

CAPTAIN MELCHEN: I believe it was the fifteenth of July.

ERNEST CALLENDER: How long have you been working on this case with Captain Barker?

CAPTAIN MELCHEN: Since the eighth of July.

ERNEST CALLENDER: YOU accompanied him from Nassau to Miami after your investigations together?

CAPTAIN MELCHEN: Yes.

ERNEST CALLENDER: When did you next see Captain Barker?

CAPTAIN MELCHEN: I did not see Barker again until we left Miami for Bar Harbor on Tuesday.

ERNEST CALLENDER: When did you reach Bar Harbor?

CAPTAIN MELCHEN: On Wednesday afternoon.

ERNEST CALLENDER: When was the funeral?

CAPTAIN MELCHEN: On Thursday morning.

ERNEST CALLENDER: Did you and Barker travel together?

CAPTAIN MELCHEN: Yes.

ERNEST CALLENDER: Did you discuss the case?

CAPTAIN MELCHEN: Yes.

ERNEST CALLENDER: Did you discuss fingerprints?

For a moment Melchen paused, staring owl-like through his thick glasses at his questioner. Then he said, "No, we did not discuss the fingerprints."

Jury and spectators stared at him in amazement. The Chief Justice had been making some notes. Now he looked up, frowning. Could he have heard aright? These two men had been together Wednesday and Thursday discussing the case and yet had not talked about the single — in fact, the only — piece of damning evidence they had discovered?

ERNEST CALLENDER: Would you say that the discovery of the fingerprint at the scene of the crime was a most vital piece of evidence?

CAPTAIN MELCHEN: Yes, I would say that.

ERNEST CALLENDER: When did you first hear that the fingerprint of the accused had been found at the scene of the crime?

CAPTAIN MELCHEN: I say definitely that the first time I heard this was at Bar Harbor on the afternoon of the funeral, when Barker told Lady Oakes.

ERNEST CALLENDER: YOU had travelled together all the way from Nassau on the tenth of July?

CAPTAIN MELCHEN: Yes.

ERNEST CALLENDER: You have been called in together and worked together?

CAPTAIN MELCHEN: Yes.

ERNEST CALLENDER: Barker must have known that the fingerprint found at the scene of the crime was the accused's. When would you say he knew that?

CAPTAIN MELCHEN: He must have known it before we left Miami.

ERNEST CALLENDER: He claims he knew it on the ninth of July, when the accused was arrested. He gave out an interview to the Press to that effect. And yet you are now willing to swear on your oath that you travelled with him from Nassau to Miami and from Miami to Bar Harbor — arriving there on the fourteenth — and yet in all this time Barker never mentioned this important fact to you?

CAPTAIN MELCHEN: Yes.

As Callender finished his cross-examination, Sir Oscar Daly put down the pen with which he had been making notes and addressed himself to the witness. "Captain Melchen, do you not now consider it strange that Captain Barker did not tell you about the fingerprint on your journey to Bar Harbor?"

Melchen nodded. "Yes," he agreed weakly. "I do now."

4

"The Defence Rests"

WHEN CAPTAIN MELCHEN took the stand on the following day, he announced that he wished to alter something else he had said earlier.

"I got a little confused yesterday," he admitted.

"Aren't you used to giving evidence in court?" the Chief Justice asked him.

"Yes," Melchen replied. "But not this long. I guess I was tired."

He now wished to say that Captain Barker and Major Herbert Pemberton, the Acting Deputy Commissioner of the Bahamas Police and head of their Criminal Investigation Department, had gone to the local Royal Air Force station, which possessed photographic facilities, and processed the print on the screen that was *thought* to be that of the accused. But they had not said why they thought it was Marigny's fingerprint.

THE CHIEF JUSTICE: That is very different from what you said yesterday. Don't you know the very great importance of this piece of evidence? Have you a good memory?

CAPTAIN MELCHEN: A fairly good memory.

THE CHIEF JUSTICE: Tell me, now that you are not tired, have you talked to Barker about this matter since you gave evidence yesterday?

CAPTAIN MELCHEN: No. I talked about it in the Attorney General's office with the Attorney General, in the presence of Captain Barker, after I gave evidence yesterday.

Melchen said that Captain Barker told him that the print was of what he called number ten digit, the fifth and little finger of the right hand. Melchen now said that in his opinion the first fire in Sir Harry Oakes's bedroom had been started by liquid thrown on the bed, not sprayed by the insecticide gun as had previously been suggested. He thought that whoever had thrown the liquid must have had a receptacle of his own in which to carry it.

"Was there any way of tracing the footprints of a man in the building or in the grounds after a rainy night?" the Chief Justice asked.

"There was no trace inside or outside the house of any person who might have thrown the liquid," Melchen replied.

"If you had been on the scene first," the Chief Justice continued, "would it have been possible to trace the footprints of a man going through the house on a rainy night?"

"There might have been footsteps on the wooden floors, footsteps on the rugs, that could have been processed. There might also have been impressions on the ground outside, but too many people had been there before I arrived."

"If a car left the highway, would it have been possible to trace the tracks of the tyres on a wet night?" Sir Oscar asked him.

"It would," Melchen agreed, "if the rain was not too heavy. If I had been informed of the alleged track of a car, it might have been possible to follow its course and ascertain whether it stopped at any particular place."

Captain James Otto Barker was the next Prosecution witness. He had seen how his colleague and Harold Christie had both wilted in the witness box, whether from tension, the humidity, or for reasons known only to themselves, and he had no intention of appearing at a disadvantage. He had eaten sparingly for days before he was due to appear, and on that morning he ate nothing at all and drank only a glass of fresh lime juice and soda.

Barker was physically much more impressive than Melchen; tall, grey-haired, broad-shouldered. And although both officers had frequently declared outside the court that they were of equal rank and importance, no one in court had any doubt that Barker was the stronger character, just as he was the stronger man. Barker was the leader; Melchen, the led.

Captain Barker now described his actions after arriving at Westbourne from Miami. He explained that he had taken the fingerprints of Mr. Christie, Dr. Quackenbush, and Major Pemberton. He then fingerprinted shelves, books, magazines, the door into Harold Christie's bedroom, and the windowpanes, but because of the humidity, he decided to postpone further work until the next day. Not until then did he "lift" the fingerprints from the screen.

Because of the fire, he felt certain that whoever had been in the room at the time of the murder must have burned hairs on his hands or head. Mr. Christie had no such burns, but Barker found traces of burned hair on the backs of both of Marigny's hands, as well as on his moustache and eyebrows.

After Marigny was arrested, Barker took nearly seventy prints from the screen, lifting them with Scotch tape and transferring them on to cards. Indeed, he took so many that he used up all the Scotch tape he had brought with him and had to use a patch of rubber for the last three. One of these was an impression that was similar to the fingerprint of the accused.

Godfrey Higgs now began to cross-examine, and under his searching questions, Captain Barker seemed increasingly uneasy. Gradually, his confidence started to wilt.

"The piece of rubber is not the best evidence," Godfrey Higgs began, "and I know of no case in which it has been produced in court before. The proper evidence would be to produce the print on the article on which it is found, and I submit that there is no print now on that screen. We have only this witness's word to suggest that the print in question came from that screen.

"We for the Defence are in a position to prove that a photograph of a lifted print cannot be produced as the original latent raised print of number ten digit of the accused, and that the best evidence is the screen itself, on which the print should be produced, and on which there is now no sign of a fingerprint."

THE CHIEF JUSTICE: You would not object to a photograph of a raised print on that screen?

GODFREY HIGGS: I would not, my lord, and this is precisely my point. By a "raised" print, I mean a print that has been dusted with powder and is visible. It can then be photographed *in situ*. The original fingerprint can be preserved by covering it with Scotch tape. The original fingerprint in this way is not destroyed. It is there for all to see, and, in addition, if need be and helpful, the photograph of the print *in situ* may be received.

THE CHIEF JUSTICE: Your point is that they should have powdered the print, left it there, and taken a photograph?

GODFREY HIGGS: That's it precisely, my lord.

THE CHIEF JUSTICE: What you say is that since they did not powder the print and leave it on the screen, it might be a forgery?

GODFREY HIGGS: That is exactly my fear and contention. Whether this print came from that point on the screen which the witness now describes depends upon the uncorroborated evidence of the witness himself.

THE CHIEF JUSTICE: It seems strange to me that no case on this exact point has come before the courts, either in England or America.

GODFREY HIGGS: I have searched the authorities, my lord, and assure the court that I can find no case in point.

THE CHIEF JUSTICE [to Captain Barker]: Why was the print not powdered, photographed, and left on the screen?

CAPTAIN BARKER: I did not have my fingerprint camera with me, so I had to lift the print from the screen.

THE CHIEF JUSTICE: And why did you not have your fingerprint camera with you?

CAPTAIN BARKER: As I was proceeding originally on the theory that the case was a suicide and did not involve any criminal act, I saw no need to bring the latent-fingerprint camera with me from Miami.

THE CHIEF JUSTICE: Would it not have been easy to powder the print and leave it there?

CAPTAIN BARKER: There is always a chance that it will be accidentally smudged or destroyed.

THE CHIEF JUSTICE: Could you not have had a latent-fingerprint camera flown over from Miami in a relatively short period of time?

CAPTAIN BARKER: Yes, I suppose that I could have.

THE CHIEF JUSTICE: So, by your process of lifting this print on the rubber matting, you deliberately destroyed the best evidence, which was the print itself?

CAPTAIN BARKER: This manner of lifting the print does destroy it, yes.

THE CHIEF JUSTICE: And a photograph of this print *in situ* taken with a latent-fingerprint camera would also have shown the background, so that there would be no doubt now where the print came from?

CAPTAIN BARKER: Well, the background doesn't always positively tell you exactly where the print came from.

THE CHIEF JUSTICE: I have no hesitancy in admitting that I am taken by surprise. It seems highly unlikely that no court has ever been called to pass upon this exact question in the past, but if Counsel assure me that they find no cases of precedent, I accept their representations. It occurs to me that I may well admit this print, Exhibit J, into evidence and let the jury decide whether it is legitimate and what weight to give it. If they have reason to doubt its genuineness, they can discard the print and, for that matter, the testimony of this witness altogether ...

So a print that may or may not have been found on the screen was admitted as evidence. The threat to Marigny, which had eased slightly after Melchen's confused testimony, now increased.

Next day, Captain Barker continued as a witness, and described how he had sent duplicates of the prints to Detective Frank Conway, Chief of the Identification Bureau in the New York City Police Department, to have his expert opinion on whether the print on the screen was made by Marigny's right little finger or not.

GODFREY HIGGS: You are not prepared to say that the fingerprint came off the area marked five in the second panel?

CAPTAIN BARKER: I am not.

GODFREY HIGGS: Do you know what portion of that top panel you took the print from?

CAPTAIN BARKER: I can only say with certainty that it came from the top portion.

Godfrey Higgs now invited the witness to walk over to the screen, where it stood in a corner of the court, and point out to the jury the part marked in blue pencil. Barker crossed the floor and stood for a moment, staring incredulously at the screen. Then he turned towards the Chief Justice, cleared his throat, and said: "I wish to inform the court that this blue line which I now see on the screen was not made by me."

GODFREY HIGGS: I beg your pardon?

CAPTAIN BARKER: There has been an effort to trace over a black line with blue pencil. That is not my work. I made the black line in the presence of the Attorney General in the police station on August the first.

No one spoke for nearly thirty seconds, and then Barker, with everyone staring at him in amazement, said hesitantly: "I now withdraw what I said about the alteration of the blue line. I find my initials where the blue line is."

"My sympathies to you, sir," said Sir Oscar. "I have often been confused in such a way myself."

Higgs was grateful for this quite unexpected — and inexplicable — mistake by the witness, and followed it by asking about the black and blue pencils.

GODFREY HIGGS: You have marked that area in two colours, in black pencil and blue?

CAPTAIN BARKER: The area was marked by me on two occasions, the first time in black and the second time in blue.

GODFREY HIGGS: And in what colour did you mark the spot where your initials are now visible?

CAPTAIN BARKER: That was in black.

GODFREY HIGGS: You have the date 7/9/43 marked in black pencil?

CAPTAIN BARKER: Yes, the American way of writing July ninth. That is the date on which I found the print. I made the inscription on August first at Nassau police headquarters. At the same time, I marked the figure five with a black pencil within the area marked on the black line.

GODFREY HIGGS: So, until August first, there was nothing to indicate where that exhibit came from?

CAPTAIN BARKER: Nothing except my memory.

GODFREY HIGGS: On August third, in the Magistrates' Court, you swore on your oath: "I marked the spot on the screen where latent impression of the print above referred to was found with pencil and it is now within the area marked with blue pencil and signified by the number five and initialled and dated 8/3/43."

CAPTAIN BARKER: Yes.

GODFREY HIGGS: Will you look again to your marking on the panel under the date 8/3/43? What colour does that now appear to be in?

CAPTAIN BARKER: I marked this area in blue in the Magistrates' Court, and that is where the print in question comes from.

GODFREY HIGGS: You were certain then that that print came from this area?

CAPTAIN BARKER: I certainly was.

GODFREY HIGGS: And why are you not certain now?

CAPTAIN BARKER: Detective Conway of the U.S. and I last Saturday examined the area marked five, but we could not find evidence of ridges which enabled us to say with certainty that that print came from within the marked area. Therefore, I had to confine myself to saying that it came from the top of the panel.

GODFREY HIGGS: You say you cannot say that this print, Exhibit J, came from that area number five on the screen?

CAPTAIN BARKER: I cannot say with certainty.

GODFREY HIGGS: Are you not saying positively that it did because you know it did *not* come from that area?

CAPTAIN BARKER: I doubt very seriously if it would be possible for the fingerprint to have come from area number five.

GODFREY HIGGS: Don't you think the Defence should have been told that you were going to move the location of the print?

THE CHIEF JUSTICE: I believe, sir, that that matter is for the Prosecution to say, rather than the witness.

GODFREY HIGGS: Very well, my lord. Thank you.

He turned to the witness. "Did you know that the Defence had also photographed area number five for experimental purposes?" he asked.

CAPTAIN BARKER: I did not know that.

GODFREY HIGGS: You made a trip to Nassau in September?

CAPTAIN BARKER: Yes, about this case. I came on a Saturday.

GODFREY HIGGS: I put it to you that this was two days after the Defence conducted these experiments.

CAPTAIN BARKER: That is a coincidence.

GODFREY HIGGS: I would say it was highly coincidental. Was it on that trip to Nassau that you realised that you could not get the print out of this area?

CAPTAIN BARKER: No.

GODFREY HIGGS: When did you first discover that Exhibit J could not have come from the area marked?

CAPTAIN BARKER: A week ago last Saturday.

GODFREY HIGGS: What made you re-examine the screen that day?

CAPTAIN BARKER: I knew that I would be called upon to produce the exact spot. Therefore, I examined the screen.

GODFREY HIGGS: Did Mr. Conway tell you that it could not come from here?

CAPTAIN BARKER: He agreed with me.

GODFREY HIGGS: Realising that you would be called upon to say where the exact spot was the print came from, you did not find out until two days before the trial began that you could not find the exact spot?

CAPTAIN BARKER: That is correct.

GODFREY HIGGS: When did you decide to change your evidence?

CAPTAIN BARKER: Immediately.

GODFREY HIGGS: Where do you say today that Exhibit J came from?

CAPTAIN BARKER: From the top portion of the end panel with the mark five, but I cannot locate it any closer.

GODFREY HIGGS: I believe you told us you have been with the Miami Police Department since 1925?

CAPTAIN BARKER: That is correct.

GODFREY HIGGS: What was your first assignment?

CAPTAIN BARKER: I was a motorcycle patrolman.

GODFREY HIGGS: And then what?

CAPTAIN BARKER: I became an emergency-call dispatcher.

GODFREY HIGGS: Are the duties of the Superintendent of the Bureau of Criminal Investigation in Miami the same as Captain of Detectives, except that the rank of captain gives the officer control over subordinate officers in examining crime scenes?

CAPTAIN BARKER: Yes, I think that is a correct explanation.

GODFREY HIGGS: You were assigned to the Bureau of Criminal Identification as a clerk in 1929?

CAPTAIN BARKER: Yes.

GODFREY HIGGS: How long did you remain in that post?

CAPTAIN BARKER: For five months.

GODFREY HIGGS: And what was your next assignment?

CAPTAIN BARKER: I was ordered back to uniform duty, and about a year later I was named to the position of Superintendent of the Identification Bureau.

GODFREY HIGGS: Is it customary in Miami to appoint superintendents with such meagre qualifications as you have described to us?

CAPTAIN BARKER: No, I do not think that it is.

GODFREY HIGGS: Why were you ordered back to uniform duty?

CAPTAIN BARKER: Because the work in the department had been brought up to date. There were only two of us, the boss and myself.

GODFREY HIGGS: And how long did you continue as Superintendent?

CAPTAIN BARKER: Until March, 1933.

GODFREY HIGGS: And what was your next assignment?

CAPTAIN BARKER: I was sent back to uniform patrol duty.

GODFREY HIGGS: And why was that?

CAPTAIN BARKER: It was claimed that I had been insubordinate to a superior officer.

GODFREY HIGGS: How long did you remain out of the Bureau of Identification at the time of this assignment?

CAPTAIN BARKER: For eleven months.

GODFREY HIGGS: Do you term yourself a fingerprint expert?

CAPTAIN BARKER: As the term applies, I think I am.

GODFREY HIGGS: Have you ever, in testifying, produced the object in court with the print on it?

CAPTAIN BARKER: Yes, when the objects were moveable.

GODFREY HIGGS: Would it not be highly advantageous to have the print in this courtroom today still on the screen?

CAPTAIN BARKER: Yes, I suppose it would.

GODFREY HIGGS: Have you ever introduced as evidence a lifted fingerprint without first having photographed the actual impression as it was found on the object?

CAPTAIN BARKER: Certainly, scores of times.

GODFREY HIGGS: Give me the names of the cases.

Barker paused for a moment, then shook his head. "I can't," he admitted.

GODFREY HIGGS: Why did you not introduce the screen in this court? Is it not moveable?

CAPTAIN BARKER: It can be moved.

Higgs now asked about the equipment the two captains had brought with them.

GODFREY HIGGS: Did you not come prepared to look for fingerprint evidence?

CAPTAIN BARKER: Yes.

GODFREY HIGGS: But you left your fingerprint camera behind?

CAPTAIN BARKER: Yes. I thought the kit I brought sufficient to take care of a murder case. The fingerprint camera would have been desirable, but I did not know the conditions.

GODFREY HIGGS: When you examined the screen on Thursday afternoon, did you not know that you were investigating a case of homicide at that time?

CAPTAIN BARKER: Yes.

GODFREY HIGGS: Could you not easily have got a camera flown over from Miami by Friday morning?

CAPTAIN BARKER: I believe I could.

GODFREY HIGGS: And you never made that effort?

CAPTAIN BARKER: No.

Godfrey Higgs picked up from the Registrar's desk a photograph of the area on the screen they had been discussing and showed it to the witness.

GODFREY HIGGS: I put it to you, sir, could not the camera that took that picture have been used to photograph the fingerprint *in situ* on the screen?

CAPTAIN BARKER: Yes, of course it could have.

GODFREY HIGGS: I tell you that the camera which took this photograph belongs to Mr. Stanley Toogood, a commercial photographer here in Nassau. Could you not have borrowed a camera from him to photograph the fingerprint on the screen before you lifted it?

CAPTAIN BARKER: Yes, I suppose I could.

GODFREY HIGGS: I suggest that there were numerous objects in that room that you did not process.

CAPTAIN BARKER: I suppose that is correct.

GODFREY HIGGS: If accused left a fingerprint on the screen, don't you think it likely that he might have left other prints in the room?

CAPTAIN BARKER: Yes, under ordinary conditions. But the very nature of the crime, in my opinion, would most likely prevent the assailant, in his emotion and hurry, from handling a lot of objects in the room. In this case, there was no necessity for the assailant to handle many objects, in my opinion.

Higgs now returned to Barker's statement that he had dusted various magazines in Sir Harry's bedroom for fingerprints.

"Did you think that the assailant was reading books and magazines in Sir Harry's room?" he asked.

CAPTAIN BARKER: I thought he might have touched one.

GODFREY HIGGS: But you didn't think he might have touched the headboard of Sir Harry's bed, since you didn't dust there?

CAPTAIN BARKER: He might have touched it. I did not dust the headboard of Sir Harry's bed. The heat from the fire would have destroyed the latent friction ridges.

GODFREY HIGGS: Why would a latent fingerprint be preserved on the screen, which is blistered due to heat, and not on the headboard of Sir Harry's bed?

CAPTAIN BARKER: I could tell by looking for certain that there would be no fingerprints left on the bed.

GODFREY HIGGS: And you did not dust the footboard of the bed either?

CAPTAIN BARKER: There is no footboard of the bed there.

Godfrey Higgs walked over to the Registrar's desk and picked up another photograph, this time of Sir Harry's bedroom. He held it up for Barker to see.

"What, pray, is that?" he asked him.

CAPTAIN BARKER: I see that the bed does have a footboard. I did not dust it.

GODFREY HIGGS: Well, why did you process in the downstairs powder room?

CAPTAIN BARKER: We could not exclude anything in an investigation of this type.

GODFREY HIGGS: But you did exclude a number of articles in Sir Harry's room?

CAPTAIN BARKER: In my opinion, yes.

GODFREY HIGGS: Had you excluded the possibility that accused might have had an accomplice?

CAPTAIN BARKER: I have not excluded the possibility of accomplices, nor have I advanced the theory that he had accomplices.

GODFREY HIGGS: In identifying a criminal, you require the rolled impressions of as many persons as possible who were at the crime scene?

CAPTAIN BARKER: Yes, for elimination purposes.

GODFREY HIGGS: And on Thursday, you only got the rolled impressions of Major Pemberton, Dr. Quackenbush, and Harold Christie?

CAPTAIN BARKER: That is correct, and the right hand of Sir Harry Oakes.

GODFREY HIGGS: Why did you not obtain the rolled fingerprint impressions of Dr. Fitzmaurice?

CAPTAIN BARKER: Because I was informed that he had not touched anything and had arrived only a short time before.

GODFREY HIGGS: Did you roll the fingerprints of Mrs. Henneage?

CAPTAIN BARKER: No, I did not.

GODFREY HIGGS: Why?

CAPTAIN BARKER: I was not told that she had been in the room.

GODFREY HIGGS: Did you roll the prints of Mrs. Kelly?

CAPTAIN BARKER: No.

GODFREY HIGGS: Why?

CAPTAIN BARKER: I was not told that she had been in the room.

GODFREY HIGGS: But you now know that she had been in the room several times?

CAPTAIN BARKER: I know it now, but I did not know it then.

GODFREY HIGGS: You did not find a single fingerprint of Harold Christie in that room?

CAPTAIN BARKER: No, I did not.

GODFREY HIGGS: You knew that Mr. Christie handled the glass and the Thermos?

CAPTAIN BARKER: I knew at the time.

GODFREY HIGGS: Is not a glass considered to be an excellent surface on which latent fingerprints can be found?

CAPTAIN BARKER: Yes, but I found no identifiable prints on the glass.

GODFREY HIGGS: Although Mr. Harold Christie and Sir Harry had been living there together for several days, you found no fingerprints of Mr. Christie?

CAPTAIN BARKER: No.

Barker now admitted he had not taken fingerprints of any of the policemen, or of Frank Christie, Mabel Ellis, the maid, or the Duke of Windsor, although all had visited Sir Harry's bedroom.

Now Higgs questioned him about the handprints on the walls. Barker thought they were the hands of an average adult of medium height. At Higgs's request, Marigny now stood up to his full six feet five. He held up his hands.

GODFREY HIGGS: Would you say these were long hands?

CAPTAIN BARKER: Yes, I would say that those are long hands.

GODFREY HIGGS: Did you see the bloody prints on the southern door of Mr. Christie's room?

CAPTAIN BARKER: Yes.

GODFREY HIGGS: Did you dust those prints?

CAPTAIN BARKER: Part of them.

GODFREY HIGGS: Was the blood moist or dry?

CAPTAIN BARKER: I'm not sure. It appeared to be dry.

GODFREY HIGGS: And doesn't dusting bloody prints obliterate them?

CAPTAIN BARKER: A portion of the marks on the south door of Mr. Christie's room were clearly bloody to the naked eye. Another portion appeared to be a delta formation, which is favourable for identifying fingerprints.

GODFREY HIGGS: And did you try to identify fingerprints on the door before you processed them?

CAPTAIN BARKER: Yes. I could not identify them.

GODFREY HIGGS: And so you then processed and obliterated them?

CAPTAIN BARKER: A portion of them.

GODFREY HIGGS: And did you dust all the marks on those doors?

CAPTAIN BARKER: I dusted the outside of the glass door, but I cannot recall dusting the screen door.

GODFREY HIGGS: I suggest that you examined both sides of the door and obliterated the marks.

CAPTAIN BARKER: If I had powdered around the area where the print was lifted, it might have been possible to discover whether the rest of the fingers of the hand touched the screen.

GODFREY HIGGS: Did you powder the area?

CAPTAIN BARKER: No.

GODFREY HIGGS: Prints left on the screen by others were destroyed by the humidity. If the accused were there that night, would not his be destroyed, too?

CAPTAIN BARKER: We were fortunate to have found it.

GODFREY HIGGS: I don't believe "fortunate" is the word. Let us say, "It was
a coincidence we found it." Do you recall seeing a bloody towel in Sir Harry's
bed?

CAPTAIN BARKER: Yes.

GODFREY HIGGS: Did this towel appear to be burned along the edge?

CAPTAIN BARKER: I would not say it was burned, but it appeared to have been subjected to heat. It should be examined under a microscope to give a definite answer.

GODFREY HIGGS: Have you made such an examination of the towel under the microscope?

CAPTAIN BARKER: No.

GODFREY HIGGS: This would not appear to you to be an important part of your investigation?

CAPTAIN BARKER: No, not at that time.

Captain Barker now accepted the Defence's invitation to show.the jury how he could lift fingerprints. He asked them to press their fingers on the table or the bars surrounding the jury box, and then lifted them with dusting powder and Scotch tape. Their fingerprints came up perfectly. Barker's competence here was in marked contrast to his apparent ineptitude at Westbourne, which is what Godfrey Higgs wished to demonstrate. He then turned to the question of the burned hair on Marigny's hands.

'I suggest that you never examined accused's arms." he said.

"That is correct," Barker agreed.

GODFREY HIGGS: Why didn't you show these hair burns to Major Pemberton, head of the local C.I.D.?

CAPTAIN BARKER: Our highest authority in the United States is the chief of police, and I therefore showed the hairs to Colonel Lindop.

GODFREY HIGGS: Colonel Erskine Lindop is now conveniently out of the colony?

The Chief Justice interrupted before Barker could answer. "This is not within the purview of knowledge of this witness," he said.

Godfrey Higgs bowed in acknowledgement and rephrased the question. "So the only person who can corroborate the fact that you even examined the accused's arms for burns is no longer available in the colony?" he asked. CAPTAIN BARKER: I don't know about that.

GODFREY HIGGS: Did you not take specimens of hairs from the accused's arms, from his beard, from his moustache, and from his hair?

CAPTAIN BARKER: Yes, I did.

GODFREY HIGGS: Was this so that these hairs could be examined under the microscope?

CAPTAIN BARKER: Yes, and to preserve them as evidence.

GODFREY HIGGS: And where are those hairs now? Do you propose to let us all see them here in open court?

CAPTAIN BARKER: The hairs were in Captain Melchen's custody.

GODFREY HIGGS: He has already testified, and there was no mention of the hairs. Do you know what happened to them?

CAPTAIN BARKER: If Captain Melchen does not have them, I don't know where they are. It could be that they have been misplaced.

GODFREY HIGGS: Would these hairs from the accused's body not be important evidence to you in this case?

CAPTAIN BARKER: No, not really. I saw them myself, so I know that he had varying degrees of burned hairs on his arms, face, and head.

GODFREY HIGGS: But we now have no other witness to corroborate what you tell us you saw.

CAPTAIN BARKER: I know what I saw, and I know that I saw burned hairs from his body, and I know that I clipped off a substantial number of these hairs.

THE CHIEF JUSTICE: Who was in charge of the investigation?

CAPTAIN BARKER: Captain Melchen and I were working together, but neither of us was under the other.

THE CHIEF JUSTICE: That's so! That's so!

GODFREY HIGGS: I put it to you that the accused told you he could not identify the shirt he was wearing that night.

CAPTAIN BARKER: That is untrue. I can remember his exact words: "It is very funny that I cannot find the shirt I wore."

GODFREY HIGGS: And isn't it very funny that you can remember those identical words but cannot remember his description of the shirt?

"It isn't very funny," retorted Barker sharply.

Godfrey Higgs now questioned him about Marigny's jacket and trousers, which had already been identified and which bore no trace of burns, and then turned to the discussion the two detectives had with Lady Oakes and Nancy Marigny at the family home in Bar Harbor, after the funeral of Sir Harry Oakes.

"Did you not tell Lady Oakes and Mrs. de Marigny, and whoever else was present, about finding a fingerprint of the accused on the screen?" he asked.

CAPTAIN BARKER: I believe I may have mentioned that we found such a fingerprint.

GODFREY HIGGS: And the funeral and your conversation were on July fifteenth?

CAPTAIN BARKER: Yes, that is correct.

GODFREY HIGGS: But you have told us not once, but several times, that you did not positively identify the accused's print, Exhibit J, until July nineteenth. How do you account for your statement to Lady Oakes and Mrs. de Marigny on the fifteenth that you had found a fingerprint of the accused on the screen? CAPTAIN BARKER: I knew of this legible print on the screen, and I thought it was the accused's.

GODFREY HIGGS: Yet you told Lady Oakes and Mrs. de Marigny *positively* that you had found the accused's fingerprint on the screen?

CAPTAIN BARKER: I believe I did.

GODFREY HIGGS: When did you first tell Captain Melchen that you had *positively* identified Exhibit J as the fingerprint of the accused's right little finger?

CAPTAIN BARKER: I believe he heard it for the first time when I told Lady Oakes and Mrs. de Marigny.

GODFREY HIGGS: I put it to you, if you were in a position to tell Lady Oakes *positively* that a fingerprint of the accused had been found on the screen, you must have made your identification before you left for Bar Harbor on July thirteenth.

CAPTAIN BARKER: Well, I wasn't entirely one hundred per cent positive at the time. I thought it was the accused's print, but I did not make sure until July nineteenth.

GODFREY HIGGS: Yet you told Lady Oakes and Mrs. de Marigny that you had positively found the accused's print on the screen. I put it to you that the only possible reasons that you could have made this allegation to them on July fifteenth was to prejudice them against the accused in order to arouse their hatred of him.

CAPTAIN BARKER: I would not say that.

GODFREY HIGGS: I suggest that you chose the psychological moment to prejudice Lady Oakes's mind against the accused.

CAPTAIN BARKER: I would not do that.

GODFREY HIGGS: After you returned to Miami from Nassau on your first trip, did you see and consult with Captain Melchen?

CAPTAIN BARKER: Yes.

GODFREY HIGGS: And you rode together on the plane to Bar Harbor from Miami?

CAPTAIN BARKER: Yes.

GODFREY HIGGS: Did you not think the discovery of the accused's fingerprints on the screen was an important item of evidence in this case?

CAPTAIN BARKER: Yes, I did.

GODFREY HIGGS: Do you think it was quite the proper thing for you not to mention this fingerprint to your co-worker, Captain Melchen, after you found it, until this conference with Lady Oakes and Mrs. de Marigny?

THE CHIEF JUSTICE [to Captain Barker]: Isn't it strange that you did not tell Captain Melchen about the fingerprint of the accused that you found on the screen?

Captain Barker did not reply.

THE CHIEF JUSTICE: You did not answer that question, Captain Barker.

Barker cleared his throat. "Yes, it is strange," he admitted.

GODFREY HIGGS: Did not His Royal Highness visit you at Westbourne and come to Sir Harry's room at the time you were processing for fingerprints?

CAPTAIN BARKER: Yes, he came up to see the crime scene.

GODFREY HIGGS: I do not think it would be proper for me to enquire as to why he came or what was said. While you were working on that screen on Friday morning, did not Captain Melchen bring the accused upstairs?

CAPTAIN BARKER: I understand he did.

GODFREY HIGGS: And did Captain Melchen take the accused into the north-western bedroom?

CAPTAIN BARKER: I understand he did.

GODFREY HIGGS: Did you not go to the door of that room and open it while they were there together?

CAPTAIN BARKER: I did not.

GODFREY HIGGS: I put it to you that you did, and that you asked Captain Melchen if everything was O.K.

CAPTAIN BARKER: I did not.

GODFREY HIGGS: I put it to you that Captain Melchen said, "Yes."

CAPTAIN BARKER: I did not even know he was in that room until the next day, I believe.

GODFREY HIGGS: Wasn't accused's latent print, Exhibit J, obtained from some object in that north-western bedroom?

CAPTAIN BARKER: Definitely not.

GODFREY HIGGS: But it was *after* he left that room that you claimed to have discovered his print, was it not?

CAPTAIN BARKER: Yes.

GODFREY HIGGS: I suggest that you and Captain Melchen deliberately planned to get the accused alone in order to get his fingerprints.

CAPTAIN BARKER: We did not.

GODFREY HIGGS: I suggest that Exhibit J did not come from that screen.

CAPTAIN BARKER: It did come from that screen. From the number five panel.

GODFREY HIGGS: You can show me one of that scroll-work from the screen on Exhibit J, can you?

CAPTAIN BARKER: I cannot.

GODFREY HIGGS: Do you usually withhold a lift? You never told Captain Melchen about it, did you, until the day at Bar Harbor?

CAPTAIN BARKER: No, I did not.

GODFREY HIGGS: This is the most outstanding case in which your expert assistance has ever. been requested, is it not?

Captain Barker nodded. "It has developed into that," he agreed.

Godfrey Higgs now passed to the witness photographs of fingerprints that Professor Keeler had lifted as an experiment, to demonstrate how it could (and should) be done. The professor had removed them so skilfully that marks of the lacquered figures on the Chinese screen showed clearly behind each fingerprint. Yet in the case of the single fingerprint that Barker insisted he lifted from the screen, no background whatever was visible. That print was clear and clean — as it would be if it had been lifted not from the thickly painted screen but from a smooth surface.

Melchen was at the back of the court during this demonstration. Suddenly, he stood up, pushed his way hurriedly past others, and rushed out into the square, which was still packed with people hoping to hear something through an open window. They now saw the Chief of the Homicide Bureau of the Miami Police Department lean against the warm wall of the courthouse and be violently sick. In between his spasms, he gasped angrily: "The bastard! Wait till I get him back in Miami!"

People stared in surprise at the scene. They did not know what Melchen feared Marigny might reveal when he gave evidence.

Meanwhile, in the court, Godfrey Higgs had a further question to ask Captain Barker.

"May I suggest that your desire for personal gain and notoriety has caused you to sweep aside truth? I put it to you, sir, you have fabricated evidence."

"I emphatically deny that," Barker retorted.

Lady Oakes now gave evidence. She was tall, almost matronly in appearance, and spoke in a quiet voice. Now and then she paused, too overcome by emotion to continue. She described how she had first learned of the marriage of her daughter Nancy to Alfred de Marigny after their wedding in the previous May. Her daughter was then exactly eighteen years and two days old.

Marigny had not told either Lady Oakes or her husband of his intention to marry Nancy, and neither of them knew that marriage was even being discussed.

"We were fearfully upset," she admitted. "We did not break with her. We had to make the best of a bad situation. After all, she was our daughter."

Shortly afterwards, the newly married couple stayed with Lady Oakes at Bar Harbor, and her other children liked Marigny and went sailing with him. After two weeks, he and Nancy went to New York and then on to Mexico, where Nancy became very ill with typhoid fever. Lady Oakes was informed that she needed blood transfusions, and she and her husband travelled to Mexico in the middle of August and stayed there until October to be near the hospital where their daughter was a patient.

Lady Oakes supplied blood for three blood transfusions for her, and Marigny, who, she agreed "was extremely attentive," gave two more. Nancy later received two further transfusions from a blood donor. Lady Oakes also gave money to Marigny to pay for the medical expenses. He offered to return £3,000 of this to her, but she refused to accept it, because she believed that the money he was going to give her was not his but belonged to his former wife.

Towards the end of 1942, Sir Harry and Lady Oakes were in Palm Beach with Nancy when she told them that she was pregnant.

"After much discussion, it was decided to terminate that pregnancy on account of her health."

Nancy did not wish to tell her husband of this decision herself, so she asked her doctor to inform him. Marigny at once flew to Palm Beach and took a room in the hospital next to hers. Nancy Marigny then underwent an operation to her mouth as well as an abortion, and her father was very concerned about her state of health. So was Freddie Marigny.

"I felt how any mother must feel under those circumstances," Lady Oakes told the court. "When we left Mexico I told him to take the utmost care of Nancy. There was no question what my meaning was."

The implication was plain: she expected them to refrain from what had earlier been referred to as "marital relations," which to everyone in the court meant sex.

Largely as a result of Marigny's having made his wife pregnant, and of a letter Nancy wrote to her mother, begging her family to accept her husband and accusing the family's American lawyer, William Foskett, of influencing them against him, relations between Marigny and his wife's parents became extremely cool. In fact, Marigny never stayed in their house again.

Walter Foskett next took the stand. He was a middle-aged lawyer who had acted for Sir Harry for the previous thirteen years. Mail addressed to Sir Harry or Lady Oakes was generally sent to his office in Palm Beach when they were out of the States. Foskett would open these letters and forward on any that he thought they should see.

He told the court that after Nancy Marigny's illness in Mexico, he had opened a letter addressed to Lady Oakes from Marigny's former wife, Ruth, in which she made a number of accusations against her ex-husband. He did not forward this letter, because the allegations had shocked him. When Marigny and Nancy came to Palm Beach for her operations, Marigny called on him in his office to discuss the rift that was developing between himself and Sir Harry.

According to Foskett, Marigny told him that he felt he was being treated with indifference and hostility; and as Nancy's husband, he believed he was entitled to be accepted as a member of the Oakes family. Marigny said that he would be very grateful if Foskett could use his influence with Sir Harry to do anything to remedy the unhappy situation.

Foskett told him that this was not a legal problem, but a personal one, and he took the opportunity of their talk to express his own disapproval of the marriage of a girl of eighteen to a twice-divorced man of nearly twice her age.

He then told Marigny that he had received a letter from his ex-wife, but he did not let him read it. Marigny replied that Ruth was jealous of Nancy and would do anything she could to injure him. He said that she had frequently told lies about him in the past, and he was sure that if she made serious allegations against him now, she was telling lies again.

Foskett waited for a further six months after their discussion before he sent the letter on to Lady Oakes. It reached her only days before Sir Harry's murder.

Marigny now went into the witness box.

For weeks he had sat in the dock, a saturnine figure, with a black policeman on either side of him. For much of this time, he chewed a match, on several occasions almost swallowing it and choking with amazement or disbelief as allegations about his character, his intentions, his motives, were discussed. Sometimes he caught his wife's eye and smiled or grimaced at her.

Jurors and spectators now watched in fascination as Marigny's tall, slim figure towered above the sides of the box. He was pale but composed and wore a lightweight suit, a cream shirt, and a dark tie. When he spoke, many were surprised that his French accent was so strong. It had been barely noticeable in conversation, but now that he spoke slowly and deliberately, so that his voice would carry across the court, it seemed almost like a stage accent. He sounded as he looked, very much a foreigner.

He said that when he married Nancy Oakes, he had nearly £8,000 in his personal bank account and owned property in Nassau, as well as about a hundred acres with two houses at Governor's Harbour in Eleuthera. He and Sir Harry and Lady Oakes had been on good terms until after Nancy's operation in Palm Beach. Afterwards, he saw Mr. Foskett to ask for his help in re-establishing friendly relations. Mr. Foskett, however, was hostile, and told him that this was his own business.

Marigny had for some time suffered from sore throats, and since his wife was already in hospital he decided to have his tonsils removed. Accordingly, he took a room adjoining hers in the same hospital. He arrived one night, in preparation for the operation on the following morning, and was immediately telephoned angrily by Sir Harry Oakes.

"He told me to 'get the hell out of that room,' and added, 'If you don't get out, I'll come and kick you out.' "

Nancy Marigny had overheard part of this conversation and was upset by it. To save further family friction, Marigny cancelled his operation and left the hospital. Next morning he spoke to Dr. Sayad, who was his wife's specialist, and told him that, for the time being, Mrs. Marigny did not wish to see any visitors, especially her mother and father, because a visit from them would only upset her. She had already told the nurse this herself, and Marigny wanted Dr. Sayad to confirm the instructions.

Dr. Sayad replied that he could not agree, and if Mrs. Marigny's parents arrived, he would allow them to see her.

"I was annoyed with Dr. Sayad," Marigny explained to the court, "and told him that if he insisted on allowing Sir Harry to come and disturb my wife, I would have to lock,Sir Harry out of the room. I did not tell him I was going to 'crack Sir Harry's^ head.' "

When Nancy Marigny recovered, she telephoned to her parents, and they visited her. Relations by then between Lady Oakes and Marigny were not exactly strained — "cold" was how he described them — but gradually Sir Harry and he became more friendly.

"Sir Harry was very impulsive and moody and would be friendly one day, but not the next."

Marigny explained that he did not wish to accept the Jones property from his father-in-law, because it was sixteen miles out of Nassau, and if he took it over, he and his wife would rarely see their friends. A great deal of money would also be required to develop the land, which was all bush. He had discussed another possibility with Sir Harry, involving several waterfront buildings, which he would have liked to acquire, but someone else had prior consideration there.

THE CHIEF JUSTICE: At this time, you would not have turned down any offer that was acceptable from a business point of view?

ALFRED DE MARIGNY: Oh, no. There was no animosity between us. The proposals were considered solely on business grounds.

In mid-March, Marigny and his wife went to Governor's Harbour and returned on March 25. On the following morning, Sir Harry and Sydney, his eldest son, came to see them at their house in Victoria Avenue. Marigny and his wife had received an invitation to a cocktail party at Government House on March 27, but they had not accepted.

"When Sir Harry came to see us," Marigny recalled, "he spoke of the Duke having invited us. After the cocktail party, Sir Harry and Sydney came to dinner with us at my house in Victoria Avenue. That night, Sir Harry was rather rude to everybody. He left around ten o'clock and I walked with him to the car. He told me that Nancy and I were a couple of asses for not going to the cocktail party and that we had made things very difficult for him and Sydney and Lady Oakes.

"He said: 'If you don't go out and meet people, you don't get anywhere... As far as I am concerned, Nancy's going to get nothing from me at any time.' To emphasise it, he spelled the word NOTHING in a very loud voice.

"When we got by the door of the car he told me, 'You have written a filthy letter to Lady Oakes. Your lawyer has done the same thing, too. And if ever any of you two repeat such things, I will have both of you whipped. As far as that girl in your house is concerned [referring to Nancy], she has caused enough trouble to her mother, and I don't want to have anything to do with you.'

"He was so angry I thought he was going to hit me. I told him, 'Sir Harry, you must either be drunk or insane.' Then I left him. He shouted, 'Sydney!' and they both left.

"March twenty-ninth was my birthday. That morning I received some glassware from Lady Oakes as a present. I had a party that night. Sydney was there. The party broke up about twelve o'clock, and Nancy asked Sydney if he would like to stay the night. At that time there were two beds in a guest room.

"About four o'clock in the morning there was a terrible pounding on the front door and somebody was shouting: 'Open the door or I'm going to break it down!'

"When I opened the door, Sir Harry walked in and asked me where Sydney was. I took him to the guest room. He pulled Sydney out by his foot and told him: 'Get your clothes and get the hell out of this house.' They left. Since that morning, the thirtieth of March, I never spoke to Sir Harry again."

Marigny had mentioned this incident to Newell Kelly and added jokingly, "If Sir Harry doesn't leave me alone, I'll introduce my big foot to him."

On the evening of July 6, Marigny met Mrs. Ainsley and Mrs. Clarke in the bar of the Prince George Hotel, through Mr. Freddie Cerretta, an American engineer employed on airfield construction, whom he had known for some time. He invited them all to dine with him, with several other guests, on the following evening, the seventh. That morning, he started work at half-past six and took three hundred chickens, hatching in an incubator in his garage, out to his farm. From the farm he telephoned Harold Christie at around nine-thirty, talked business briefly — he was still operating his farm without an official permit, and wondered when he would receive it — and asked Mr. Christie to join them for dinner that evening.

"Mr. Christie told me he could not come, because he was busy and had an engagement with Sir Harry and was staying with him that night."

That afternoon, Marigny entered his yacht in a race, returned home for a bath, changed his clothes, and then collected Mrs. Clarke and Mrs. Ainsley from the cottages they rented beyond Westbourne. He had intended to serve dinner outside, but changed this plan because of the mosquitoes. His dining room was lighted by three candles with hurricane shades, and two candelabra

with six candles in each.

"I lit the ones on the right with my right hand, the ones on the left with my left hand," he explained.

"I use either hand because I am ambidextrous. When I lit the candles in the hurricane shades, I burned my hand."

The party lasted until half-past twelve. Among the guests was Georges's current girl friend, Betty Roberts, an usherette in the Savoy cinema. Marigny drove Mrs. Clarke and Mrs. Ainsley home, and invited Mr. Cerretta to accompany him, but he did not wish to do so. Marigny left his house at about one o'clock. On the way, Mrs. Clarke mentioned that it must be one-twenty or one-twenty-five. Marigny looked at his own watch and the car clock, which both gave the time as one-five. Mrs.. Clarke then admitted that her watch was fast. He was home again by about one-forty.

At three o'clock he was awakened by Georges's Maltese cat, Grisou, which came into his bedroom. At the same time, he heard Georges's car leave the driveway, and thought that he must be driving Betty Roberts home. As Georges liked his cat to be in his room, Marigny waited until he heard him return, about fifteen minutes later.

"I called to him. He came into my room and took the cat out."

Marigny suffered from indigestion and woke up some time later to take a Maclean's Stomach Powder in a glass of water. At six-thirty, he checked the incubator to make sure it was working, had his usual breakfast of Ovaltine and dry toast — toasted in the oven — and drove out to his chicken farm.

Just after nine o'clock he went to the police station to ask about the necessity of reregistering a car he had converted into a truck. He was certainly not there at seven-thirty. At half-past ten, he passed Mr. Anderson in the street, and Anderson told him that Sir Harry had died.

"He did not look very serious, so I said, 'You're kidding me?' He said, 'No. I'm serious. I've had it confirmed by Dr. Fitzmaurice.' "

Marigny asked Anderson whether he knew how Sir Harry died. Had he suffered a stroke, "or something like that?" Anderson replied that he did not know. They both went to tell Georges, who at once said, "Let's go and see what happened."

They then realised that they were not sure in which house Sir Harry had been staying, for he owned several on the island. As they drove past Westbourne, they saw a number of cars parked in the drive, so they went inside. Mrs. Kelly was there, with Frank Christie, who explained that Sir Harry had been found dead with a wound in his head, and badly burned. Marigny sent a telegram to his wife, with the news that her father had died suddenly, and then drove back home with Anderson, who stayed to have lunch with him.

In the afternoon, they returned to Westbourne, where Captain Melchen and Captain Barker said that they wished to question him. With a magnifying glass they examined his head, moustache, and beard, his hands and the lower part of his forearms. They then asked him to leave the room for a few moments while they discussed the matter.

They called him back and declared that he had areas of burned hair on his hands and face. How could he account for this? Marigny replied that he smoked half a dozen cigars a day, and since the climate was damp, he frequently had to relight them. Melchen agreed that this could account for burns on his moustache and his beard. But what about his hands?

Marigny explained that he had a gas stove at home, where he sometimes did the cooking — and made toast — and he also had an open fire at the chicken farm, where he boiled drums of water to scald chickens.

The two detectives then wanted to know what clothes he had been wearing the night before, and went back with him to his house. There, they examined a number of cream-coloured shirts in the laundry basket. Marigny explained that he had worn one of these shirts on the previous night, but he could not say which one, since he had so many — possibly a dozen — of the same colour and style.

Before they left, Marigny was asked if he would mind having Lieutenant Douglas as his guest for the night. He agreed. Douglas complained that this was to have been his night off, and instead he had to spend it watching Marigny. Next morning, they returned to Westbourne. On the way, Douglas remarked: "What boils me is that they're making all this fuss over Sir Harry because he had plenty of money. If it was some poor coloured fellow in Grant's Town, I just would be asked to go and take information about it, and that's all there would be to it."

Marigny added: "I know Douglas very well, and we talked about the trouble Sir Harry and I had had about Ruth de Marigny. I never said to Douglas, That guy Sir Harry, the old bastard, should have been killed anyway.'

"I never used the words 'guy' or 'bastard' at all. I remember this expression being used by Douglas. He seemed to be dissatisfied."

Marigny did not know at that stage how Sir Harry had been killed, and he asked Douglas whether he had been shot or stabbed. Douglas said that he did not know, either, so Marigny, making conversation, asked him, "If they can't find the weapon, can the police proceed with the case?"

Douglas replied that they could.

They then discussed another murder case, in which someone had been arrested purely on circumstantial evidence. Marigny was of the opinion that under French law this could not have happened. Douglas replied that under British law it could. They walked up and down the beach for some time, but the sandflies became troublesome, so they went into the house. It was then about eleven o'clock. Melchen took him upstairs on his own, into Sir Harry's bedroom, and asked him whether he knew Mr. Christie and whether Christie was indebted to Sir Harry or had any grievance against him. Marigny replied that Christie was one of his best friends, and also one of Sir Harry's best friends, and he should ask Christie himself for any information.

Melchen then pointed his finger at him and asked, "You're *sure* you didn't come to Westbourne last night? Didn't you want to get even with

Sir Harry, and came here to see him and had an argument with him and hit him?"

Marigny replied, "If I wanted to talk to Sir Harry, I would do that in the day, not in the middle of the night."

"You were up that evening about three o'clock and your friend [meaning Georges] was up, too," retorted Melchen. "How do you account for that?"

"I might get up in the middle of the night but not to kill anybody."

"You were seen coming into Westbourne that night," said Melchen.

"I defy you or anybody in Nassau to say any such thing," Marigny replied vehemently. Melchen then offered Marigny a packet of Lucky Strike cigarettes.

They were both sitting at a table with a bottle of water and two glasses on a tray, and Melchen asked Marigny to pour a glass of water for him. Marigny did so and at the same time poured another for himself.

Captain Barker now put his head around the door and asked, "Is everything O.K.?"

Melchen replied, "Yes."

As Marigny described this incident, many recalled that when Professor Keeler had demonstrated to the jury how to lift a fingerprint from the Chinese screen, the lacquered, scrolled background of the screen showed clearly. In contrast, the print that the American detectives claimed they had taken from the same screen was clear and clean, as though lifted from a totally smooth surface.

Was it not possible, in the light of Marigny's account, that in fact it *had* come from such a smooth background: either the glossy wrapper on the cigarette packet that Melchen had handed to him, or the glass of water that Melchen had asked Marigny to pour for him?

Marigny said that when he came downstairs, Mr. Anderson was still there with his wife, so he drove them back to his home, and they stayed to lunch. Afterwards, Mrs. Anderson left, but Anderson returned with Marigny to Westbourne at around four o'clock. Melchen took Marigny into the empty living room.

"Have you anything more to say?" he asked him.

Marigny shook his head. "I don't know what else you want me to say," he replied, puzzled.

"You don't?" said Melchen. "Well, I want to warn you about one thing. In this case, nobody is too big or too small to be arrested, and even after we've gone away, we'll come back and keep investigating the case."

"That's all right with me," said Marigny, not fully understanding the significance of the conversation.

That same evening he was arrested and charged with the murder of his father-in-law.

As he finished his testimony, Godfrey Higgs asked him two final questions.

"Did you go to Westbourne on the night of July seventh or the early morning of July eighth?"

MARIGNY: I did not.

GODFREY HIGGS: *Did* you kill Sir Harry Oakes?

MARIGNY: No, sir!

Georges Visdelou, still described as "Marquis," came into the witness box, looking not as his friends knew him — urbane and sophisticated — but like a nervous, worried man. The transformation was as surprising as it had been with Harold Christie.

He agreed that he had spoken to Marigny at one-thirty on the night of the murder, and had gone to Marigny's room and taken Grisou, his cat, back to his own bedroom at three o'clock in the morning.

ALFRED ADDERLEY: Did you go to the accused's room for the cat?

GEORGES VISDELOU: I may have done, but I cannot recall if I did.

ALFRED ADDERLEY: If you had done so, would you say so?

GEORGES VISDELOU: Yes.

Alfred Adderley picked up several sheets of paper, clipped together, and held them up.

"Do you see these five sheets?" he asked Visdelou.

"Yes."

"Do you see your signature on them?"

"Yes."

"I shall read the statement to you," Alfred Adderley continued. "It says: 'I did not see de Marigny from eleven P.M. until ten A.M. the following morning.' Is that what it says?"

Georges Visdelou nodded nervously, face pale, lips dry. "Yes," he said.

From the dock, Marigny stared in horror at his friend. It did not matter now that Captain Barker and Captain Melchen had been totally discredited, for here, in a written statement, Georges was denying he had seen him throughout the night of the murder.

ALFRED ADDERLEY: Do you not think it strange that you now contradict this statement you made when the facts were fresh in your mind?

Georges Visdelou agreed. "I cannot understand it, Mr. Adderley."

During the lunch recess, Higgs and Callender examined the document. Why had it not been released to them before? Both agreed that there could only be one reason: something was wrong with it. But what? Could it be a phrase, even a single word that did not quite ring true, that could conceivably have two meanings? It took them all that lunch recess to find what this was.

In the afternoon it was Ernest Callender's turn to question Georges Visdelou.

"I shall read the statement to you," he said." 'I and my girlfriend left and went upstairs. I was not feeling in a party mood. About one-thirty A.M. de Marigny came to my apartment door and asked if he could take my girlfriend home. I replied, "No." ' Is that what it says?"

GEORGES VISDELOU: Yes.

The Chief Justice asked to see the papers. They were handed up to him and he read them quickly and then called to Mr. Adderley.

"You gave me and the jury to understand that Mr. de Visdelou's statement was a contradiction of his evidence," he said. "What we have here puts a completely different light on the matter."

"If you will pardon me, Your Honour," Alfred Adderley replied, "I was showing that the witness stated he did not *see* de Marigny from midnight on. The statement just read by my learned friend does not contradict that. The statement merely says that the witness *talked* to the accused."

"I don't appreciate the fineness of the distinction when a man's life is at stake, Mr. Adderley," said the Chief Justice sternly. "The impression you tried to convey in your examination was that the witness had said in that statement that he had neither seen *nor* talked to the accused from midnight until ten the next morning."

So now, after months of waiting and weeks in court, Marigny's life pivoted on the jury's interpretation of one word.

Hundreds of people crowded the square outside the court, straining their ears at the open windows, when Nancy Marigny appeared as the final witness for her husband. Wearing a white hat, a black suit with white polka dots, and white gloves, she was an appealing figure, composed but pale.

Godfrey Higgs asked her what reason she could give for the coolness that had arisen after her marriage between her and her parents.

NANCY MARIGNY: I attribute it solely to the attitude of my parents. My husband and I tried hard to change that attitude, and we had still hoped to change it.

GODFREY HIGGS: Did you at any time ever hear your husband make any expression of hatred toward your father?

NANCY MARIGNY: No, never. He never spoke ill of my father at all. When the differences and disagreeable episodes occurred, he was always sympathetic towards my father, attributing it to his age and health.

GODFREY HIGGS: At any time during your married life did the accused ever try to obtain money from you?

NANCY MARIGNY: No, never.

GODFREY HIGGS: Did the accused at any time make any offer to you in connection with any money you had?

NANCY MARIGNY: No. I invested three thousand pounds sterling in the chicken farm. This was from my savings account, and I made my own decision to make the investment after he and I talked it over. I became half owner in the chicken farm. It was not a loan of money to him.

GODFREY HIGGS: What money did you and your husband use to live on after your marriage?

NANCY MARIGNY: He had some money of his own, several thousand pounds. I had some savings funds. My mother gave us some money for the Mexican honeymoon trip. We were not destitute or dependent upon my parents or anyone else. We had planned to make our own way, and the chicken farm appeared to be a profitable enterprise.

She was then asked about the visit the two American detectives paid to her mother's home at Bar Harbor after her father's funeral.

GODFREY HIGGS: Did Captain Melchen and Captain Barker tell you anything about who murdered your father?

NANCY MARIGNY: Yes. Both on the telephone and at Bar Harbor, they gave me to understand it was my husband.

GODFREY HIGGS: Did they tell you why they thought it was your husband?

NANCY MARIGNY: Yes, they said there could be no doubt about it. His fingerprints had been found on the screen next to my father's bed.

GODFREY HIGGS: Did they say fingerprint or fingerprints?

NANCY MARIGNY: They definitely said fingerprints. I understood there were several, or many, of my husband's fingerprints on the screen.

GODFREY HIGGS: Did they imply any doubt as to whether these fingerprints had positively been identified as your husband's?

NANCY MARIGNY: There was no doubt whatsoever. As a matter of fact, they assured me that the prints positively were those of my husband.

The Attorney General now read to the court a letter Nancy Marigny had written to her mother on May 26, about five weeks before her father's murder. In this she said that she would be returning £2,000 worth of British War Loan Bonds that her mother had bought her.

... Under the circumstances, it is impossible for me to accept from either you or Father such gifts that have the smell of charity to a poor relative.

At the time that you and Father left Mexico, you both seemed to hold my husband in high esteem. In fact, you both took him into your confidence in many matters of a personal nature, indeed, much more so than you had ever done with your own child.

As things were then, even you were very happy and looking forward to a normal family life of trust and good fellowship. However, since our return from Mexico, the picture has changed erratically. You choose to believe the insinuations of third parties, in preference to inquiring frankly the truth and facts of certain matters of your own people ...

When Father came to Nassau with Sydney he was most insulting in his behaviour towards us. At that time, he expressed in the most forceful terms his desire for us to sever further connections with the Oakes family. Painful as it was, I was forced to choose between my parents and my husband. Under the circumstances, there could be no question in my mind as to where my decision lay.

For this wholly unnecessary and unhappy situation, I place the responsibility on Walter Foskett, who has been, I believe, deliberately misguiding your judgement. His conduct throughout has been most unethical... I want you to know that both of us can forgive this whole painful affair if you and Father can wash away your prejudices against my husband, and you can regard him with respect and trust to which he is entitled. Otherwise, I can never again feel any love or respect for you or Father or accept any of the natural advantages usually given to children by their parents.

Sincerely, I am praying that you will not misunderstand the plain language of this letter. It may appear hard at first reading, but no insulting or bitter feeling is intended. It is simply the bare truth as seen through my eyes. I pray God that you will also see the truth and justice in these statements.

Your loving daughter, Nancy

The Attorney General suggested that if this letter did not change the situation between her husband and her parents, then she was prepared to break off relations with her parents.

NANCY MARIGNY: I was afraid that I probably would have to sever relations with my father and mother, but I was hoping that they would change their attitude.

THE ATTORNEY GENERAL: After you wrote that letter to your mother, did either your mother or father send you any communication in an effort on their part to make friends?

NANCY MARIGNY: I did not receive any communication whatsoever again from either my father or my mother.

THE ATTORNEY GENERAL: I take it then that you were cut off by your parents?

NANCY MARIGNY: I do not consider myself cut off by them or from them. We just had no more relations afterwards.

The foreman of the jury now asked a question: "Did Mrs. Marigny know whether her parents had changed their wills in February?"

NANCY MARIGNY: They might have, but I did not know anything about it.

THE JURY FOREMAN: Did you ever discuss the question of your parents' wills with your husband?

NANCY MARIGNY: No, never. That would not be a proper subject for us to talk about.

As Nancy Marigny stepped down from the witness box, Godfrey Higgs turned to the Chief Justice and bowed.

"The Defence rests, my lord," he said.

The hands of the courtroom clock pointed to five-twenty-five as the jury filed out of the court and went upstairs to consider their verdict. The case had lasted for twenty-five days. How long would they take to pronounce Marigny guilty or innocent?

Outside, policemen linked arms to hold back the huge crowds that had poured into the square beneath the silk cotton tree to await the verdict. Every approach road was packed. Now, the spectacle was all but over. How would the last act end — with a hanging or an acquittal? Bookmakers took huge bets on both possibilities.

Lady Oakes did not wait for the result of the trial; she had already left Nassau for the United States.

Mrs. Nancy Marigny waited for the verdict in a room on the second floor of the police station, looking out over the familiar courtyard and the cotton-wood tree towards Bay Street and Rawson Square and the harbour.

Marigny was in another room in the same building, forcing himself to make conversation with policemen as minutes ticked by at the pace of hours. As he heard the excited hum of the hundreds of people outside, he remembered a French proverb from his school days that now seemed apt: *"Les gens brulent ceux qu'ils ont adores et adorent ceux qu'ils ont brules"* ("The crowd loves to burn what it adores and adores what it burns").

Questions chased answers around his exhausted mind.

Why had Barker and Melchen perjured themselves in a desperate attempt to convict him of a crime they must know he had not committed?

Who had deliberately posted Colonel Erskine Lindop away from Nassau, virtually on the eve of the trial, so that he could not give evidence in his favour?

Why should Captain Sears insist he had seen Harold Christie being driven through Nassau in his car on the night of the murder — when Christie just as vehemently denied he had ever left Westbourne? Why did Christie also deny he had told Marigny he was staying that night in Sir Harry Oakes's house?

Although the Chief Justice called before the court the two Bahamian police constables who had sworn false evidence about the time

Melchen had taken Marigny to Sir Harry's bedroom, no one asked who had suggested — or, more likely, ordered — that they tell lies on oath. Was this because no one cared — or was the question deliberately not asked because the answer might prove embarrassing?

But of all the unanswered questions, three concerned Marigny most gravely.

Why had he been deliberately selected to stand trial for the murder of his father-in-law on false and manufactured evidence?

Who *had* killed Sir Harry Oakes? And for what conceivable reason?

5

A Proposition is Proposed

ERLE STANLEY GARDNER, the distinguished advocate who created the fictional character Perry Mason, part lawyer, part detective, reported the trial for an American newspaper group. During the proceedings, a police officer showed him over Sir Harry's house, and Gardner saw the table where Sir Harry and his guests had played Chinese chequers, and suggested that this had not been used since then.

"I'm sorry to spoil that story," replied the police officer, "but our policemen have been playing chequers here for several months."

"Don't let that worry you," replied Gardner cheerfully. "Facts should never spoil a good story."

Bearing this half jocular remark in mind, but using facts since made available in Washington and elsewhere, and adding some conjectures, a possible answer emerges to the question: Who killed Sir Harry Oakes?

First, a link appears between his murder and the loss of the French liner *Normandie* in New York docks 18 months earlier. On Monday, February 9, 1942, *Normandie* suddenly began to burn fiercely at her pier off West 48th Street. Steam from fire-hoses spewing jets of water on her red-hot hull hung in the air like bitter, acrid fog. Then, at precisely twenty-five minutes to three in the following morning, under a blaze of searchlights that transformed the curving cascades of fireboats' hoses into rainbows, *Normandie* slowly turned over and sank at her moorings.

For more than twelve hours she had blazed furiously, incandescent with heat, a floating iron torch over a thousand feet long. Smoke was so thick that throughout the daylight hours street lamps were kept burning, and at noon fire engines needed headlights to find a way through the gloom.

Firemen with the most modern equipment from twenty-four New York stations had proved powerless against the fury of the fire. Mobile water towers and cranes directing high-pressure hoses from three fire-fighting tugs, pouring millions of tons of water on the blaze, had almost as little effect. As fast as they subdued one part of the inferno, another erupted elsewhere. Alloy superstructure buckled, and metal ran liquid into the boiling sea. Finally, the weight of thousands of tons of water within the ship made her capsize. Her own gross bulk, and not the efforts of the firemen, finally defeated the blaze, and *Normandie* lay like a bloated sea-beast, her carbuncled, rusting hull green with slime beneath the lights, the rims of her three funnels only inches above the water.

As the crowds began to drift away, many recalled how, seven years earlier, *Normandie* had arrived in New York on her maiden voyage. Everything about her, even the drama of these final hours, seemed cast on an heroic scale. One of the world's largest liners, she had cost *$56* million to build in 1935, an unprecedented sum, more than the annual revenue of many countries. She displaced 83,428 tons, yet on that first voyage she crossed the Atlantic in the record time of four days, eleven hours and thirty-three minutes, an average speed of 29.68 knots. Furniture and fittings in saloons and staterooms were valued in millions of dollars; dining rooms alone contained $150,000 worth of silver. Her main passenger lounge was so large that the ceiling was as high as a three-storey building. Bronze entrance doors weighed six tons, and walls were covered not with paper or wooden panels, but with giant slabs of Algerian onyx. The world's largest Aubusson carpet covered a floor the size of several tennis courts. *Normandie* could carry 2,170 passengers in unprecedented luxury. They had their own hospital, church, library, even a theatre, with swimming pools and famous Paris shops on either side of promenades broad as city streets.

Now she had made her last voyage. She left Le Havre in the summer of 1939, days before the European war broke out, and since arriving in New York, she had lain uselessly at anchor, rusting and uncared for. Then, weeks after Pearl Harbor, the United States Maritime Commission requisitioned *Normandie* as a fleet auxiliary and renamed her *Lafayette,* after the French nobleman who had commanded a division in the American War of Independence. Two thousand dockyard labourers came aboard to work in shifts around the clock, transforming the liner into an enormous troopship, capable of transporting an entire division across the Atlantic. Now these ambitious plans had to be summarily abandoned. She would never sail again.

On the fourth floor of a brownstone building in Manhattan, 90 Church Street, formerly a private hotel and now the wartime headquarters of Number 3 District, the U.S. Navy, an admiral sat listening to a news flash on a 'portable radio.

"Nazi Germany, broadcasting from Berlin, has just claimed that its agents destroyed the *Normandie*" the newscaster declared excitedly. The admiral pursed his lips in annoyance, switched off the set, and glanced enquiringly at the lieutenant commander who hovered uneasily at his elbow.

"We have immediately denied that report, of course, sir," the commander assured the admiral nervously.

"So what are you saying caused the fire?"

"What several independent sources have already corroborated, sir. Two workmen were cutting through an iron pillar with acetylene torches. Sparks set light to piles of mattresses and life jackets. Their inflammable fillings suddenly caught fire. Because there are a lot of air currents in a ship that size — long corridors, companionways, port-holes open, and so on — once the fire took hold, nothing could put it out."

The admiral nodded reflectively. This explanation could well be true, but it did not say much for naval safety arrangements. Why the devil had those piles of kapok lifejackets been lying around in the first place? The recital of possible causes did not augur well for his own career as a professional sailor, which, now that his country was finally at war, had seemed bound to prosper. He was not a wartime naval officer, like the commander; the navy was his career, and if he wished to advance it, he needed quick convincing action to assure the public that such a catastrophe could never happen again.

Even before this German claim, which doubtless would be repeated and expanded in every news bulletin unless or until the navy could scotch it, rumours were spreading in New York that a fire of such extraordinary ferocity aboard an iron ship, largely stripped of inflammable furnishings, must be sabotage.

Once more he looked enquiringly at the commander, who only months earlier had been creative director in a New York advertising agency. He in turn regarded the admiral as a difficult, sometimes stubborn, client who needed convincing that the campaign he was proposing must be the best.

"I've put out a story that the navy has stationed extra guards on every ship in our district," he went on hastily. "From now on, dockyards will be floodlit and security patrols doubled."

The admiral nodded again. This was obvious and routine stuff, but far too late. He had to accept responsibility for the loss of what would have been the U.S. Navy's largest troop carrier. His best hope of avoiding a severe reprimand, and almost certain setback to promotion, perhaps even premature retirement, lay in securing immediate and powerful political backing. The commander also realised this, and so had deliberately kept his most important news until last.

"One other thing, sir," he went on casually, as though he had just remembered some trivial matter. "I've had three telephone calls that I think are potentially important. One was from Mr. Dewey's office, sir, early this morning. The second was a person-to-person call from Judge William O'Dwyer of Kings County. The third from another judge, Philip McCook. All were eager to help the navy, sir. And, so I gathered, wanted to assure you personally that no one held you in any way responsible for what's happened."

The admiral's pleasure and surprise showed in his face. This could be the break he needed. Thomas Dewey, an ambitious, aggressive lawyer of thirty-nine, would without doubt be New York's next Governor. He had only narrowly missed being chosen as the Republican presidential candidate in the last election, and such was the prestige in which the Republicans held him that he was virtually certain to receive their nomination in two years' time.

In the mid-1930's, Dewey had abandoned a lucrative private practice to become Special Prosecutor during a state campaign against racketeers and gangsters. This had understandably made him enormously popular with the public and extremely influential politically. It had also made him wealthy, for commercial institutions and corporations engaged him as their attorney to show gratitude for what appeared to be a brave and selfless disregard of all underworld threats as he relentlessly pursued his campaign against corruption.

O'Dwyer was another very successful lawyer, a Roman Catholic with equally strong political ambitions, who, according to the newspapers could be New York's next Mayor when Fiorello La Guardia stepped down. O'Dwyer was said to control the critically important Irish vote. Political backing from him could help to push through the most forlorn campaign, and his doubts about any project could mean instant and virulent criticism and almost certain abandonment.

Judge McCook was O'Dwyer's Protestant equivalent, a stern and incorruptible judicial figure, well-connected socially, who had sentenced many important gangsters found guilty after Dewey's masterly prosecutions, again always without fear of threats or reprisals. He stood for what the admiral felt was best in his country's judiciary: absolute impartiality and total integrity.

How typical of these three men of eminence (and between them carrying enormous political clout) to telephone his headquarters on the same day to wish him well. His heart warmed to their charity and judgement. If they were for him, who would dare to be against him?

"They wanted to speak to me?" asked the admiral, unable to keep surprise and relief entirely out of his voice.

"Yes, sir. But I said you were down with the fire chiefs. They'll call again later today."

"Did they leave any messages?"

"Only Judge McCook, sir. He told me that the others were calling with the same purpose — to suggest an almost certain way to stop sabotage at the docks."

"We've had dozens of calls about that already," said the admiral drily. "Cranks, most of them. What exactly do these gentlemen propose?"

"An extremely ingenious suggestion, sir. That we approach leaders of the Italian-American community and seek their help and support as loyal American citizens. The judge told me he knows that some of them feel insulted because, since they were born in Italy or Sicily or have relatives there — and we're now at war with Mussolini — they haven't been asked to contribute to the war effort in the one way they can help us immeasurably. Dock security."

"I assume that what you call the Italian-American community includes those Italian and Sicilian gangsters who, according to the Press, control the dock unions?"

"Judge McCook didn't exactly put it in those terms, sir, but I assume that's what he meant. After all, the best way to stop any sabotage on the docks would be to get the workers wholeheartedly on our side. And that could produce a very positive public response. All Americans together. One America. One war. One victory. That sort of thing."

"I see. And how does the judge suggest we set about this?"

"He proposes that we contact a gangster in Dannemora State Penitentiary. He's one of the leaders Dewey prosecuted successfully. Judge McCook personally gave him a thirty to fifty years' sentence.

He's already served six years in Dannemora. The judge says he'll be pleased to organise a meeting."

"Kind of him. But what makes him think this guy will want to help ws?"

"McCook is convinced he will. So, apparently, according to him, is Dewey. And they *should* know what he thinks. After all, one prosecuted him, and the other put him away for what amounts to the rest of his life."

"So we'll see him. What's his name?"

"Salvatore Luciano."

"You mean Charlie 'Lucky' Luciano?" asked the admiral doubtfully.

"Could be lucky for us too, sir," the commander pointed out.

The admiral paused for only a moment. Then he nodded agreement and reached for his telephone.

Lucky Luciano sat in his cell at Dannemora Penitentiary, New York State's maximum-security prison, reading the sports section of the *Daily Mirror.*

Eighteen thousand people were expected to see Notre Dame face N. Y.U. in a basketball double-header in Madison Square Garden.

Sitting in his cell, Luciano found it difficult to recall the excitement of being in a capacity crowd. Chill winds, sweeping south from Canada, had coated the prison's outer northern walls with ice. Yet in summer, by contrast, the grey building would shimmer with heat, airless as a brick oven. Because of these extremes of climate, and its remoteness, the convicts referred to Dannemora as "Siberia."

Lucky Luciano was a shortish, thick-set man with curly black hair that grew low on his forehead. He had broad shoulders and very strong hands. He might have become a boxer, a ball-player, or even a day labourer, like many of his contemporaries, had he not followed the infinitely more lucrative career of professional gangster.

Now his legendary luck seemed to have deserted him, but he did not appear downhearted, although for the past six years he had been confined to this green distempered cell with its metal bed, armoured ceiling light, and Judas spyhole in the sliding door. Luciano had been convicted for living off immoral earnings, and for such a crime his sentence was unusually heavy. In fact, this crime was about the only one against which he had no convincing defence. Just as Al Capone, who for years had successfully side-stepped charges of murder, extortion, and bribery on a prodigious scale, finally went down for a relatively minor tax offence, the charge against Luciano was totally false and selected with infinite guile, for the political advancement of the New York Prosecutor, Thomas Dewey.

Luciano, like Capone, had been criminal from boyhood (virtually from the day after he landed, at the age of nine, in New York from Sicily with his parents), but it was his boast that he had never taken a cent from the earnings of any whore.

His name was Luciana then, and his parents were peasants, grateful for the chance of a new life in the New World. On landing, they did not understand what was instantly obvious to him; they had simply exchanged poverty in the sunny streets of Lercara Friddi, where everyone knew everyone else, for poverty of a harsher and lonelier kind in the chill, sunless world of tenement and ghetto.

Here, groups of immigrants — Italians, Jews, Sicilians, Irish — lived in wretchedness and squalor. Luciana spoke no English, and so took several years to understand what school teachers were attempting to teach him. By then, he had learned his most abiding lesson: what you wanted, you took, with violence or without. If you were caught, then you lied, fought, or bought your way to freedom. This would bring the opportunity to do the same thing again, but this time with greater planning and care — and for a larger prize.

As long as you had enough money, you could always buy the best professional brains to advise you, defend you, guide you through the labyrinth of rules that lawyers had deliberately constructed in as complicated a manner as possible to ensure that they would also never go short of fees. A Sicilian proverb said it all: *"Cu avini dinari e atnicizia tent la giustizia"* ("He who has money and friends has justice as well").

Luciana changed his name to Luciano, because he thought that his real name sounded effeminate in his new language, and Charlie seemed more American than Salvatore. Then he started his career by picking pockets. An early friend was Benjamin Siegel, whose parents came from Kiev. Benjamin's nickname was "Bugsy," since his contemporaries said he must be mad — bugsy — to carry a gun before he was even in his teens. Another associate from those days was Meyer Lansky, formerly Maier Sucholjansky, from Grodno, in Poland. Luciano, a Catholic, was attracted to these two Jews. Like him, they were strangers in a harsh and hostile land, and he admired Siegel as a fist-fighter, and Lansky — known even then, because of his size, as the Little Man — for his brilliance with figures. They, in turn, admired Luciano because he was a born organiser. They formed a gang to pool their diverse talents and divide the spoils.

During the First World War they were so successful that they decided it would be unthinkable for Luciano to be called up. Instead, it was agreed that he would deliberately contract clap, which would automatically prevent his recruitment on medical grounds.

From then on, the trio became more ambitious in their targets, for where profits were greater, the risks were paradoxically less. Individuals might go to the police when they were robbed; companies did not always care to do so. They could lose more by the disruption this caused — and even more again when the gang returned a second time, as they invariably did in such cases. From robbing door-to-door insurance agents, the three young men now began to raid banks and jewellery shops. They organised a profitable protection scheme for restaurants and bookmakers. If their clients did not pay an agreed percentage of all takings, then their offices, houses, cars would be wrecked. When the terms of this agreement were explained to them, most paid immediately; all, eventually. In return, they were promised the monopoly of their trade in that neighbourhood.

Then, in the 1920's, Prohibition brought an opportunity of making money on a scale that reduced aft this to the level of petty cash. The Volstead Act might make illegal the sale of alcoholic drinks in the United States, but it did nothing to lessen the demand, which gangsters of all types determined to supply — a situation that the high-minded legislators had never imagined.

Gangs smuggled into the States rye from Canada, rum from Nassau, whisky from Scotland. Soon all the genuine alcoholic beverages they brought in could supply only a tiny part of the vast market. They therefore started to distil their own illicit — and sometimes lethal — brews in warehouses and factories. At first, they worked individually in cities and towns across the United States, but this situation soon produced two consequences. First, bitter disputes arose over territories and agreements, and these led inevitably to feuds and fights and murder. Soon, some gangsters were spending as much time in such profitless diversions as in making and selling the merchandise, which was absurd.

Luciano's solution was simple: combination, a lesson that the Mafia had proved successful during the two thousand years of foreign occupation Sicily had endured before it became part of Italy, in the nineteenth century. No one was quite certain how the organisation, or even its name, had come into being; some did not care to believe that it existed at all. Others claimed that it dated from the Dark Ages, when an Arab tribe, Ma Afir, occupied Palermo. Others said that it came from the Arabic word *mahias,* meaning courageous, or that it had yet another Arabic base: raw, meaning safety, and *afah,* to protect. All agreed that it was very old, and its teachings had not weakened with time.

Provincial gang leaders with Luciano's Sicilian background had observed that when successful business corporations grew larger, their profits increased proportionally. This principle, Luciano assured them, could also prove true in crime. Instead of gangs operating individually, often in rivalry, everything would be planned: they would all become partners in organised crime.

Lansky proposed that areas of interest, with new sources of high revenue and low risk and then a total monopoly of crime, could be created, coast to coast. The details were agreed at a meeting of all concerned in Chicago, and to pacify older members who feared change, it was also agreed that an almost forgotten name should be resurrected, a reminder of their ancient tradition: Unione Siciliano. This met with overwhelming approval, although Luciano preferred his own all-embracing title: the Outfit.

As a Jew, Lansky could never be a full member, for that was a matter of blood, family, and whether you or your forebears came from the Old Country. This did not worry him. He was content to direct the financial strategy, to calculate where money would be made, not only now or next year, but in the next decade. He knew the value of what later graduates of business schools (some of whom attended at the Unione's expense) called forward planning.

Luciano organised buildings to make and store the Unione's products; bottling plants; printers to produce coloured labels; fast motor launches capable of eluding customs cutters on the run from Nassau to Florida. He bought fleets of trucks to transport crates of bottles, and guards to prevent their theft. He arranged for bundles of used bank notes to be available to bribe police and politicians and to pay the lawyers who would energetically defend anyone unfortunate enough to be caught.

The Outfit was soon making $12 million a month from bootlegging. To this they added another $6 million from betting. Luciano was technically in charge, with the Little Man at his elbow. No one would go against Lansky's views, for he never had been known to give bad or even indifferent advice. Therefore, when he advised against involvements with drugs or prostitutes, Luciano agreed. Everyone in the Outfit knew this — which made Luciano's arrest and sentence on such a charge so bitter to bear. Extortion, kidnappings, maimings, bribery on a huge scale, complicity in many murders — on any or all of these charges he was guilty. But Luciano was so adept in covering his tracks, at threatening (or eliminating) witnesses, at bribing or blackmailing judges and jury foremen, that earlier attempts to bring such charges against him had always failed.

It took another man on the make to devise a scheme to trap him.

Thomas Dewey had also known poverty as.a boy, and like Luciano, had neither the wish nor the intention to renew its acquaintance. As a poor law student, he was forced to sing in church and synagogue choirs for a few dollars a time to help pay his college fees. Now his aim was for high political office — eventually, the presidency — and the wealth and prestige that would accompany such success.

Dewey realised that if he could convict Luciano, who had escaped so often before, he would be hailed as a crusader by the same Press and public that had hitherto marvelled at Luciano's years of good luck. He therefore threatened sixty worried, ageing whores with long terms of imprisonment on charges of habitual prostitution and drug-pushing if they refused to testify against Luciano. They testified, reluctantly but with devastating effect. Individually, their testimony might have been worthless; collectively, it secured a conviction and a thirty to fifty years' sentence for Luciano.

Until that moment, Lucky's luck had seemed perpetual. He had acquired his nickname in 1929, when a fellow gangster, Salvatore Maranzano, asked to meet him alone in a deserted warehouse on Staten Island. He wanted to persuade Luciano to kill a third Sicilian gang leader, Giuseppe Masseria.

Now, by ancient Sicilian Mafia tradition, a member who killed a superior could not immediately succeed to his place — and Luciano was determined to become top man in the Outfit. He therefore saw this request as an ingenious way of preventing his advancement, so he declined the assignment. But Maranzano had not come alone, as he had promised, and he now whistled up reserves hiding elsewhere in the building.

They strung up Luciano by his wrists against a wall and beat him with sticks and belts, burned him with cigarette butts, slashed his face with knives, to make him change his mind. He refused. Finally, they cut him down and bundled him into a car and then threw him out on the pavement as they gathered speed, hoping that the fall would kill him and obliterate any traces of his torture. The crew of a patrolling police car found Luciano unconscious and took him to a hospital. The cuts on his face alone needed fifty-five stitches, but he recovered.

When Lansky visited him, Luciano told him how lucky he felt, just to be alive.

"Lucky," repeated Lansky. "Lucky Luciano, that's you."

The name had stuck. Now he might be lucky again, for Lansky had sent word to expect a special visitor that afternoon, and had explained what this visitor's proposition would be and suggested how Luciano should react.

At half-past two, a guard opened the cell door and beckoned him outside. Luciano followed him to a windowless interview room, where Lansky and Siegel and others would regularly come to visit him to settle matters of policy for the Outfit. To give these meetings the gloss of legality, they generally would bring at least one lawyer, on the pretext that they were discussing an appeal against Luciano's conviction. Now a young man wearing civilian clothes was waiting for him: the lieutenant commander from naval headquarters. The guard, also on the Unione's payroll, considerately left them alone in the room.

"I've come to ask your help," the officer began diffidently, after he had introduced himself. "Not for me, but for the country."

"How?" asked Luciano innocently.

"You see any newspapers in here?"

Luciano nodded.

"Then you've read about *Normandie,* burned out at her pier?"

"Yeah. I saw that."

"Maybe you also read how we've denied rumours of sabotage, though it does seem pretty clear that the fire *was* arson. A lot of workers on the docks have German or Italian backgrounds. It only needed one man — one out of two thousand aboard *Normandie* — to be an Axis sympathiser. Now a ship worth millions of dollars, totally irreplaceable as a troop carrier, is reduced to scrap metal."

Luciano shook his head sympathetically; life, he agreed, was tough.

"The navy wants to prevent any further incidents like this. I'm told — and please don't take this wrong, Mr. Luciano — that you were one of the top men in, well, the underworld before the war. I've come here to ask you to use your great personal influence with union leaders at every port in the U.S. to help stop sabotage and arson."

The lieutenant commander paused, conscious that he was asking a lot from a man in jail. But he had said his piece; he had been frank. Luciano could only say no.

"You're making it sound like I got more influence than I really do," said Luciano gently. "But, after all, this *is* my adopted country, and anything I ever made of myself, I owe to America. That's a big debt, and even in here I know it. If I can help you, sure I will. But tell me, who said I could help this way?"

"You may find it difficult to believe," the officer replied, "but it was the man who sentenced you, Judge Philip McCook. And two even more prominent people."

"Now why would the judge do that?" asked Luciano in amazement. "You know he put me in for up to fifty years?"

The commander nodded, not wishing to comment. He did not guess that the question was totally rhetorical. Luciano knew precisely why the judge had done this — he had specifically asked McCook to do so several weeks earlier, when the judge had paid Lucky a totally unexpected visit.

Luciano had not seen McCook since the sentencing, six years earlier, but he remembered him as a vigorous man in middle life. At the recent visit, however, McCook looked ill and thin. His hair was grey; his face lined. He seemed broken in spirit, a man grown old before his time.

"You bear me no hard feelings, I hope?" he asked Luciano nervously, as soon as they were alone. "I was only doing my duty. What I was trained for — what I was paid for."

"You came here just to tell me that?" Luciano asked him sarcastically.

"No. This may sound strange, almost impertinent, but I've come to ask a favour. I want you to lift the spell from me."

"The spell?" Luciano looked at him sharply. What the hell did this old man mean? Was he mad?

"Yes. It can't be anything else but an ancient Sicilian spell. I've heard of such things, of course. The evil eye, evil spirits, the black mass. But, thank God, I've never encountered anything like that myself — until now."

"What do you mean? What's happened?" Luciano asked him, carefully concealing his amazement. There might be some mileage for him in this fool's delusion.

"Since I passed sentence on you, Mr. Luciano, everything in my life has gone wrong. First, my house was burned down and all its contents destroyed. Books I've treasured since my college days, furniture and paintings that had been in my family's possession for generations. All lost. I could have accepted that simply as bad luck. But not the rest.

"My wife became sick. Every kind of specialist examined her, but none could diagnose the disease. She simply wasted away and died. Then my oldest son, the healthiest boy you could possibly imagine, developed tuberculosis and was dead within three months.

"Now, friends of mine have suddenly begun avoiding me. My career has suffered; so has my health. I've reached the stage where I feel I have nothing left to live for. That's why, after much thought and prayer and inner conflict, I've come to beg you to help me.

"I am a Christian. I go to church every Sunday. I give you my word I did not sentence you out of any personal animosity — but simply because it was my duty to administer justice. And the evidence against you *was* overwhelming. Sixty witnesses, as I recall. But if you've suffered, so have 1.1 implore you to release me from the Sicilian spell you've placed upon me."

Luciano nodded gravely. "I didn't put a spell on you," he replied. "I swear it. But maybe people in the Old Country did it without telling me. I promise I'll do what I can to find out who's behind it. But it could take a long time, because I'm here in jail and have to deal through other people, and the war makes it a lot harder to get in touch. Meanwhile, you can do a Christian act for me."

"What's that?" McCook asked him eagerly.

"Tell anyone — everyone — in authority that I don't hold a grudge against the state for sentencing me. Tell them that I love this country, and I'll do everything I can to help it win the war — if they only give me the chance."

Luciano asked the judge for a pen and a piece of paper and wrote down two names.

"Ask them to help, too," he told him. "Tell them you spoke to me. If they need proof, show them this note — my handwriting. If this spell is going to be lifted, God will let me help my country. That will be a sign to us both."

After the judge left, Luciano sat until dusk, wondering how he could use this extraordinary and unexpected visit to his own advantage. Of course he hadn't put a spell on the judge, nor had anyone else. The old idiot must be lonely and imagining it all. But he felt instinctively that he should be able to extract some benefit from the judge's belief.

At last, Luciano decided on his course of action, and through the prison authorities he asked his colleagues and the obligatory lawyer to visit him to discuss a new approach to the question of his parole. For the first time since he was sentenced, this would be the true matter of their discussions.

"I want a fire," he told Lansky. "Big enough to worry the authorities and make them see just how much they need the help of the Italians and Sicilians in this country."

"What kind of fire?"

"Try the docks. It's controllable there — all that water* And in New York. What about that French liner I read the navy's taken over? The *Normandie* or *Lafayette}* She's not even American, so we're not hurting our country's property."

"That ought to be easy enough. Then what?"

"Then we lean on Dewey. Then on that bum O'Dwyer and this lunatic McCook — and anyone else we can think of who owes us a favour or needs one. Get them all to contact the navy brass. Tell them the best way to stop other things like this is to ask for our help. And we can make sure that all the goddamn docks are safe."

"And our price?"

"My parole."

"Ingenious," admitted Lansky, admiringly.

"Foolproof," retorted Luciano, confidently.

Now, events had happened just as he had hoped. Here was a naval officer begging for his help. Well, he could have it — on one condition. But Luciano was too wise to take the bait too soon.

"You said others also told you about me?" he asked tentatively.

"Yes. Thomas Dewey and Judge O'Dwyer."

Luciano showed suitable gratification and surprise. Those were the two names he had written down for McCook.

Luciano knew that Dewey had very strong hopes of being nominated Republican candidate for President in 1944. To be certain of this he first had to be elected Governor of New York in November, a post often considered the second most important in the country. The Outfit could deliver almost all of Manhattan, which would practically ensure Dewey's election. The price would be Luciano's parole.

It was obviously essential for Dewey to keep any such arrangement completely secret, because it would mean political death for him if it was known that he was consorting with gangsters he had so often pledged to eradicate. This worked strongly in Luciano's favour; Dewey could not afford to break any promise he made, in case this secret was revealed.

O'Dwyer also had important reasons for staying on friendly terms with Luciano. As a District Attorney, O'Dwyer had been in the Outfit's pay for years, and only months earlier, this secret had almost been uncovered. An unusually unsuccessful and unpleasant gangster, Abe Reles, formerly of Murder Inc. and then serving his seventh jail sentence after forty-two previous arrests, suddenly decided to reform. He promised to tell all he knew about organised crime in exchange for freedom and the chance to go straight.

O'Dwyer realised that he would immediately be implicated if Reles's disclosures were ever made public, for he could name the men behind most major crimes over the past ten years and list everyone in authority who had taken bribes over the same period.

The state considered Reles such a vital witness that six police officers were assigned to guard him in Room 623 of the Half Moon Hotel on Coney Island, under the command of Captain Frank Bals. One morning, despite this twenty-four hour guard, Reles's body was found on the ground, six floors below and more than twenty feet from the hotel wall. Captain Bals explained that Reles had attempted to climb a short way down from his window on a rope made from two knotted bedsheets as a joke to amuse his police guard — and then had fallen.

The position of the body disproved this instantly, and indeed the truth was rather different. Luciano had arranged for Bals, also an Outfit beneficiary, to receive $50,000 in five-dollar bills to share with his colleagues. One policeman then knocked Reles unconscious, and they all threw him out of the window with such force that he landed far away from the wall.

No blame whatever was attached to Captain Bals or to William O'Dwyer for the death; but both men knew how much they owed the Outfit. Now was the time for them to repay their debts.

"If Mr. Dewey and Mr. O'Dwyer think I can help, I'm honoured," Luciano told the commander. "But if I do what you want, what'll I get in return?"

The commander looked doubtful. No one had suggested that Luciano would require a *quid pro quo.* He had somehow and naively assumed that Luciano would act purely out of loyalty to his adopted country.

"What do you want?" he asked at last.

"Parole."

"That's not in my power to give," the commander pointed out. "But of course I'll do all I can. It may take time, though."

"I've already been in here for six years. At least get me transferred to someplace better than this goddamn hole while the deal's being worked out. *That* can't be so hard."

"There is one difficulty," the commander said. "You'll need a judge to sign your transfer papers."

"No problem. We got one, ready, willing, and, I happen to know, eager. Judge McCook."

Like the Dannemora interview room, the equivalent room in Sing Sing Prison, on the Hudson River, thirty-one miles north of New York City, smelled strongly of drain disinfectant. Here, across a scrubbed wooden table, convicts whose lawyers had failed to save them from imprisonment now listened to their legal explanations and excuses. Wives faced erring husbands, and accomplices in crime who had not escaped detection confronted colleagues who had. So that a visitor could not pass a weapon or a hacksaw to a prisoner, a strong wire mesh screen separated the callers from the inmates.

On this particular day, the screen had been removed and a freshly starched white linen cloth covered the table. Plates of lobster and cold ham and sliced chicken, rolls and butter, salads and green pickles, and bottles of Chianti were set out — even his favourite Dr. Brown's Celery Tonic. Luciano regarded the unexpected transformation with amazement.

"All for you, Lucky," said Meyer Lansky, delighted at his surprise. "I stopped by the pickle place on Delancey Street for those small ones you like, from the top of the barrel. When I told them it was for you, they sent their regards."

"But why all this?" Luciano asked him.

"Because I'd like you to meet a gentleman from Mr. Dewey's office. Our lawyers, of course, you know. And you met the naval commander in Dannemora."

They shook hands solemnly, then Luciano sat down, shook out a folded napkin, stuffed one corner in the open neck of his shirt, and began to gorge himself on the unaccustomed food. The others sat and picked at the meal, waiting for him to finish. They were here not to eat, but to negotiate.

"O.K.," said Luciano at last, pushing away his plate. "What did you guys work out?"

"I think we have agreed on something that will satisfy you, Mr. Luciano," one of the lawyers said cautiously. "In fact, I feel so confident that I suggest our naval friend here telephone his office now to tell his superiors that, subject to our discussion, you'll do all you can to help this country's war effort along the lines proposed."

Luciano glanced sharply at Lansky, who gave an almost imperceptible nod.

"Sure," said Luciano easily.

"There's a telephone in the warden's office, commander," the lawyer explained. "I've made arrangements for you to use it."

"Do you want to see me here later?" the commander asked him.

"Why don't you wait for ten minutes in the warden's waiting room after making your call? If we have any problems — and I don't foresee any at all — we'll contact you before then. If we don't, you can assume that we have a deal that should minimise all risk of enemy sabotage in the docks, no matter how long this war lasts."

The commander looked at the men around the table. They nodded agreement. He left the room.

"Had to get that guy out of the way," the lawyer explained almost shamefacedly.

"Yeah, I could tell," said Luciano. "But what does it matter if he's here or not? How the hell can I help anyone when I'm locked up in the can — with probably another forty-four years to go? What about parole? That's my condition. Is that agreed?"

Mr. Dewey's envoy cleared his throat. "I've talked to my office about that," he said carefully. "As you'll understand, Mr. Dewey is not as yet in a position to offer you parole immediately, because he has no authority to do so, even though that course would be very desirable. But when he's Governor of New York, he'll have the necessary authority."

"And he'll use it to parole me?"

"That's his intention."

"The hell with his intention. Is that his promise?"

"As far as I am empowered to give an assurance, yes."

"Seems goddamn vague to me," Luciano said, disappointed.

"It's as good as you'll ever get from a politician before he's been elected," Lansky pointed out.

"Doesn't sound so good to me — not after six years. So what do I do until he *is* elected? *If he* is? He could lose."

"Not if you hand him Manhattan," said Dewey's representative quickly. "And I understand that you can virtually guarantee to do that?"

"Say I can. Am I supposed to rot in Dannemora — or here in Sing Sing — until the election, almost nine months from now?"

"No. We'll arrange for you to be transferred to Great Meadow Prison in Comstock. Life is so easy there, it's the next best thing to freedom. The cons call it the Country Club, because the rules are so lax. You'll have your own room there, Mr. Luciano. Clean sheets every day, meals sent in from outside, as many visitors as you want. Maybe we could even arrange for you to spend evenings out in the town."

"That's the best you can offer?"

"It's pretty good, Lucky," said Lansky.

"It's better than this, but it's still not freedom. And why should I trust Dewey? He set me up with those hookers. I'm in here because of that bastard. He could do me in again."

"He needs you, Mr. Luciano."

"So that's the difference, huh? Then, he needed me inside. What else does he need besides Manhattan?"

"Two hundred and fifty thousand dollars, in notes of small denomination. Toward his election expenses."

"Jee-sus. And that's all?"

"That's all. So what'll I tell him, Mr. Luciano?"

"Tell him from me he's a shit. Like he always was. You can also tell him that if he double-crosses me, I'll cancel anything we agree to do about the docks. And I'll throw everything I got at him. I know those broads were bribed. I got signed affadavits from a lot of them to prove it. The newspaper boys would love that — and we'd give them all the facts. I don't mind him being elected Governor on my back, but he sure as hell isn't going to be President. Not unless he delivers."

"I don't think any of that will be necessary, Mr. Luciano," Dewey's emissary assured him nervously. "I promise you."

"Great," replied Luciano ironically. "It's almost as good as his promise. Now, gentlemen, what else do you want to discuss?"

Lansky said, "I got a couple of private things I want to talk to you about, Lucky." He looked pointedly at the other men. They stood up, said their good-byes, and filed out the door. Luciano poured himself another glass of Chianti.

"Well?" he asked Lansky when they were alone.

"Thought I'd keep you informed about how things are going outside," Lansky went on. "We've just taken a share in four hundred gas stations from New York to Louisiana. With gas rationing, that's the best news. We're already making a mint with forged ration stamps. Now Tony Lucchese has taken over all the restaurants Schultz used to control, so we're making money both sides of the street, selling meat to the restaurants *and* stamps so they can buy it!"

"Sounds good. How's the gambling?"

"Never been better. Everyone's happy, even the losers. They're optimists. All sure they're going to win — next time."

"And we win every time?"

"Sure. That's why we're in it. And with more money floating around because of the war, trade'll only get better. After the war, it'll be phenomenal."

"How come you're so sure?"

"Look at the facts. Servicemen now going overseas will have gotten a taste for travel. Right? Dozens of bombers fly the Atlantic every day of the week. So what's going to happen? After the war, someone will buy up those planes, put in rows of seats, and then they'll be flying tourists to places they've only ever read about. It'll be a whole new ball game for us. We'll have to move overseas with them."

"But we done that already. Cuba. The Hotel Nacionale in Havana has been buttoned up for years."

"Sure, and that dictator there, Batista. No problem. But that's only one territory — and Batista won't always be top man. Nobody ever is.

At the last election, he used the Reds to help him. What if next time they dump him and try to help themselves? They could have different ideas. So we got to broaden our base. United States troops will land in Europe before too long, and a lot of their families originally came from Germany or Italy or Poland or wherever. Once they've seen the Old Country, they'll want to go back for vacations. We need hotels for them to stay in. Casinos where they can lose their money."

"That's a long time ahead," Luciano pointed out bleakly. "What's for now?"

"The Bahamas. They're a natural. Nassau's only a hundred and eighty miles from Florida, and it's better than Cuba because it's not *really* foreign. Everybody speaks English. And another plus, it's part of the British Empire, so everything works. You've got law and order and a wonderful climate, warm ocean for swimming, flowers, beaches, everything. Also, we got good contacts there, people we dealt with during Prohibition..So probably they'd like to do business with us again. I'm going to establish a base there first. Then, after the war, we go into Europe."

"What do you have in mind for Nassau?"

"One hotel for a start. With a casino. Pan American already has regular flights from Miami, only an hour away. They'll have dozens more after the war. So will other airlines, and cruise ships. Fellow there we made some liquor deals with, Harold Christie, has plans to make the islands a sort of paradise for rich tourists. And where the rich go, the others'll follow. We might even go into the travel business, guarantee an airline or a shipping company every place is taken. Then they'd give us a good price, and we could fly in whole planeloads of suckers for a weekend of gambling. Put them up in *our* hotels — we'll have more by then — so they can lose money in *our* casinos. Then we fly them home — or ship them back — and take down the next bunch."

"So what's holding you back?"

"Nothing."

Lansky glanced at his gold wrist watch. "In fact, Lucky, allowing for time differences, our man should be landing in Nassau around now."

As the aircraft came in low over the ocean, the islands stood on end, a vast amber and emerald necklace shimmering in a sea of jade.

Frank Marshall remembered the coral and diamond necklace he had bought for Carole when he was last in Nassau — how long ago?

Ten years, twelve, a lifetime? It had cost him $5,000, absurdly over-priced, a fortune then — or now; especially now. But he thought nothing of spending money in those days, for he could always make more so easily; a thousand bucks a trip up to Florida, coaxing the big engines of the launch, hull forced down in the water by the dead weight of rum aboard. Then the same fee for the run south, travelling fast and empty to pick up another load. Now, he had barely $1,000 in the world.

His wife's people said, "Easy come, easy go; that's Frank." They were right, of course, but that only made their remarks so much harder to take. What would they say about his trip now, for instance? What he admitted to himself, but to no one else: that he was too old still to be a leg-man; that at his age he should be giving orders, not taking them. Worse, Carole had married the man he was being sent to see, the last person of their old crowd he would ever have imagined to hold any attraction for her, or who would have become so rich while he was still so short of money.

Marshall had a sudden view of waves breaking white against a pink coral reef. A beach lay pale as bleached bone beneath him, then acres of green scrub, with the occasional splash of flame-tree petals, red as newly spilled blood. Palm trees nodded deferentially as the aircraft came down with a roar of reversed pitch on the propellers and the drum of fat tyres on hot concrete. A wind sock fluttered lazily; half a dozen new RAF bombers waited, wings roped to rocks to frustrate any unexpected breeze. The steward opened the cabin door, and the passengers walked down aluminium steps into bright, eye-aching sunshine.

Marshall had been to Nassau many times in the old days, but everything was different then, even his name. He had been Francesco Castellianchi in those days, single, no ties whatever; and he had always arrived and left by boat — never one of the white cruise liners anchored off Prince George Wharf, but in the long fast launches he remembered so well.

This was his first visit by air, and, looking back, he could not remember ever having travelled far out of Nassau. He remembered prodigious drinking sessions in the Prince George Hotel on one side of Bay Street, or in Dirty Dick's across the road. Always, there had been at least half a dozen bottles on the table. It was such a contrast to be allowed to drink legally, after the elaborate furtiveness of speakeasies, that everyone drank far too much. In the background, beyond the laughter, the boasting, and the rum, a steel band would bang away; then the inevitable limbo dancer, shining with sweat and concentration while everyone cheered and clapped. And girls, girls, girls, around his table or leaning across from other people's tables, smiling, wanting to spend his money for him, with him. And Carole in the background, the girl he liked more than any other, more than the sum of all the others.

By dawn, he would be at sea again, with the over-loaded launch feeling her way sluggishly through the shallow northern channel between Nassau Harbour and Hog Island. Only inches below their feet, razor-edged coral spears waited to rip the hull to shreds if the skipper missed the marker buoys. Then, miles beyond the reef, the sea would turn black as squid's ink with depth, and up went the launch's bow as he opened both throttles. He was the engineer; he understood engines as though they had souls of their own. If only he could understand people one tenth as well. If only he had understood Carole and what she had never said, what he should have realised: that he loved her.

The Bahamian policeman, boot-black face against a white bush shirt, blue trousers, red stripe down each leg, examined his passport casually: Frank's profession was simply "business." He was thirty-three, six feet, one inch tall, with a scar over his left eye. When anyone asked him about it, he explained that in his teens he'd been involved in a motorcycle crash. Actually, it was the result of a shoot-out with Maranzano's lot; a ricochet had nicked him.

"Nothing to declare," he told the white customs officer, who nodded him through.

Jack, his contact and Carole's husband, waited in the shade on the far side of the little airport building, fanning himself with a copy of *The Tribune*. Beyond him, the perimeter trembled with heat. Frank was sweating, and to his surprise, he was also trembling slightly. This would be the first time he had seen Jack or Carole for at least ten years, probably longer. As he shook Jack's hand with forced heartiness, he found himself imagining Jack caressing Carole, holding her, touching her, as she liked to be touched.

"Good flight?" Jack asked him.

"Smooth as honey."

Jack opened the door of a blue Buick convertible. Its paintwork glittered, and the canvas top was scrubbed white as a racing yacht's mainsail. Jack had always been so lazy, he'd never even cleaned his shoes in the old days. Must have plenty of servants now, of course. Carole would like that; *he* could never have given her such luxury. Not unless he had saved his money, made it work for him, as Jack had done. How almost unbelievable that Jack had become so successful; he had always been so cautious then, so careful, never taking the slightest risk if someone else would take it for him. Frank had been the one who picked out the prettiest girls, and then Jack would make sure he was introduced. Frank had even introduced him to Carole.

"Booked me in somewhere nice?" he asked to take his thoughts off such regrets.

"It's a long time since you've been here," replied Jack reprovingly. "You're out of touch. Fort Montagu Hotel's full of British troops sent over to guard the Duke of Windsor. British Colonial's packed with American engineers building a new airfield. Royal Victoria's requisitioned by the government. I thought it would be best if you stayed with us. And Carole will be glad to see you after all this time."

"I don't want to put you out," said Frank, thinking of his own cramped apartment.

"No chance," Jack assured him easily. "We've got servants to do everything. At less than a dollar a day, who wouldn't?"

The road shimmered ahead of them like a river. Whitewashed stones marked its neat edges, and beyond them lurked green forest, thick with plantains and sea-grape. Huge casuarina trees dangled long, dried fronds, like hair, in the hot wind. Around the next corner Jack stopped to let a truck turn, in a shroud of sandy dust, across the road into a newly cut track that stretched into the trees.

"The new airfield," Jack explained.

An orange-painted tractor backed out from this track and turned noisily, exhaust barking. The driver was a stocky, broad-shouldered man wearing breeches, high-top lace-up boots, and, curiously, in the heat, a collar and tie. Under a brown straw hat with a colourful checked band, his face was strong and sun-tanned. He was old but tough, and he did not look like any tractor driver or day labourer Frank had ever seen. Even in that brief view, he commanded instant respect. Just for a second Frank's eyes met his, and then the tractor was across the road and crashing its way into the bush. The driver waved them past casually, without even looking over his shoulder.

"Who's that?" Frank asked, turning in his seat to look back at him.

"Harry Oakes."

"And who's Harry Oakes when he's at home?"

"He's at home here. Has been for about eight years. Owns ten thousand acres on this island alone — about a third of the whole place — and God knows what else. You've just landed at Oakes Field. He's building the new one called Satellite. The British Colonial. He owns that — and of course he has several houses here and in the States. Westbourne is probably the finest place on Cable Beach. That's the smart beach, in case you've forgotten."

"I never even knew. Didn't have much chance to leave town in the old days, you know. We were only here for hours at a stretch. What does he do, this guy Oakes, that he's got all this?"

Jack smiled, looking across at him almost pityingly, the old hand explaining basic facts to the new arrival.

"He doesn't have to *do* anything. He owns his own goddamn gold mine. In Canada. He's a baronet now. British title. Sir Harry Oakes, Bart."

"I thought Canadians couldn't take titles."

"Right. And Oakes was born in the States. Sangerville, Maine, which makes it even more unlikely. But he discovered gold in Ontario. Then he came on down to the Bahamas and became a Bahamian citizen. There's no law that says a Bahamian can't be a baronet, or a lord or an earl or any damn thing."

"Quite a guy," said Frank. "So why is he driving a tractor?"

"Because he wants to. That's why he does anything now. Why he dresses like that — like he did when he was prospecting. He doesn't have to wear a fancy suit to impress you."

"So he's got no problems?"

"Not money ones."

"Then what?"

Marshall could not imagine any worry wholly unrelated to financial difficulties. Surely the rich must always be happy. It helped to even the balance if this wasn't so.

"His oldest daughter, Nancy. She's just eighteen, a pretty girl, and she's married a foreigner, fourteen years older than herself. Mind you, her mother is twenty-four years younger than Sir Harry. So you'd think that would make them quits."

"But it didn't?"

"Right," said Jack. "It didn't. Her husband's actually a French count. He's also about a foot taller than Sir Harry, and, from what I hear, pretty big with it. None of which helps any."

"So you reckon the old man's jealous?" Frank asked.

Jack shrugged. The matter was of no concern to him.

"I haven't got any pretty daughters, so I wouldn't know," he replied. "But I reckon he *could* be. He's a smooth fellow, this Marigny. All the continental charm. Kisses your hand, bows, that sort of crap."

"But Sir Harry's got a lot of muscle here?"

"The most."

"What about the Duke of Windsop, the Governor? How does he rate?"

"The King Who Never Was. He's head man in name only. And if he's head, his wife is the neck that turns the head. He's a weak little guy, seems anxious to please. Always very civil."

"Wonder what Wallis thinks of him for giving up his kingdom?"

"If you were a woman, what would you think of a man who did that for you — just before you married him?"

"I see what you mean," said Marshall, thinking about his own wife and her shrill voice in their walk-up apartment. Then a thought cheered him: mention of the King brought back another memory.

"Remember that song we used to sing in Dirty Dick's about the King when we were running rum?" he asked.

Jack nodded and began to beat time with one hand as they shouted tunelessly together:

"Four and twenty Yankees, feeling very glum, Sent down to the Bahamas to buy a keg of rum. When the keg was opened, the Yanks began to sing: 'God bless America — but *God Save the King!*'"

"That King was his father," explained Jack drily. "The Duke of Windsor has what they call ExCo, the Governor's Executive Council, but the real power belongs to the Legislative Assembly. They've got the money and the influence. Merchants, lawyers, dealers. Most of them have their offices on Bay Street."

"That's where we used to deal with the guys who supplied the booze."

"Yeah. The Bay Street Boys, they're called. But how come you're so interested in who runs this place?"

"I'll tell you in good time," said Frank.

Jack drove inland, along a narrow lane between palms growing wild. Some had clusters of green coconuts high in their branches like huge eggs; others, big red berries, as though nature had run amok. Everything was rich and lush and overgrown. Outside a single-storey village school a giant bell hung from a wooden frame. Houses here were only crude shelters made from old metal advertisements for Typhoo Tea and Pratts High Test petrol, leaning together to support a roof of dried palm fronds. They all had brightly painted front doors: blue, purple, jade.

A one-armed black man, thin and emaciated like a cartoon character, scrabbled through an oil drum of rubbish for scraps of food. The rotting keel and ribs of a boat lay in a field like a giant's skeleton. Trees sprouted through the windows of abandoned, burned-out cars.

"Typical village in this sun-drenched tourist paradise?" asked Frank sarcastically.

"In the centre of the island, yes. Remember when we used to go over the hill, where the real bands played, and the rum was so strong it evaporated in your glass?"

"I remember."

"This is what that's like in daylight. The underside of glamour."

Three sapodilla trees stood close together, as though for company. Two barefoot boys had stripped the first two, smashing the branches carelessly, but they did not touch the third, which hung heavy with egg-shaped fruit.

"Why don't they rob that one?" Frank asked.

"Obeah," explained Jack. "The old black magic from Africa. Someone's put a spell on that tree. The other day, I saw a bottle hanging in it, stuffed with bark and hair. No one will risk touching the fruit when they see that, in case they die."

"Like protection?"

"Right. Just as effective and a whole lot easier."

"You've got a lot of obeah here?"

"More than any tourist ever imagines."

Ahead, sea suddenly blazed a comforting blue beyond a lattice of bright green branches; they had crossed the narrow island to its north shore and were safe in rich man's territory. The road followed the beach, past pink-walled houses built high on rocky promontories, overlooking the ocean. The acres of prickly bushes, pushing plants with unnaturally fleshy leaves, rattling palm fronds, were all behind them now. The feeling of menace, sullen and only half-concealed, that Frank had sensed strongly in the village had no place among watered palm trees and closely mown grass verges along the road. Even so, it had not entirely disappeared; it had simply been left in the background. Obeah was still only yards away.

Jack turned off between a red blaze of bougainvillea. A black gardener weeding a flower bed stood up and saluted respectfully as they passed; a guard dog barked on a long, rattling chain.

Carole came to the front door, plumper than Frank remembered her. He saw surprise in her eyes; she was remembering him as he had been ten years earlier. Reality was different; nothing could ever be the same, but she still held attraction for him. She always would.

Now she gave him a perfunctory kiss of welcome, and a maid carried his bag upstairs to a bedroom overlooking the sea: chintz curtains and plain wood furniture; fitted cupboards with flowers painted on sliding doors; a wash basin cut from a huge slab of marble, with gold-plated taps. Frank had a nose for money, and he could see nothing cheap here. How unlike his own apartment, with holes in the carpets and stained chair covers.

He hung up the only other suit he had brought, threw shirts, pants and socks into a drawer, and then walked to the window. The beach was a few yards away, a crescent of fine white sand with a rim of dark seaweed, washed up by the tide. To the right, a spit of land stretched into the sea. Palms and sea-grapes framed white roofs of white houses, otherwise hidden. Ahead, half a mile out, he recognised the once familiar rim of breakers, with the ocean beyond them. The reef.

He remembered watching for the dim lights on swinging buoys that marked the north entrance channel of Nassau Habour, the sweep of the solitary searchlight on the tip of Hog Island. And even when they had crossed the reef safely, other dangers awaited them — not least an attack by armed men aboard another launch. Not a U.S. customs cutter, but mobsters, carrying on the old pirate tradition of the Bahamas. Even recalling the risks he had so casually accepted then still made him uneasy. He must be growing soft or old or both. If he was ever going to change his dreary life, he must act soon. Perhaps on this trip?

Jack and Carole were sitting outside under a green canvas awning, waiting for him.

"I've mixed you a Nassau special," said Jack, handing him a glass frosted with ice. "Rum. Coconut rum. Fresh pineapple juice. Remind you of the old days."

"It's always the old days," complained Frank. "Too much thinking about the past's a bad thing. Let's drink to the future."

"Here's to that," said Carole approvingly, raising her glass. "Our future."

Was there any emphasis on "our"? Both men wondered, for different reasons, as they toasted themselves seriously, then began to dredge for conversation. Nice place you have here. Pity you couldn't bring your wife down. You have a little boy now, don't you?

Frank's arrival had disturbed them both for different reasons: Jack, because he knew of Frank's affair with Carole; and Carole, because she feared the Outfit's long reach, its unfading memory, and she wanted no part of that life again. She and Jack had been lucky. All the fiddles and the bribes and the shootings lay behind them, and until Jack told her that Frank was coming here on what he vaguely called "business," she had optimistically hoped such troubles would never return.

Now she knew differently: the only way you left the Outfit without their permission was in a wooden box.

"You can't still be living here like this on what you made on our trips," Frank said, thinking aloud.

"No way," agreed Jack. "I do other things. Bit of real estate — though that's fallen off because of the war. Mainly, right now, I'm backing people."

"What people?"

Jack paused for a moment, toying with his drink. Ice tinkled against the glass like a tiny temple bell.

"If you must know, Royal Air Force pilots."

"Doing what, exactly?"

"What we used to do ten years ago, but in more style and total safety. Rum-running. They fly out of here, heading for Britain or North Africa. They ferry bombers, usually empty, except maybe for spares. I put up money so some can stack their aircraft with crates stencilled 'Engine Parts' and such. They contain booze, and the fliers stop off on the way."

"There isn't much on the way, though, is there? Only sea."

"There's Recife in Brazil," Jack corrected him. "And then Ascension Island. They sell for dollars when they can, pounds when they can't, then give the money to someone flying back here. Money changes currency very easily in Nassau. Marks, francs, escudos, lire, dollars, pounds. Sometimes they'll take a load on to Accra and buy diamonds. Always useful. Easy to carry, make a profit anywhere."

"And you take a cut?"

"That's what I'm in it for. Fifty per cent. Equal shares for capital and labour."

"Don't they swindle you?"

"One or two tried. After all, not everyone wants to get involved. Only a few. But smuggling is a court-martial offence, you know. They haven't tried it again."

"So it's pretty easy money? For you, at least."

Frank thought suddenly of an aircraft ditching; the splutter of a dying engine, the chill of an endless, heaving sea, not the placid blue water beyond this patio.

"You could say that. And it'll go on as long as the war lasts. So who cares how long that is?"

"Room for any more to come in?"

"If you've got money to put up, sure. Some pilots do it on their own, but they can only buy as much as they can afford, so usually they can't fill the whole aircraft. They might split with you. Half a loaf is better than none. How much are you thinking of?"

"Fifty thousand dollars. Maybe more."

Jack looked impressed. "Whenever you like, Frank," he said. "I'll give you some introductions. My pleasure."

Frank nodded, held out his empty glass. He had nothing like $50,000 in all the world. If he threw in the entire contents of his little apartment, his shabby Chevrolet, the few War Bonds he had bought in his wife's name, they would still only add up to a tiny fraction of the sum. But in the back of his mind he had an idea, a way in which he could swing this amount into his pocket. He would be free then, his own man, like Jack. And if this soft bastard could do it, so could he.

Jack glanced at Carole. She recognised her cue, stood up.

"I'll just check everything's all right in the kitchen," she said brightly and walked into the house. Jack turned to Frank, eyebrows raised. Now was the moment for his visitor to explain why he had arrived so unexpectedly. Frank let him wait; the man's obvious prosperity annoyed him. Frank's envious eyes hung price tags on white garden furniture and striped sun blinds. He remembered once, when they had first been offered $1,000 for the trip to Florida, he had gratefully accepted at once, but Jack held out for twelve hundred.

"What's two hundred more against their profit of a quarter of a million clear?" he'd asked Frank afterwards, and Frank could find no answer.

Now Jack asked him another question. "So what brings you here?"

"You got a portable radio set?" Frank asked in reply.

"Yes. Why?"

"I'd like you to play it."

Jack went into the house, came back with a portable in a fawn Rexine case, switched it on. The Ink Spots were asking, "Do I worry, do I?"

"Makes a background," explained Frank. "I don't want to be overheard."

Just for a moment he saw worry and fear on Jack's face. Then the shadow was gone. But it had been there. Frank felt the same sour, pointless pleasure at Jack's being uneasy that he had experienced when he learned of Sir Harry Oakes's doubts about his daughter's marriage.

"The Outfit sent me," Frank began. Jack's fingers drumming on the white metal table beneath the awning betrayed his nervousness. "They want your help."

"Doing what? I wouldn't think there are many openings for them here. Nassau's pretty well buttoned up by the Bay Street Boys."

"Possibly — now. But there's the future we just drank to. They've got some ideas that will pay off. They reckon you owe them a favour."

"I don't owe them anything," retorted Jack. "I did my job. Like you, I was paid. I don't want to get back into that business."

"It's not a question of getting back," said Frank quietly. "Once you're in, you're in for life. You got to die to beat it. Like insurance. This could be an insurance premium for you. If you play things right."

"How do you mean?"

"I mean they wouldn't trouble you again."

"What help do they want? What do they have in mind?"

Frank noted instinctively the word *they,* rather than *you.* He was an outsider still, not one of the principals; the messenger, not the man who sent the message.

"The idea is that after the war a lot of people will want to come down here for vacations."

"Tourists did that before the war. We had a good season most years."

"But those were rich guys. These will be ordinary people taking a few days off. They'll fly in a group so they can get competitive rates on the planes, and stay in hotels with a casino right on hand."

"The government will never allow gambling in Nassau," said Jack at once. "Used to be a bit in the Bahamian Club before the war, but not much. Gambling's against the law here."

"So I'm told. But laws can always be changed."

"This law won't be," replied Jack firmly. "The Bahamas are very strict about things like that. You ought to hear the radio on Sunday. Nothing but services, religious meetings, revivalists, hot Gospellers."

"I've come to get permission to build a new hotel here with its own casino."

"Nassau has all the hotels it needs. Fort Montagu three miles east. British Colonial and Royal Victoria in town. Plus several smaller places and lots of apartment houses. Big and small, I tell you, they all have one thing in common. They're almost empty out of season."

"The plan is to change that. Have a year-long season. Pack them throughout the year. Bring in tourists by aircraft and cruise ships every week, maybe twice a week. They're met by taxis and coaches, taken to casinos. Served cut-rate beverages, gourmet meals, just so long as they spend their money. They can do that in the off-season — probably better, because there's not so much else to do."

"What if they don't gamble?"

"Only a few won't, because big winnings will be one of the main attractions. That's mostly why they'll come in the first place."

"So what do they want me to do?"

"They want you to tell me the quickest way to change this damn stupid law."

6

Honi Soit Qui Mai Y Pense

HAROLD GEORGE CHRISTIE, the most ambitious and imaginative man in the Bahamas, and after Sir Harry Oakes one of the most generous, faced Frank Marshall across his desk in his real estate office overlooking Bay Street.

Christie was slight in stature, with receding hair, a high domed forehead, small piercing eyes that were always watchful, ever wary. Like many men of his size and muscular build, he exuded an extraordinary aura of power, authority, and determination. He wore a lightweight suit, while Marshall sweated in grey worsted, experiencing, as he always did in the company of men infinitely more successful and ruthless than he, an almost panicky sense of inferiority and insufficiency.

He had already reminded Christie that they had met on several occasions years before, when Marshall arrived in Nassau from Florida to pick up crates of rum. Christie, whom he remembered working in shirt sleeves and cotton trousers, had then appeared almost as an equal, a man eager to make a deal. Now he showed no sign of recollecting any of these meetings. Rum-running was a part of his past he preferred to forget and, if need be, deny. For him, the next deal was always more important than the last: how it could be best arranged, what it would involve. The loose ends of contracts, like dates and specifications, he could always leave confidently to his brother Frank. Setting up the project initially was his special forte. Prohibition belonged strictly to the past.

Harold Christie was not simply a bootlegger turned businessman who had struck lucky, like many others in Nassau. He was a visionary, probably the only one in the Bahamas, whose working life was dedicated to realising a dream that only a few others could even appreciate, let alone believe. He intended to transform this second-rate colonial outpost, with its long history of violence and inertia, into the world's most important and exclusive tourist resort.

He peddled this dream to anyone who would listen or, he hoped, had money to buy land; he never admitted discouragement, never allowed No to be the final answer.

He had inherited from his father his ability to visualise clearly what others could not imagine, and from his mother, his tenacity and business sense. His father had won second prize in a British Empire competition for the ode he wrote on the accession of King Edward VII. He was a good poet, known locally as "the Poet Laureate of the Bahamas," but he lacked the staying power and resilience every creative person needs almost as much as talent. As a young man, he became chief of advertising for the General Electric Company, moved to New York with his family, and then resigned after only a few months and returned to Nassau. He was a member of the religious sect, the Plymouth Brethren, and on the impulse would abandon whatever job he might be doing and leave home for several weeks on a preaching trip around the Out Islands. He was not much interested in money or any material things, but lived more and more in fantasy. After his death, his widow brought up their eight children on her own, without complaint and without self-pity.

She frequently had to sell embroidery that she had made to visitors at the gates of the Royal Victoria Hotel. Sometimes, neighbours said that, out of the tourist season, the children virtually begged for food; but they were a proud family, and gradually she built up a business exporting locally made straw baskets and hats to Georgia. She also bought and sold houses — and then lost her savings in the financial crash of 1929. Christie was devoted to her. Friends said that while he admired his father, he worshipped his mother.

Harold Christie served briefly in the Royal Canadian Air Force in his late teens, then for a few years worked as a journalist in New York before he returned to the Bahamas. He could not afford the fare, so he worked his passage as a steward aboard a cruise liner and jumped ship in Nassau. The only suit he possessed was his steward's uniform, so another brother, Percy, lent him a pair of trousers so that he could go job-hunting.

Christie had heard that an Englishman had recently bought the Grove Estate, west of Nassau, and planned to divide it up into building plots. Christie cycled out to offer himself as a salesman, prepared to sell these plots on commission. He succeeded so well that he took plots of land himself instead of money. He knew that, although money could melt away, as had happened to his mother's savings in 1929, land remained, and its value could increase dramatically.

Looking at Marshall now, Christie wondered about his background, whether he had ever gone barefoot, or been hungry or humiliated as a boy. He was big but looked flabby, a little blurred round the edges, the sort of man for whom Christie did not greatly care.

He must find out more about Marshall, of course, before he agreed to anything. This would be easy enough, for Harold Christie maintained what was practically his own private intelligence service throughout the Bahamas. Each island contained at least one person who was indebted to him, for Christie's generosity to people in adversity seemed boundless: he never forgot that once he had also been poor as the poorest.

Fishermen or day labourers down on their luck, with wives or children ill, and in desperate need of a few pounds, would give Christie the option to buy strips of land that they or their family owned, if they could not repay his loans. The pieces of land were invariably small and useful only for chickens or goats. Put together, however, with the care of a mosaic-maker, they added up to something much more valuable, and with vast potential in Christie's plans for the Bahamas.

In return for his generosity, one of these men on each island, often known locally as "Mr. Christie's man," would report to him on any newcomers and unusual happenings or developments, good and bad luck, that might in any way interest Mr. Christie, either personally or professionally.

Marshall's reference to bootlegging brought back to Harold Christie recollections of shadowy figures he preferred to forget. Not the tough carousing extroverts of the bars, a girl on each arm, and wads of dollar bills jammed carelessly in back pockets of their trousers, but quieter and more sinister visitors with sallow skins and soft voices. They kept out of the sun, like creatures of the night, and carried their own aura of menace, so that their presence could make other people feel uneasy. They possessed the power to empty a room quickly when they came into it. Were men like these behind Mr. Marshall's interest in the Bahamas?

"You're interested in purchasing real estate, here on New Providence, Mr. Marshall?" Christie asked him directly, lighting a cigarette. He was a heavy smoker.

"Not for myself," replied Marshall. "But, as you'll see from my card, I represent a consortium in New York that wants to purchase a site facing the ocean in the Bahamas. After the war, they plan to build a modern hotel with its own casino."

"We already have three large hotels in Nassau," Christie pointed out. "Pre-war, they were not always full, even in the season, which lasts only from December to April. And a casino would be quite out of the question. Gambling is against the law for Bahamians."

"Drinking alcohol was also against the law for Americans when we first met, Mr. Christie. That law was changed. Couldn't this one be?"

"Most unlikely," Christie replied. "There's a very strong puritanical element in the islands, you know. Religion plays an important part in people's lives. Opposition to gambling would be very strong. A hotel is a different matter, of course. But tell me, how do you propose to fill it? We would then have *four* large hotels here, remember. If we can't fill three, how will we fill four?"

"My principals calculate that after the war there'll be a great increase in air travel. Regular flights at cheap prices could possibly fill more than four."

"That's a possibility, of course," Christie agreed cautiously. He had helped to found the local airline, Bahamas Airways, seven years earlier, with Pan American Airways as a substantial investor. Their amphibious planes linked outlying islands, and they planned to expand after the war. If what this American said was true, that might help him to realise his dream — after nearly a quarter of a century of struggle.

From the start, he had sold houses and land to the very rich, because they were the only people with time and enough money for sea voyages from the States, Canada, and Europe. Air travel could cut a voyage of days to hours, and if sufficient people travelled, then the costs would drop in proportion. The very rich were, of necessity, limited in number. The potential in Marshall's proposition quickened Christie's blood, but he must be sure of the men with whom he would be dealing.

"Who exactly is backing your consortium?" he asked bluntly.

"Businessmen active in other fields. Trucking, garbage disposal, laundries, printing, bottling, concessions for beverages."

"Any people or companies I might know?"

"I think that's unlikely, though they're all respected in their own areas," replied Marshall carefully.

"Would by any chance their founders have made money from our joint enterprise here during Prohibition?" Christie asked innocently.

He raised an eyebrow quizzically as he spoke, stubbed out his cigarette, lit another.

Marshall allowed himself a slight smile. "That's a pretty educated guess, Mr. Christie."

"So, to put it bluntly, there are, shall we say, men and money of dubious repute behind your consortium?"

Marshall frowned. "I wouldn't say that."

"There's no need for you to do so. You've told me enough for me to make my own deductions. I don't think such influence would be welcome here in Nassau."

"Money is always welcome," replied Marshall earnestly. "Just consider for a moment what such a development would mean to these islands. First, there would be direct work for builders, electricians, and contractors of all kinds. Then regular year-round employment for maids, cooks, waiters, cleaners.

"Assume that an average stay for each vacationer will be one week. Just think what this could mean to local shopkeepers. To taxi drivers. To restaurants — and the people in the food and beverage business. It could also benefit people in the small Out Islands. Fishermen. Fruit farmers. Boatmen to take tourists on fishing trips.

"The fact that investors made money during Prohibition would not in any way diminish the immense good that could come from this project. After all, we both made money then. So, as I recall, did nearly everyone else in Nassau, directly or indirectly. Even the old women who sit out there on the sidewalks selling straw hats to tourists did very well out of it, sewing bottles of rum into canvas covers to cut down the risk of breakage."

Marshall paused, confident that this was the correct response. Also, he had been well briefed. Like an actor or an advocate, he had learned his lines.

"Put like that," agreed Christie slowly, "your proposal certainly is interesting. But, again, there's the question of gambling. That just won't go here. I could probably influence the Governor's Executive Council to allow a new hotel *without* a casino. The Governor has the best interests of the Bahamas at heart. With cheaper air travel, he would see its possibilities."

"But my consortium wouldn't," replied Marshall shortly. "Without a casino, you're left with just another big hotel by the ocean. Now why should Americans fly down here for that? They've got lots of similar hotels in Florida. But add a casino, and it has the special attraction of big money — plus the foreign atmosphere here. Those old cannons outside Government House. Columbus's statue. The Union Jack flying. Policemen in funny white helmets and uniforms. There are different laws, customs, food. But it's a British colony, so it's well run. Orderly. And above all, *safe.*

"The Hotel Nacionale in Havana has its own casino and does good business. But not everyone's crazy about Cuba or the Cubans. And the potential here is much greater. With respect for all you've done already, Mr. Christie, in selling real estate, the surface has barely been scratched."

"So what do you want me to do?" asked Christie.

"I want your help in getting permission for a casino."

"That's the Governor's prerogative, through his Executive Council," replied Christie. "They are the only people who can change this law."

"What if the House of Assembly were for it?"

"That would be helpful, of course. But I cannot imagine such a situation. As I say, Bahamians consider gambling to be a bad influence."

"What if some of the more important members thought otherwise? Like Sir Harry Oakes? Or yourself?"

"I don't believe they would think otherwise. And even if we both did, we would be two against the rest."

"Could I ask that you do at least your best — in the long-term interests of the islands?"

"I will consider what you say," said Christie carefully, and stood up to show Marshall that the interview was at an end. He waited by the window watching Marshall walk up Bay Street under the overhanging upper storeys.

Years ago, such a proposition might have excited him, but now he was above such political manipulations, which, in any case, he had never cared for. He did not like the prospect of Marshall's anonymous backers involving themselves in the Bahamas. Before he reached any decision,'lie would make some necessary enquiries. Not only about the possibility of success, but, more important, about Marshall and the men behind him.

Government House was not the largest building in Nassau nor the highest nor even the most expensive; the Crown had paid £4,000 for it in 1800. But because of the intense interest in the Duke of Windsor, the Bahamas' first Royal Governor, who had willingly surrendered the throne for a middle-aged American divorcee, it was the one most visited by tourists. All hoped for a sight, however brief, of him, or even, more exciting still, of her.

Four tall white columns supported a high carriage porch, recalling the "plantation" style of architecture more usual in Kentucky and Virginia. Walls were pink, the colour of the conch, the shell-fish that provided food for most Bahamians. Each window had white shutters, and a pink and white cupola crowned the roof. From a distance, the effect was of a pink and white iced cake, topped by a fancy decoration, a fairy-tale setting for a fairy-tale romance.

On either side of the main entrance, two cannons stood sentinel, and a long flight of stone steps led down to the town. Halfway up this stone stairway, as though pausing for breath, stood a statue of Christopher Columbus, one hand on hip, the other on his sword hilt, looking over the rooftops towards the sea and the country from which he had come.

In an upper room, now, the Duke of Windsor looked over Columbus's stone shoulder, beyond a Union Jack, which drooped like his spirits, towards the narrow channel that separated Nassau from Hog Island. At moments like this, it was difficult to believe that he had given up his heritage and his crown for a run-down outpost, so unimportant and remote that in twenty-five years of travel around the British Empire, as Prince of Wales, he had never paid it even the shortest visit. His kingdom now comprised a rash of tiny islands, some so small that they were totally uninhabited: New Providence, the most important, was only four miles across by twenty-miles wide. A fetid smell from piles of old conch-shells, dumped by fishermen near the harbour, drifted towards him on the morning wind, as though to reinforce the feeling of decay.

If he had been exiled by uprising, revolution, even a violent change of government, as had happened to other European Kings — Boris of Bulgaria, Carol of Rumania, Zog of Albania — he might have accepted the situation more readily, for these were accepted hazards for every ruler. Instead, he had somehow naively imagined that to step down from the destiny for which he had been born, to share his life with Wallis Simpson whom he called "the woman I love," would mark the start of an idyllic new existence. What he had not realised until too late was that in abdicating his responsibilities, he had also forfeited respect.

Sometimes, when mist lay like candy floss on the sea, he remembered another, colder fog, which had shrouded Fort Belvedere, his favourite house in England, on the eve of his abdication.

Wallis had been in the south of France, and for days she was almost impossible to reach by telephone because of atmospherics, bad connections, and eavesdroppers in remote French exchanges. Then, suddenly and unexpectedly, they had been able to speak clearly. Her voice echoed now in his ears, metallic over seven hundred miles of wire, insistent, beseeching. *"Anything,"* she said desperately, *"anything* would be better than abdication."

He did not realise then — indeed, had never even imagined — that she might be more entranced by the pomp and pageantry of monarchy than by the monarch. Its magic captivated her, as he had been bewitched by what he thought was the prospect of love. Each had followed a personal vision and found it to be a mirage. All they had now was each other, and a shared emptiness of purpose, a filling-in of days. The former King, from whose audiences courtiers would respectfully back away — for no one turns his back in Royalty's presence — would now pause, irresolute, outside a locked bedroom door.

He stood, a small, slight, peculiarly and incongruously boyish figure, wearing a grey suit, with loosely knotted tie (the Windsor knot) and light blue shoes.

When he became Duke of Windsor, he was suddenly forced to find new ways of passing time, which could march with leaden feet. In France, at the outbreak of war, he was appointed liaison officer to the French commander-in-chief, General Maurice Gamelin, a post without definition, responsibilities, or even properly defined working hours. At first, he had reported diligently to the general's office at eleven o'clock every morning. After a chat with the general or other officers of high rank, he would leave for an early lunch. He had no real reason for returning to the office, so soon he was spending most afternoons at home in Paris. Gradually, these daily office visits dwindled to twice a week, and then finally, fell away altogether, except for an occasional lunch with Gamelin, a commander referred to caustically by some brother officers as "the best general the Germans ever had."

When the German armies over-ran France, the Duke and Duchess hastily moved south to the Riviera villa they rented, to remove and secrete furniture and other valuables that the Nazis might otherwise seize. Then they drove in two cars, with a truck behind for luggage, to Biarritz, on the way to Spain. At each roadside stop the locked boxes containing the jewels that the Duke had given to his wife on marriage would all be taken from the car boot, counted, and set down beside their owner.

In Spain, he was warned of a German plan to kidnap him so that when Hitler invaded Britain, the Duke could be coerced to return as a puppet King. Sir Samuel Hoare, the British Ambassador in Madrid, persuaded him to move on to the relative safety of Portugal, Britain's oldest ally. The Duke was reluctant to do so, but in the end, he agreed. Spanish aristocrats and foreign diplomats in Madrid had appeared delighted to have him in their midst, and he was flattered by this now rare attention.

In Lisbon, he telegraphed to Mr. Churchill, newly appointed Prime Minister, that he would not leave Portugal unless he was promised a definite job in Britain and his Duchess granted the style of "Her Royal Highness", as were the wives of other Royal Dukes.

Churchill replied by sending two flying boats to Lisbon to bring them both back and earnestly urged him not to quibble about terms, but to return while he had the chance. Kidnapping was a very real possibility. Still the Duke vacillated. Arguments continued, with each request he made and every government response being laboriously encoded and decoded by British Embassy officials in Lisbon.

Finally, the Duke announced that since the government — and his younger brother, King George VI — could not accede to his requests, he would not return to Britain. Instead, he declared himself willing to serve anywhere else in any suitable capacity. This boiled down to becoming Governor and commander-in-chief of the Bahamas, an undemanding post — and far away from Europe. The existing Governor was retired early and the Duke and Duchess set sail aboard an American liner with luggage that by now filled two trucks.

Nassau, the capital of the Bahamas, contained only fifteen thousand people, the vast majority of them coloured, Negro, or mulatto. The Duke recalled without affection his first sight of Nassau, with Government House on top of a grassy hill, shimmering in humidity.

He had no tropical uniform, and in his cold-weather khaki he perspired so much that damp patches stained the back of his jacket. His hand was so moist that when he attested the Oath of Allegiance to his younger brother, sweat almost obliterated his signature. This seemed somehow symbolic of all that had happened since his abdication; he was only a shadow of what he had been. What was even more galling was the fact that he signed this oath next to a statue of his great-grandmother, Queen Victoria, remembered clearly from childhood meetings at Windsor. What would she have thought if she could see him now, his kingdom shrunk so humiliatingly?

The Duchess declared on arrival that she could not live in Government House, with its dark mahogany furniture, slow-turning fans, dim paint, and walls lined with indifferent portraits of past Governors. So until it was redecorated, she and her husband accepted the hospitality of Sir Harry Oakes.

The House of Assembly voted £2,000 for the decorations, but she insisted that a New York interior decorator be called in to refurbish the whole building to her ideas. So far, this bill amounted to £7,000, along with other expensive items, such as a dining room table bought for $1,500 in New York. The Colonial Office in London and the House of Assembly refused responsibility for such expenditure in time of war.

As a result, some bills were still unpaid, not an unusual situation as far as the Duke was concerned, for he was never one to spend his own money readily. As Royalty, he did not carry cash himself, for an equerry always picked up every bill. By custom, all Royal personages would naturally discharge this debt when they returned home, but the Duke was not always quick to follow this procedure.

He was reluctant to spend such small sums as a tip to a golf caddie or a waiter. When servants or other members of his staff sought any increase in salary, however small, they would be reminded of the honour it was to serve Royalty.

Previous Governors of the Bahamas invariably refused to accept their salary of £3,000 a year. They saw the poverty on the islands and used this money to help local charities. The Duke did not follow this example; he had infinitely greater expenses than any of his predecessors. Few of them could have visited New York and taken a whole floor of the Waldorf-Astoria Hotel, for a prolonged stay, bringing more luggage than the customs officer said he could count, along with a full staff, including pet dogs. Neither could their wives spend several times their husbands' official salaries on clothes in a twelvemonth, or buy hats by the dozen or eighteen pairs of shoes at a time.

Even if they had been able to indulge in these expensive whims in peacetime, when the pound sterling could be freely exchanged for any other currency, in wartime the Exchange Control Regulations made this very difficult.

The Governors of the Bahamas and their staffs could not claim any allowances for travelling outside the region, so how could dollars be found to fund the Windsors' visits to the United States?

The Duke felt concerned about such financial matters, as about his failure to ensure that the Duchess should be addressed officially as Her Royal Highness. However, with the help of Sir Harry Oakes and Harold Christie, a way had been proposed for dealing with the former problem, if not the latter. Strictly speaking, the solution was illegal in time of war, but, of course, no one knew about it except the two others involved. And the fact that they were involved would surely ensure their silence.

Like his grandfather, King Edward VII, the Duke was fascinated by great wealth, and especially by men who could create it. To inherit a fortune and great estates was purely a matter of chance. To acquire both from a humble start showed unusual gifts, denied to him, that he admired enormously.

This had attracted him initially to Sir Harry Oakes, and, to a lesser degree, to Harold Christie. One had made himself very wealthy; the other was in the course of doing so.

The Duke glanced at his watch, then walked along the corridor and knocked timidly on the door of the Duchess's bedroom, which overlooked the gardens. She was arranging her hair in front of several mirrors. Beyond the windows, he could see a line of royal palms and revolving sprays on the lawn. How tough and crude the turf appeared against the well-remembered lawns of Fort Belvedere and Windsor Castle.

He usually called on the Duchess at this hour to learn her plans for the day: perhaps a Red Cross meeting, or a visit to the forces' canteen to ladle soup or to be photographed handing a plate of eggs and bacon to. a soldier. His arrangements must be subsidiary to hers. Having been ruled from childhood by autocratic parents, he had continually tried to appease, and now he found himself unable to contradict his wife's whims, which carried all the force of command. So the Duke stood, half in, half out of the doorway, not wishing to risk a reprimand by advancing farther. Even in such tiny matters he lacked the power of decision.

"I thought I'd play a round of golf before lunch," he said diffidently, prepared to abandon the proposition if it caused displeasure.

"You do that," the Duchess replied. "I'll go out to lunch. There will be ten tonight for dinner. Tell the butler."

"Of course. Whom have you invited?"

"The usual. Who else is there? Aren't many strangers in this lousy hole."

This was how she referred to Nassau on days when humidity caked her make-up and made her long for the life she had experienced in London and now so sorely missed. What bliss it would be to rise late, enjoy a light luncheon with friends, followed perhaps by a visit to a dress show; then tea, and home in time for cocktails; on to dinner somewhere and a night club. How long ago this civilised way of life seemed now, how infinitely far away, and, by reason of this vast gulf of time and space, how much more greatly desired.

"There *is* someone new in Nassau," her husband said importantly. "An American. He wants to meet me."

"Don't they all?"

This was probably some boring and obsequious Midwestern, middle-class officer, flattered at the prospect of meeting a Duke, a genuine ex-King. What an interesting item this would make for his next letter to the folks back home.

"Fellow represents some American real estate group, so Christie tells me. Wants to build a hotel here, a casino."

"It's against the law to gamble in Nassau, isn't it?" replied the Duchess shortly, in a tone that suggested it was illegal to participate in any enjoyment on this benighted island. The Duchess stood up; she was ready to leave. She walked past the Duke without another word. High heels tap-tapped along the corridor, beneath the slow-turning blades of fans, down the stairs. He leaned over the verandah, watching her Buick glide down the steep drive towards another day of make-believe duties and importance.

It was the same model Buick he had given to Wallis when he was still Prince of Wales. But because then he would soon be King, that car had been a Canadian-built Buick, and technically an Empire product. Hers was American. So, now, was his. Odd, he thought, how American he had become. But then, why not? His country had rejected him, had sent him into exile. Wallis was right; this place *was* Elba.

He changed into his golfing clothes, which his valet had laid out, and was driven down Blue Hill Road, past the British Colonial Hotel and then along by the edge of the sea to Westbourne.

This was a large, long, two-storey building with a crescent-shaped drive in from the road, and a garden that stretched down to the beach. There were tennis courts and a salt-water swimming pool. Harry Oakes, hands in his pockets, was waiting in the porch, wearing his usual clothes for hot weather or cold, sunshine or rain: leggings, breeches, shirt, and jacket. He was whistling, as he liked to do, hat jammed hard down on his head. He looked like a hobo, the Duke thought, unconsciously using the American word instead of the English *tramp*. No one seeing him would have imagined he was a multi-millionaire, any more, he thought wryly, than a stranger would guess he had once been King Edward VIII, by Grace of God, of Great Britain, Ireland, and the British Dominions Beyond the Seas, Defender of the Faith, Emperor of India, Sovereign of the Most Noble Order of the Garter.

The two men walked the few yards to the golf course across the road. In England, the motor magnate Lord Nuffield, who, as William Morris, had founded his business by building bicycles in a shed, had the impression, after he became rich, that he was unwelcome at a local golf club. Accordingly, he bought it and then adapted the clubhouse as his home. Sir Harry Oakes had gone one better. He laid out his own private course, here, as he had done in Canada, and supervised the construction of every green.

Oakes was the same height as the Duke, but far more strongly built, a man in a resolute mould. His shoulders were broad, his muscles still hard. The years of hunger and disappointment when he was searching for the strike that made him rich had etched lines of suffering in his face.

As they walked, the Duke instinctively fell in step with the older man; Sir Harry never felt the need to fall into step with anyone. No one ever talked to him as the Duchess addressed the Duke every day. But this morning, he appeared totally out of character. His whistling sounded morose and tuneless. He walked with shoulders hunched, head bowed, like a man carrying a great weight on his back.

They reached the first tee, drove off. Still without speaking, they walked across the short, springy turf, their two caddies deliberately keeping a discreet way behind them so that they could not overhear any conversation.

"Had some damn bad news," said Oakes gruffly.

"Bad news?" repeated the Duke. "Sorry to hear that. What about? Business?"

"Hell, no. Business is O.K. It's about my daughter Nancy."

The Duke had met Nancy Oakes, a pretty, slightly built girl with red hair, now in the States.

"She's not ill, I hope? Not been an accident or something?"

"No. Nothing like that. She's just got herself married."

"Married? But she's only eighteen."

"That's old enough," said Oakes grimly.

"I thought she was still at school."

"She was. Now she's gone and married Freddie de Marigny. He's almost twice her age — he's thirty-two — *and* he's been married twice before."

So has Wallis, thought the Duke sadly. "Where was the wedding?" he asked.

"In New York. Bronx County Court House. Stood in line with a lot of G.I.s. Then she cabled her mother to tell her. Eunice rang me."

"Have you spoken to her?"

"Of course. 'So you're married?' I told her. 'Well, how much money do you want?' You know what she replied? 'Nothing.' Got to admire the girl. Independent as hell. You know anything about him?" He looked at the Duke hopefully.

The Duke shook his head. "Not a lot. I've met him, of course. But that's all. Not really my kind of fellow."

"Wouldn't expect him to be. But there's no denying, he has a way with women. Comes from his French background, I suppose. They go for that kind of stuff."

"He is good-looking, in a foreign type of way," the Duke agreed.

He might not find Marigny particularly handsome or attractive, but perhaps his Duchess could? After the failure of her first marriage, to an American naval officer with a drinking problem, she had embarked upon an affair with a Spanish diplomat, Felipe Espil, who resembled Marigny in many ways. He was tall and dark-skinned, and he wore beautiful suits; he also danced perfectly and possessed the same indefinable sexual magnetism.

Espil did not marry Wallis; she wasn't rich enough, and he was ambitious, and when he did finally marry, he chose a wealthy wife. Someone had once told the Duke that Espil was the only man Wallis had wanted and couldn't get.

Something in Marigny's attitude, his looks, his nonchalance, called Felipe Espil to mind. This alone might have been cause to keep him at a distance, but the Duke had other reasons. He believed that Marigny was contemptuous of him. He had heard how Marigny had once remarked — for an easy laugh, no doubt — that the Duke of Windsor wasn't his favourite ex-King, and the remark rankled. He might not be King now, but he had been not only a King, but *the* King, Marigny's King. He would not be insulted behind his back by a man who had once been fortunate to be his subject.

"Marigny and that fellow Visdelou, who lodges in his house, both came here from Mauritius," said Oakes. "Marigny's said to be a Count. Frog title, I expect. But to be fair, he doesn't use it. Not like Visdelou. You know that fellow actually had visiting cards printed saying he was a Marquis?"

The Duke shook his head. "They are not British titles," he said, as though this both explained and finished the matter.

"She didn't tell her mother or me a thing about it," Oakes went on gloomily, ignoring the remark. "I said I thought that was disgraceful, after all her mother had done for her. Nancy admitted she'd *meant* to mention it to us on several occasions — the last time when we were all in Canada together. But somehow she just couldn't bring herself to do it."

"I know how she felt," the Duke agreed instantly. He could well appreciate how Nancy Oakes had lacked courage at the last moment. When he had finally told his mother, Queen Mary, and his three brothers, the Dukes of York, Gloucester, and Kent, that he intended to marry Mrs. Simpson, although this would cost him the crown, and saw the amazement and disbelief with which they greeted this news, he realised he should have told them all earlier. He should have done so many things earlier; maybe then he would not be in this wretched situation now, chained by the myth of a great romance, the King who had stepped down to marry the commoner of his choice.

"I'm sure she didn't mean to hurt you," he said lamely. He hadn't meant to hurt anyone, either, but events had hurt him.

Oakes grunted. "I wouldn't have thought any living person could hurt me," he admitted. "But she did. You see, I want the best for her. To see Nancy happy, above all else. You know why? I love her."

He addressed himself to the ball, as though he had said too much about a private matter. The two men played off again, and then walked on purposefully and in step, as though their game were important and it genuinely mattered to both who won.

They came back to the clubhouse when they had played only nine holes, for despite all efforts, neither man had his heart in the game. The Duke now cautiously raised the matter he wished to discuss. It was not the best time to do so, not even a moderately good time, but he did not want to delay.

"Saw Harold Christie the other day," he said brightly. "He tells me a chap's just arrived from the States. Wants to build a hotel here."

"We've already got three," Oakes pointed out, thinking of the vast British Colonial Hotel he owned. Its mock-Palladian front, pillared and conch-pink like Government House, marked the end of Bay Street. The story was that soon after his arrival in Nassau, he had visited the restaurant for lunch. The white head waiter did not greatly take to this strangely dressed visitor in dusty leggings and shabby jacket, and so showed him to a table out of sight of the more smartly dressed regular customers. This treatment annoyed Oakes, and a few weeks later he returned, still in the same odd clothes, and once more was given a place at the same obscure table. This time he refused it, and told the waiter he was fired; for between Sir Harry's first and second visits, he had bought the hotel.

The story was rubbish, of course, but he did not bother to deny it, because it added to his legend, to the aura of ruthlessness and waywardness he appeared to cultivate deliberately.

In fact, the British Colonial had been losing money for years, and Harold Christie, always on the look-out for a possible commission, persuaded Sir Harry to buy it. The intention was to pull it down and extend Bay Street through the grounds with more shops, more houses, more offices, more commissions for Harold Christie. But now this would have to wait until after the war, along with so much else. In the meantime, Oakes had hired coloured waiters, cleaners, and clerks for the hotel to replace Europeans. When it was pointed out that locals were totally untrained, he opened a special training school for them.

"He's also got the idea of starting a casino," went on the Duke.

"Gambling's against the law here."

"He knows that, too. But, as he says, laws can be changed."

The law had not changed for him so that he could keep his throne and marry a woman twice divorced, but it *could* have been. The thought of what could have been, if only this or that course had been followed, was never far from his mind. Regurgitations of what actually happened, what might have happened, if only he had taken a different course before the abdication, formed an abiding and sometimes abrasive source of discussion between the Duke and Duchess.

"His scheme could bring a lot of trade and prosperity to the Bahamas," he said stubbornly, not wanting to admit defeat so easily. "Help the people here very much indeed."

" *You* haven't been so lucky with that so far, have you?" retorted Sir Harry.

The Duke coloured. As Governor he had a Colonial Secretary, an Attorney General, and a Receiver General who dealt with official finances. His small Executive Council, with its non-official members, could, in theory, decide policy, but always real power lay with the House of Assembly, whose members were almost all of white extraction, the Bay Street Boys. As rich men, they hated to see money spent on what they considered inessentials. Accordingly, they consistently vetoed the Duke's attempts to benefit the humbler coloured citizens of the Bahamas. The Colonial Office in London was willing to advance money for various developments and social purposes, but the House of Assembly refused to accept it. If the Colonial Office paid for improvements, they could then insist that they were carried out. This could mean a rise in wages for the islanders, and consequently less profit for the employers. The Duke had repeatedly clashed with The Assembly and had always lost.

The Executive Council also could, in theory, approve applications for a gambling licence or a new hotel — but would these recommendations be passed by the House of Assembly? Not if any of the honourable members considered that they impinged on any of their own business interests. If Harry Oakes and Harold Christie approved, however, other members might fall in behind them, as they had done on other occasions.

"The best way to help the poor people in the Bahamas," the Duke continued, "would be to introduce income tax among the rich."

Oakes stretched himself up to his full height of five feet six.

"If you introduce income tax on this island, I will go to China," he retorted emphatically.

The Duke smiled. "You would, too," he said admiringly.

"The best way to help most poor people here is to give them work," said Oakes firmly.

"You sound like Harold Christie."

"What's wrong with that? If he can sell enough houses, the buyers will employ servants, gardeners, chauffeurs. That would help the economy."

"So would this fellow's scheme."

"You seem to think so. What does Harold say about it?"

"He mentioned it to me. If you and he backed it, the measure could go through. Others would follow your lead."

"Gambling never did anyone any good," retorted Oakes. "It's providing money without work. Degenerate."

"You gambled on finding a gold mine," pointed out the Duke.

"Like hell I did. I gambled nothing. I deliberately spent years in a scientific search. When you were sailing round your Empire in a battleship surrounded by flunkeys, I was making an Empire tour of a different kind. I worked my way across Canada, South Africa, Australia, New Zealand. The only helping hands I had were right here on the ends of my arms.

"For nearly a year I sweated in Death Valley. I froze during the Nome gold stampede on the Bering Straits. Gold was said to be off-shore, so a Dane and I bought a boat between us to search for it. The wind got up and blew us right across the Straits —— into Siberia. The Russians arrested us and let us go only because we looked so wretched, we weren't worth killing.

"I knew the sort of rock formations that *should* contain gold, and I looked for them until I found them. No gamble there."

"But you did find gold in the end," the Duke said, trying to avoid losing another argument.

"Sure I did — after years and years of looking, seven days a week, fifty-two weeks a year. Leap years, I worked an extra day. No gamble there, either. Just hard work."

"Agreed," said the Duke meekly. "But a lot of people here don't even have the chance to work to buy enough food to eat."

"And you think this fellow could change things with a hotel and a casino?"

"It must do — eventually. They would attract more tourists, who'd spend more money."

"So what do you want me to do?"

"Have a word with members. Try to bring them round to the idea."

"I'll think about it," Oakes promised, his thoughts elsewhere. "But I don't like gambling. In the meantime, *you* think what I should do over my daughter and Marigny."

"I know nothing about problems of parents and children," the Duke replied. He had always stood in awe of his own father, and could not remember a single word of praise or kindness the old King had ever said to him. He vaguely assumed other children must feel the same way about their parents.

"You never regret not having children yourself?" Oakes suddenly asked him.

The Duke smiled wanly. There was a cruel island answer to this question: The Duke was not heir-conditioned.

The room in Great Meadow Prison where convicts could talk to visitors was understandably less austere than its equivalent accommodation in Dannemora or Sing Sing. This was the prison known jocularly as the Country Club and its interview room might have been the waiting room of an unfashionable provincial physician of the old school.

On this particular Thursday, Luciano sat in an armchair, facing two visitors. One was the naval commander who had originally come to see him in Dannemora. The other was introduced as a colonel in the American army. Both wore civilian clothes, and the colonel carried a locked briefcase, which he held across his knees as they talked. He looked nervous, almost ill at ease, like a supplicant about to make a request which he fears will be refused.

"I've told my friend here how valuable your co-operation has been over the matter of security in the docks," the commander was saying.

"It hasn't brought me parole yet," Luciano pointed out drily.

"It will. I'm certain of that."

"I wish I felt like you do. Anyhow, what does the colonel want? He's got to want something, or he wouldn't be here."

"He's come to ask for your co-operation on another matter. Not in this country."

Luciano raised his eyebrows. "Then where, seeing I'm kept strictly confined in this particular part of this country?"

The colonel took a deep breath. "Mr. Luciano;" he began, "I'm going to ask you to accept what I am about to say as conjecture only. Nothing definite, nothing agreed, just one of several possibilities open to the Allied high command. No doubt you've seen in the newspapers various articles theorizing about where we *could* strike next to facilitate an Allied advance into Europe. I'd like your advice on one possibility — only one, I repeat, of many. But obviously, the more options we have, the better the all-round picture."

He unlocked his briefcase, took out a large-scale map of the Mediterranean, unfolded it across the table.

"You see Sicily here, the toe of Italy up here," he said, pointing them out. "Our forces are on the North African coast. No secret about that. Now if — and I stress the if — it's decided to advance through Southern Europe, we *could* land first in Sicily and then move on to Italy. Alternatively, we might go straight to the Riviera or head for the Adriatic. Or we might not go for what Mr. Churchill calls 'the soft underbelly' at all."

"You want *me* to help make the decision?" asked Luciano.

"No, sir. But we'd value your assistance should it be decided to land in Sicily first and then go on up through Italy."

The colonel paused. Luciano raised his eyebrows and looked at both the officers quizzically.

"We understand you may have family or other close connections in Sicily," the naval officer said tentatively.

"You understand right, Commander."

"Could you swing any influential people you know in Sicily in favour of the Allies — *if we* decided to land there?"

"I think they're already in favour of the Allies," replied Luciano. "Mussolini's been rough on them. But how am I going to contact anyone from here?"

"We have our means," said the colonel carefully. "Emissaries could be landed by submarine. Or they could be dropped by parachute, introduced by small boats. All sorts of ways. But unless they know who to seek out, and where, and unless their own credentials are impeccable, I guess they wouldn't make much progress. Am I right?"

"You're right," Luciano replied.

"So, in the broadest sense, Mr. Luciano, can we rely on your help in preparing an assessment of Sicily as one of several options?"

"As long as you remember any help I give when my parole comes up. I been inside for nearly seven years, on a trumped-up charge. I helped the navy with security on the docks, and there hasn't been any trouble since then. I think I can help you here, too. But *you* got to promise to help me."

"I give you my word," said the colonel earnestly. "I'll do everything in my power."

"I hope so," said Luciano. "Now, what do you want to know?"

"Where exactly is the influence of your connections strongest?"

"In the centre, to the west and the north," said Luciano. "Villalba. Castellammare. Palermo."

"You know people in those places?"

"Lots. All my life I been friends with men there of influence and honour."

"Good. So there was an Allied invasion, with Canadians and British, as well as our own troops, and we had the co-operation of your contacts, it would be in our best interest to land in the west?"

"That's what I think. Though it's really rough country."

"Our information is that, although the German garrisons are on the east of the island, and can be expected to resist very strongly, the west is held by units of the Italian army. Perhaps that might make the task of your people even easier?"

Luciano nodded. "Could be," he agreed.

"Good," said the colonel. "I must repeat that this is only a possibility, of course."

"Sure, Colonel. I understand that. But at least let's look at the possibility. Sometimes a possibility turns into a probability."

For some time after his visitors left, Luciano sat, considering their request. For nearly two thousand years Sicily, the island of his birth, had been ruled by foreign absentee landlords. Gradually, local people lost faith in any recognized system of law, and formed their own secret conspiracy, the Mafia. Individually, they might be powerless; collectively, they could withstand anyone. To break their code of honour — *omerta,* silence — to be a witness to any crime, to inform one against another, was punishable by death.

Sometimes, despite everyone's refusal to testify, leaders had been arrested, deported to Italy, and had then arrived in the United States as immigrants. So the Mafia had spread. Luciano, its head in the United States, the *capo mafioso,* could appeal to his equivalent in Sicily, Calogero Vizzini, otherwise known as Don Calo. As one head of state might appeal to another friendly power, he would do so, in the certainty of getting a sympathetic response: Don Calo would help him.

Late that afternoon, Meyer Lansky came to see Luciano. They usually met at least once a month, and frequently as often as once a week. He would come to discuss business matters, sometimes bringing a colleague or a lawyer with him. They were not dealing in small change or minor ventures. The Outfit's financial resources far exceeded those of Ford and General Motors combined, and their political influence across the United States, at all levels of government and politics, national and local, was immeasurable.

Luciano told him of the army's request.

"You'll help, of course?" asked Lansky.

"Sure," Luciano replied. "Any way I can. It'll only help me. And all of us, if they go up through Italy."

"Genovese was in Rome, last we heard," said Lansky. "He could be very useful. He owes us a favour — if he's still alive."

"That bastard will live forever," retorted Luciano.

Vito Genovese was no friend of his. He had specialised in drugs and had acquired a reputation in the gang wars as a professional killer who found pleasure in the physical act of murder. Where one pistol bullet was sufficient to kill a man, Genovese would use a magazine, or even a shotgun. His growing appetite for unnecessary violence angered his colleagues to such an extent that he began to fear for his own life and asked the Outfit's permission to leave the United States and return to Italy; he had been born near Naples.

Luciano was glad to see him go. Not only did he despise Genovese, he no longer trusted him. So Genovese sailed back to Italy, rented a huge apartment in Rome, and was soon known as a generous host to important people. In due time, he met Count Ciano, Mussolini's son-in-law and Italy's Foreign Minister. Ciano was a drug addict, and Genovese was pleased to supply him at cut rates. This act of friendship brought him other influential clients. Soon Genovese was on terms of familiarity with many senior members of the government and the Fascist Party.

The advance of American forces in North Africa had temporarily cut his lines of supply. Should the Americans land in Italy, and Mussolini be forced to sue for peace, Genovese's friends and contacts could be of great help to the Outfit. Also, he would be in no position to drive a hard bargain for himself in such a situation, because a few discreet words by the Outfit to the right people could result in his arrest, and he would be sent back to the United States to stand trial on at least thirty murder charges.

But all this was looking far ahead.

"First thing, we got to get the military to put a lot of Cristianis in any force that lands in Sicily," advised Luciano.

The word did not mean Christians, but men of honour, the sons and grandsons of families still living in Sicily. The agreed proportion was fifteen out of every hundred soldiers. Then they had to arrange signs and signals that would not only assure the Sicilians that they were co-operating officially.with the United States armed services, but would also prove their own importance and their adherence to ancient Mafia traditions. And throughout the long discussion, the prospect of parole remained uppermost in Luciano's mind.

Lansky reassured him that such further co-operation with the authorities would accelerate this. It would also give the Outfit a firm base from which to expand from Sicily right across Italy and then through Europe once the war was over.

"It'll be like the United States over again — but a much more profitable operation. Because now we've learned from our mistakes."

"I don't think we've made all that many," said Luciano.

"Maybe so. But from now on, we'll make even fewer."

"What's happening on the Bahamas project?"

"There's no hurry about that. We'll get permission from their Executive Council or House of Assembly or whatever they call it, if not now, then some time. No question of that. But I've been approached through go-betweens about something else altogether. The President, no less, wants me to have a chat with our old friend Batista in Havana."

"About what?"

"To make sure Cuba stays friendly with us after their elections next year."

"And how are you going to do that?"

"The President's afraid that the Communists may take over in Cuba if Batista gets back. They supported him in the last election, and just to make sure he's re-elected, he's making very big concessions to them. Too many and too big. Even so, the President thinks the Reds may not be satisfied, and once he's elected, they'll just wait for their chance and take over the country themselves."

"How come he chose you?"

Lansky smiled.

"It seems Roosevelt thinks Fulgencio Batista is only a gangster. So on the basis that it takes one to know one, I make him an offer he won't refuse. If you weren't in the can, Lucky, maybe you'd be sent instead of me. But since you are, I'm going.

"My job is to get Batista to step aside and put up a stooge — who'll get beaten. The Cubans then will have their first honest election for years, and the whole political situation can cool."

"And what happens to Batista?"

"He retires gracefully. Bows out at the height of his fame. The voice of the people is the voice of God. Then maybe the new guy isn't so hot — and Batista bounces back."

"So what about our concessions if he doesn't?"

"They could continue, either way. Strengthened with others in the Bahamas by then."

"What about Marshall? Has he tied everything up in Nassau?"

"He thought he had, or said he had. But now it turns out he hasn't actually got a firm deal. He's spent fifty thousand bucks to smooth the way, apparently, and everything *seemed* O.K. Now there are hold-ups and difficulties, and God knows what else."

"Maybe they want a hundred thousand?"

"That they won't get. I've passed the word to take things easy, let it all coast either until Cuba's firm again or until it isn't. Your news about Sicily makes that even more important. We don't want a side-show like the Bahamas to backfire and louse everything up. Last thing we need right now is any trouble in Nassau — or any violence."

7

"Read, Tear Up and Do Not Trouble to Acknowledge"

HARRY OAKES stumped across the white carpet of his drawing room in his heavy boots, pulled off his hat, and threw it on to a chair. Then he poured himself a drink and sat down heavily, so that his heels scuffed the carpet. His wife, half a head taller than her husband, and with a placid, peaceful disposition that complemented his mercurial moods and enthusiasms, raised her own glass in a silent toast. Oakes grunted grudgingly and lifted his drink in acknowledgement.

"What's the matter?" she asked him gently.

"Saw an American in a car near the airfield the other day whom I didn't take to," he explained simply. "He's just come up to me on the beach. I told him he was on private property and to get the hell out. He only smiled."

His wife also smiled, trying to humour her husband.

"Who was he? A visitor who didn't know it was private land?"

"Said he'd flown in from Miami and wanted to see me. Been here several days, apparently."

"What did he want to see you about?"

"Some damn fool proposition, building another big hotel here in Nassau. I told him I wasn't interested. We've enough hotels here already, and can't always fill the ones we've got. Then he said this would be different. He wanted it to have a casino. I told him the Executive Council would have to decide that. And that's also nothing to do with me at all. I can't help him, even if I wanted to. And I don't."

Oakes paused, remembering the Duke of Windsor's cautious remarks on the golf course.

"He's already had a go at Windsor over this. I know that for a fact. He's also seen Christie. Made out he met him here during Prohibition. He was on the Florida run then. Name of Marshall."

"Why did he upset you so much? Was he rude?"

"In no way. Rather the opposite. Ingratiating. I just didn't take to him. Something about him, I suppose. Dark-haired, dago type. Looked as though he could easily be insolent. A bit like Freddie Marigny. Big, too, but not lean like him. Flabby. Puffy under the eyes."

"You said you also saw this man the other day," said Lady Oakes. "Did you speak to him then?"

"No. Someone was driving him from the airport. Didn't see who. I was on my tractor."

"I shouldn't think he'll bother you again," said his wife soothingly.

"He'd better not," said Oakes grimly. "He'd better goddamn not. Why is it that every guy who comes to Nassau with some mad scheme wants to see *me?* I'm only a private person here."

"You're also the richest man in the Bahamas, maybe in the Empire."

"That's not the only reason. Is it because they think I'm a soft touch? O.K. I *have* built a new wing for the local hospital. If people can't get treatment they need, I'll fly them up to Miami. So I run a bus service for labourers, organise free milk for their kids at school — and what do I get out of it?"

"You don't do any of these things for what you get out of them, Harry. You do them because you like doing them."

"Maybe you're right. I used to reckon the most important thing about money is that it allows you to do just what you want — when you want. But having it seems to invite every other guy to pester you with all kinds of idiot ideas and crackbrained schemes that *they* want."

"There's another side, too," said his wife quietly. "You're not like most rich men. You've never let money become your master, as most of them do. The more possessions they accumulate, the more frightened they become at the thought of losing them. Think how difficult it must be for someone like the Duke to adjust to living here on what to him is a pittance."

"He's always been wealthy. He still is, though he doesn't think so. I started with nothing. I can always go back to that."

"Most rich men can't contemplate such a thing. The Duke couldn't. Nor, I should think, can Axel. He doesn't seem very happy where he is."

"You saw the paper, then?" her husband asked her.

"Yes."

They had both read the news report from Mexico City about a former neighbour of theirs in Nassau, another multi-millionaire, the Swedish-born Axel Wenner-Gren. Like Sir Harry and Lady Oakes, Wenner-Gren and his American wife had settled in the Bahamas in the 1930's, but unlike them, they had taken up full-time residence only after the outbreak of war. Wenner-Gren was seven years younger than Sir

Harry, tall and blond and impressive in an Aryan way, with very white teeth and unusually pale blue eyes. When Wenner-Gren smiled, which was often, his teeth seemed surprisingly large; he did not often smile with his eyes.

His American wife, Marguerite, was the daughter of a Kansas City businessman, and described herself as an opera singer, although no one could recall actually having heard her sing professionally. She was a steady drinker at parties, and when the two were together, her husband's eyes rarely left her. As with the Duchess of Windsor, there was no doubt who was the dominant partner.

Wenner-Gren was full of charitable ideas, some on an international level, and most of them bearing his name; he had no children. He financed the Wenner-Gren Institute for Experimental and Physiological Chemistry at Stockholm University, and the Wenner-Gren Foundation for Nordic Cooperation and Research, with a grant of $7.5 million. In the Bahamas, he started a cray-fish canning factory, and lived on Hog Island in a vast house in style comparable with his wealth. To add colour and song to his estate, named Shangri-La, he imported flocks of brightly plumed exotic birds to sing in specially planted avenues of trees. A staff of thirty ran his house, exercising his horses and maintaining his fast motor boats. His yacht, *Southern Cross,* 320 feet long and formerly owned by Howard Hughes, was the largest private yacht in the world, and crewed by strongly pro-Nazi former officers of the Swedish navy.

Wenner-Gren was reticent about his family background. Some said his father was a farmer; others, that he had been in trade. Wenner-Gren said nothing. When he heard himself described as one of the richest men in the world, he would shake his head deprecatingly and say that he was not as wealthy as Henry Ford.

Like Sir Harry Oakes, Wenner-Gren had wanted from boyhood to become rich, but unlike Oakes, he had no idealism about the best means to achieve this ambition. He was born in Uddevalla in Sweden and educated in Germany, a country with whose aims and lifestyle he was always in sympathy. When he graduated from the *Handelsakademie* (an advanced school of commerce) in Berlin, he joined the Alfa-Laval Separator Company.

Dissatisfied with prospects there, he emigrated to New York in the hope that he could somehow make his fortune more quickly in the United States than in Europe. This proved less easy than he had anticipated, and he was working in a factory for fifteen cents an hour, when he was offered the post of salesman in the States for a Swedish company manufacturing electric light bulbs.

Electric light was beginning to supersede gas and oil lamps, and working for a low salary and commission in a vast country, Wenner-Gren soon recognised the immense sales potential, which his employers in Sweden had not yet begun to appreciate. Like Harold Christie, Wenner-Gren found that he was a born salesman, and also like Christie he soon realised the wisdom of taking his commission on sales in kind rather than cash.

He arranged for it to be paid in the form of shares in the company, and considering the relatively small orders for electric bulbs that other salesmen brought in, his directors considered this reasonable. But when Wenner-Gren contracted to supply bulbs to floodlight the Panama Canal when it was opened in August, 1914, and then several similar deals followed, the shares he earned gave him complete control of the company; the tail had taken over the dog.

In 1921, Wenner-Gren formed the Electrolux Company to manufacture vacuum cleaners and, later, household refrigerators, then a rarity. Soon, he had factories producing such domestic goods in Scandinavia, France, Britain, Germany, and the United States.

In the 1930's, when a second European war seemed probable, the Swedish government passed a law outlawing Nazi participation in Swedish manufacturing companies. This gave Wenner-Gren the opportunity to acquire a third share in the Bofors Munition Works, which made the famous Bofors gun, from Krupp of Germany. He soon owned the whole firm. Then he established a factory to manufacture Northrop aircraft and became his country's richest citizen, with a personal fortune estimated at around $100 million.

His yacht was a floating palace for guests, usually chosen from those politically or potentially useful to him.

On the day the Second World War broke out in September, 1939, he sailed in *Southern Cross* from Gothenburg for the Bahamas. By coincidence, he was off the north coast of Scotland, and actually in sight of the British liner *Athenia,* when a German U-boat torpedoed her — the first Allied sea casualty of the war.

Wenner-Gren at once took 376 survivors aboard his yacht and used the occasion as an excuse to send a personal radio message to President Roosevelt: "Seeing at first hand the misery, suffering, tragedy, and horror of this one incident, I recall your own expressed views, and I believe that the disaster, if properly utilised, might form the basis for new peace efforts with prospects of success." The words "if properly utilised" caused some to ask whose interests this act of war could best benefit — and how.

British Intelligence wondered why his yacht, sprouting more radio aerials than any sailing vessel needed, should have been, of all places in every ocean, in that one particular area at that crucial moment. Some even went further and speculated whether it was possible that someone aboard the yacht could have been in radio communication with the U-boat.

In the Bahamas, Wenner-Gren boasted of his friendship with Goering and declared that this had helped to keep Sweden neutral. He was cruising in the sunshine, one day in early 1940, when Goering sent him a radio message, asking him to return to Sweden urgently to attempt to negotiate peace between Russia and Finland.

"I have a good standing in Germany," Wenner-Gren explained, adding how pleased and proud he would be if he could also help to negotiate peace between the Axis and the Allies. To show his total open-handedness, he was equally pleased and proud to mention his friendship with Mussolini and the Duke of Windsor. On this particular European trip, he visited Rome and then Berlin, but nothing more was heard of any part he played in mediating between Finland and Russia. His own interest in that particular war had been to sell arms to the Finns.

For his huge white and gold yacht, he built a giant harbour pen on Hog Island. Its immense size, and the fact that it concealed any ships at anchor, caused the rumour that other less friendly vessels might also shelter there in perfect safety and seclusion. However, constructing this had provided work for fifteen hundred locals who might otherwise have been unemployed.

But why, people asked, did *Southern Cross* have such powerful radio transmitters and receivers? How was she so conveniently on hand on several occasions when Allied pilots, training in the Bahamas, crashed into the sea? And why did she need to carry samples of almost every armament her owner's companies produced?

Either ignorant of such unfriendly remarks or, more likely, ignoring them, Wenner-Gren sailed his vast yacht around the sunlit Caribbean, and sometimes the Duke and Duchess of Windsor were among her passengers. When the Duchess wished to consult a dentist in Miami, the *Southern Cross* was placed at her disposal to carry her and the Duke to Miami in infinitely greater comfort than any other vessel or aircraft, and, of course, at no cost whatever, an important consideration for the Duke.

The yacht also took Wenner-Gren to Mexico on a number of occasions, and he visited Rio de Janeiro, where he attempted to secure rights to all iron ore in Minas Gerais. When Intelligence sources showed that his backers were a German and Swedish group involving the ubiquitous Krupp, the U.S. Export-Import Bank scotched the deal at the last moment by offering a substantial loan to Brazil.

Wenner-Gren moved on to Peru, with the declared aim of financing an archaeological expedition to discover the lost cities of the Incas. During his stay, he presented the country with a million-acre park, to be known as the Wenner-Gren Archaeological Park, and in return the University of Cuzco conferred an honorary doctorate on him. Thereafter, Wenner-Gren's staff were instructed to address him as "doctor."

It seemed that the real object of this trip, however, was to buy arms for Germany, and when this became known, he left Peru for Mexico, where he had a good and influential friend in General Maximino Avila Camacho, the President's wealthy brother. Camacho presented Wenner-Gren with a gold key to Mexico City, and Wenner-Gren announced in return that he intended "to engage in economic activities in collaboration with American and Mexican financiers." In such economic activities, Camacho, a greedy, avaricious, Fascist sympathiser, who had seized his own chance for wealth and power in the Mexican revolution before the First World War, saw prospects for himself. It was already a joke in Mexico City that Camacho owned everything there apart from the National Palace and the cathedral — and, given time, he would remedy even this.

Wenner-Gren transferred the registration of his yacht to that country — *Southern Cross* had previously been sailed under the Panamanian flag — and then announced that he would use her no longer.

"If I continue," he explained, sadly, "people will only say I am using her to refuel U-boats." This was an oblique reference to the unusually large fuel tanks fitted to *Southern Cross*.

Wenner-Gren had established a bank in Mexico for reasons that interested British and American Intelligence agents; and several men of distinction in the Bahamas, Harold Christie, Sir Harry Oakes, and the Duke of Windsor, among others, ignorant or uncaring of his reasons, desperately wished to take advantage of its financial facilities.

Wenner-Gren, in turn, was just as eager to be associated with them. Immensely rich as he was, he was strapped for liquid assets; the U.S. State Department estimated that he could raise barely $250,000 in cash. Yet he talked in tens of millions, because he *was* a multi-millionaire. Wenner-Gren's money was blocked in London, Sweden, and the United States, and in a world at war, he was forced to use the names of friends as credit. Their names would guarantee his, for who would doubt the wealth and integrity of the former King of England, or the richest baronet in the British Empire? For Wenner-Gren, in his paradoxical situation of being immensely rich but having little money on hand, names like these were better than any bank loan.

To show the close terms of friendship he enjoyed with the former King and Sir Harry Oakes, Wenner-Gren invited General Camacho to Nassau. He assumed that Camacho would come alone, or at most with one or two companions. To his surprise, Camacho arrived with sixteen colleagues and luggage for twice as many. Oakes put them up as his guests in the penthouse and other rooms of the British Colonial Hotel. They wanted to meet the Duke, of course — and it was important for Wenner-Gren that such a meeting be speedily arranged.

Oakes had neither the time nor inclination for protocol. He swiftly took the Mexican visitors up Blue Hill Road from the hotel, past the sentries, and into Government House. No nonsense about appointments.

That morning Captain H. Montgomery Hyde, a British Intelligence officer, had called to see the Duke to discuss security arrangements in the Bahamas. Montgomery Hyde, who was on the staff of William "Intrepid" Stephenson, who controlled British Intelligence activities in the Western Hemisphere, was not impressed by the security obtaining in Nassau. He stayed with Captain Millar, who combined the duties of prison superintendent with those of Naval Reporting Officer, and was surprised to discover that all secret files and security dossiers, with cipher and code books, were held in the Duke's private office, and not, as was more usual, in the care of the Colonial Secretary.

Apparently, the Duke's predecessor as Governor, Sir Charles Dundas (who had earlier been Colonial Secretary), found it more convenient to transact confidential business from Government House, and, despite the war, the Duke had followed this peacetime precedent.

Oakes remembered the astonishment on Captain Montgomery Hyde's face as he introduced the Mexicans to the Duke. He could tell what the younger man was thinking: how extraordinary it was that the Duke, a former King and the present King's elder brother, should be receiving these people at all.

The Mexican government had seized British oil companies' assets without making any proper offer of compensation, and then had broken off diplomatic relations with Britain in 1938. None of the Mexicans should have been in the Bahamas, for as foreigners, they required passports bearing British consular visas. But they could not obtain these visas, because all British consulates in Mexico had been closed for years. As Oakes and the Duke knew, they had landed without showing their passports, possibly without even being asked to do so — hardly convincing evidence of security on the island.

Sir Harry Oakes was accustomed to calling on the Duke whenever he liked, and had never thought about the advisability of arranging an appointment. Great wealth allowed you to assume that your business had priority over everyone else's, and, of course, it invariably did.

The Duke covered his embarrassment by speaking in Spanish to Camacho, a language that he hoped Montgomery Hyde did not understand. He told Camacho that he would like to entertain him and his colleagues at dinner, when they would have more time and privacy to discuss matters of mutual interest.

After Montgomery Hyde finished his talk with the Duke, he called on Leslie Heape, the Colonial Secretary, and asked him to send an immigration officer to the British Colonial to check out these visitors. It was then discovered that one of Camacho's party was wanted by the F.B.I, for his "un-American activities."

The incident disturbed Montgomery Hyde, as did the sight of a telegram in the cable censor's office, signed Byers, and addressed to someone in Dublin. He recognised the sender's name, but a close check of the immigration files failed to show that anyone of that name had entered the Bahamas on the day in question. The fact was, of course, that, like the Mexicans, people were entering and leaving without any proper check being made — and not all were necessarily friendly to the Allied cause.

Wenner-Gren invited the Duke and Duchess to visit Mexico — an extraordinary invitation to make and even more ill-advised to accept, given all the circumstances, but it would underline his own importance if they accepted, which they did.

Wenner-Gren had been in Mexico City to complete arrangements, and he was aboard his yacht, heading back to the Bahamas, to pick up the Duke and Duchess for this visit, when, to his astonishment and horror, he heard on the radio that the British and United States governments had placed him on their blacklist of individuals who, while claiming to be neutral, were in fact suspected of actively helping the Axis.

This meant, of course, that if Wenner-Gren returned to Nassau, he could be jailed. He had turned his yacht about, and ever since had been in virtual exile in Mexico. His estate on Hog Island was closed, the motor launches laid up, and his staff, except for a nucleus of two or three, departed in search of other jobs. From time to time, Wenner-Gren petitioned eloquently against what he claimed was totally unwarranted treatment, and several newspapers had that day published details of yet another personal appeal he had made to President Roosevelt, again without result.

Looking out of the window, across the beach, at the darkening sea, it was easy for Sir Harry to imagine that the lights of *Southern Cross* would suddenly come into glittering view.

"He's a brilliant financial brain," said Oakes ruminatively.

"Well, he won't be using it back here for some time," replied his wife drily. "And he must miss the old days very much — almost as much as the Duke."

Sir Harry nodded; as far as he was concerned, the subject was closed. His good humour returned, for he had more interesting and agreeable matters to occupy his mind. He needed to be up early in the morning to continue work on the new airfield road.

If Sir Harry had not been so occupied with driving tractors, and if his wife had been closer to their eldest daughter, they both might have realised the importance of her growing attachment to Marigny before she finally decided to marry him.

To a young girl of seventeen, strictly brought up and therefore younger than her years, with a father already in late middle age at the time of her birth, and with a family whose conversation largely concerned trusts and shares and dividends, Marigny appeared like a guide to a golden world awaiting her discovery.

First, Marigny, like her father, was his own man, and she was more accustomed to lawyers and managers and accountants of Marigny's age, who bowed obsequiously to her father and accepted his opinions with deference simply because of his wealth.

They might discuss Sir Harry's foibles in a supercilious way, or smile at his sometimes crude approach — but only behind his back. To his face, they would never disagree with him.

Marigny was never like this. She knew about his two earlier marriages, and accepted what appeared to be the strange terms of his divorce from his second wife, Ruth. She had also heard how he replied to the Attorney General, Eric Hallinan, when it was claimed that this divorce was not legal in the Bahamas, and she admired his agile mind.

The allegation had been made after Ruth applied to the authorities to transfer some of her own money back to the United States, on the grounds that since she was once more an American citizen, British Exchange Control Regulations did not affect her.

The Attorney General took the view that because Marigny was a British subject, living in the Bahamas, he had to recognise the divorce laws of the colony, and under these laws the only reason for divorce was adultery. If this was so, then Ruth was still married to a British subject, was bound by Exchange Control Regulations, and so could not transfer her own money. This might seem logical enough, and indeed a final decision to many people, if not most, but Marigny was not among them.

One of his yachting friends, Godfrey Higgs, an ambitious barrister of about his own age, discovered a weakness in the Attorney General's argument. There was an important difference in English law between the *residence* of a person and his *domicile*. Higgs and Marigny contended that technically Marigny was still domiciled in Mauritius, even if resident in the Bahamas, and so was subject to French law, which recognised the grounds on which he had obtained his divorce. This was a fine point of law, and Hallinan called Marigny into his office to discuss the matter.

"I suppose you think you've been very clever over this?" he began.

"I don't know about that," Marigny replied. "I didn't set out to be clever; simply to find a solution. But I think you must agree we're right?"

"I do not agree," replied Hallinan shortly. "So far as we are concerned, this lady is still your wife."

"What you're saying is that my divorce is not legal?"

"Of course it's not legal, because it was not granted in accordance with the laws of the Bahamas."

"You say that because an American judge in Miami granted my wife a divorce on the grounds of mental cruelty?"

"I do."

"And adultery is the only reason that's accepted in the Bahamas?"

"You know that quite well.'

"Can I tell you that this same judge — and, by coincidence, in that very same court — divorced me from my first wife on the same grounds?"

"That has nothing whatever to do with this situation."

"I disagree. I think that it has everything to do with this situation. If you claim that my second divorce is not legal because of the grounds on which it was granted, then neither is my first! So either way, according to your reasoning, Ruth Fahnestock cannot be my wife."

The Attorney General had to accept the logic behind this, but its acceptance rankled. Marigny was not a man he could like. Shortly after this meeting, Eric Hallinan again asked to see him in his office, this time in the presence of Leslie Heape.

"I've asked you here, Marigny," he explained, "because of a letter your wife has written to *Time* magazine."

"As you already know, I haven't got a wife. I am single."

Hallinan did not reply. Instead, he handed a letter to him. It was in Ruth's handwriting and mentioned that supplies of butter were reaching Nassau from the United States at a time when advertisements were appearing in American newspapers asking their readers to use as little butter and lard as they could and to send the rest in gift parcels to people in Britain.

"The censor stopped the letter, of course," said the Colonial Secretary. "Can't have things like this interfering with the war effort.*

"But what has it all got to do with me?" asked Marigny in bewilderment. "And how is it interfering with the war effort? I simply don't understand you. Ruth is an American citizen. What she says is a matter for her own country, not for us."

"You don't appear to realise quite what this means."

"I don't. What *does* it mean?"

"Simply that we can put your name before the Executive Council as an undesirable person, and therefore subject to deportation."

"On what grounds?"

"Moral turpitude, and contravening Exchange Control Regulations."

Marigny looked at the two men with a confidence he did not entirely feel.

The right of deporting any non-Bahamian without prospect of appeal had been granted during the heady days of Prohibition. Many American gangsters had found the Bahamas so pleasant that they bought houses in Nassau; some still lived here on the island or on others in the group. Some local people, who had been willing to make large sums of money with their help, now resented their presence as residents. They feared what might happen if too many professional gangsters were allowed to remain, so this law had been hurriedly passed.

"I know you have the right to do this to me, as a non-Bahamian," Marigny agreed. "But we've already discussed the question of my divorce. I wrote you a letter about it. You replied that you accepted it. I *am* divorced. So I repeat that what my American ex-wife may do is of no concern of mine. And surely, as a member of the Exchange Control Board, you should have brought a charge against me if you had any reason to do so. But you hadn't then, and you haven't now. Gentlemen, I shall bid you good day."

Nancy knew of other occasions when Marigny had irritated those in authority. Once, the British actress Madeleine Carroll had come to Nassau for a special premiere of her film *Bahama Passage,* which had been made in the Bahamas. Afterwards she was to be guest of honour at a dinner Sir Harry Oakes was giving for her at the British Colonial Hotel, with the Duke and Duchess of Windsor as principal guests. Instead, she spent the evening with Marigny and Georges Visdelou.

This had understandably annoyed the Duke, who felt he had lost face with the Duchess. He showed his displeasure when Marigny wrote to him shortly afterwards to ask whether he and the Duchess would attend a charity dinner he was arranging at the Prince George Hotel to raise money to help dependents of Bahamian servicemen who had been posted overseas.

The Duke declined the invitation. An aide-de-camp explained that the Duchess did not like the Prince George Hotel; she remembered a scandal there that had involved two American tourists. The Duke was, in any case, too busy to attend that particular dinner.

Marigny pointed out drily that the Duke never seemed to be too busy to play golf. This rather acrimonious exchange took place in an ante-room to the Duke's office, and since the door was open, the Duke heard every word.

Such a man, able to stand up for himself, who scorned sycophancy, who could start such an unlikely business as a chicken farm in Nassau — and make it pay — had qualities of courage and independence that Nancy could only admire. After all, her father possessed them in equal measure.

"Whatever made you start that farm?" she once asked Marigny.

"Because I saw it could be profitable. There are a lot of troops on the island.

They have to be fed. So does everyone else, and we grow far too little of our

own food. I sell a dozen eggs for a dollar, and the chickens produce around

fifteen hundred eggs a month. I can get a dollar a pound eight for broilers —

and I sell three thousand chickens

every month."

"My father says you're just peddling chickens on Bay Street," said Nancy.

"I wouldn't disagree. But we all have to start small. Look how Henry Ford and Frank Woolworth began — or even your father himself."

Nancy Oakes suspected that her father secretly admired Marigny's business acumen and drive. He had even suggested buying the Bahamas Trust Company, and then Marigny could learn the business of banking and take over from the present manager, John Anderson.

Anderson was in the unenviable position of being very close to people of great wealth every working day, but not being wealthy himself. In an attempt to remedy this unhappy paradox, he gambled. He owed Marigny $4,000 he had borrowed for one session and

$2,000 from another. Of course, a gambling debt was not legally enforceable, and anyhow, in Marigny's view it was not really important.

What was important to him was the struggle, the fight, the challenge.

How could any girl of spirit not be drawn to a stranger who joined the Nassau Yacht Club and at once decided not to be just another yachtsman, but the best? In the clubhouse one day, Marigny met a visiting American captain who twice had been runner-up for the international yachting championship.

"If I buy a boat tomorrow," Marigny told him, "I bet I'll beat you within two years."

The American laughed.

"Not only that," Marigny continued. "Give me five years, and I'll *win* the international championship."

Now everyone laughed. Who was this new member who talked so big? They soon discovered. Marigny travelled to New York, brought back a yacht, and spent six months learning how to handle her properly, and then more months changing her design in his search for speed and manoeuvrability. He broke several masts, ruined several suits of sails — but finally had the fastest and most successful yacht in the colony.

Nancy was then at school in the States, but she managed to see him race at weekends on Long Island Sound. He was flattered by her attention, of course; any man would be, for she was pretty and young, and the eldest daughter of one of the world's richest men.

Marigny would sometimes fly up from Nassau to see her and take her out to dinner. Although her family was so rich, he discovered that she possessed only one evening dress —which her mother had discarded and she had altered to make it fit.

On one of these trips, they married. Afterwards, Nancy cabled her mother, who was astonished at the news. Sir Harry concealed his doubts more diplomatically, but Marigny was not the man they would have chosen for their daughter. But, then, they had not made the choice; Nancy had done that.

Marigny understood their reservations and had no wish to pretend to be what or who he wasn't. He explained simply that he loved Nancy and that he could support her on what he earned. He also believed that they could be happy together.

"I don't care a damn about a man's past," Sir Harry had replied. "No one with guts does. But what I *do* want is for my daughter to be happy. That's all there is to it."

But, of course, there was much more. Lady Oakes could not conceal her disappointment at the marriage. She had married a man twenty-four years older than herself; a man who could have been her father instead of her husband. And now their eldest daughter was doing almost the same thing, and with such an unsuitable man.

What irony to be so very rich that you could buy anything in the world that you wanted — except what you wanted most of all: happiness for your children.

Frank Marshall sat at a corner table on the upstairs verandah of the Prince George Hotel. Beneath him, in the sunshine, beyond the fluttering flags of the Allies that decorated the roof, a few open taxis threaded their way between military lorries. There were no tourists now; the passengers were servicemen and women. Chauffeurs in white duck uniforms waited by their employers' cars parked beneath the trees that lined the street.

Marshall sipped his pina colada, savouring the tang of two different rums, laced with milk, fresh pineapple juice, and sugar. The sun and the slow pace of life here suited him; he would live like this when he had made his money.

Jack came up the wooden stairs, paused for a moment, then saw Marshall and walked towards him. He sat down thankfully, dumped his briefcase on the table, and mopped his forehead with a white handkerchief. He was the sort of man who sweated at the slightest exertion, thought Marshall with distaste. For the first time, he admitted to himself how much he disliked Jack. Was this only because Jack was so much more successful — or could it also be because of Carole?

"Had a hell of a time finding you," Jack began accusingly.

"I've been around," said Marshall. "What's the hurry? Is there trouble?"

"Why must there always be trouble? You've got a suspicious mind. And you're only half right; I've good news as well as bad."

Marshall signalled to a waiter to bring two more coladas. Jack drank greedily. The creamy mixture sank in his glass, and Frank's spirits went down with it.

Jack looked around him conspiratorially. The verandah was crowded with chattering people, mostly servicemen, with pretty girls, their wives or someone else's. No one could hear what he had to say, but even so, he spoke in a whisper.

"That fifty thousand you gave me," he said. "Collected your first dividend today. Twenty thousand bucks. Forty per cent return — after all expenses."

"Can't be bad," said Marshall, impressed.

"Can't be *bad?*" repeated Jack. "That all you can say, you ungrateful bastard? If you'd put that sum in U.S. Bonds, you'd be lucky to get four per cent interest — and not in a few months, but after a whole year."

"I'm not complaining," said Marshall quickly.

"I should hope not. I've got the notes back home, but I brought a hundred-dollar bill for you. Go next door and open up an account with it at the Royal Bank of Canada. Not in your own name, though."

The reason was obvious; he could be traced. Marshall's heart gave a drumbeat of alarm at the prospect. If the Outfit ever discovered he had been using their money for his own profit, there would be only one reaction, even if he offered to pay it back at once. What if Jack knew — or guessed — he had been using their money? Marshall's fingers closed around the hundred-dollar bill; this, at least, was comforting.

"And now the bad news?"

"It is bad, too," said Jack, suddenly serious. "The casino idea of yours. It's not going through."

"What do you mean, not going through? I spoke to Christie and Harry Oakes about it. They didn't shoot it down right away."

"Maybe. But now they've thought it through, they don't like it. My information is that Oakes doesn't trust you. Don't know why. That's his way. He either likes someone at first sight or he doesn't. And if he doesn't, that's it. I don't think you have much chance of making him change his mind. The same goes for Christie. He'll follow Oakes's lead. He must have made a pretty shrewd guess who's backing the venture. Maybe that's why he wants no part of it."

"But I've told the Outfit it was almost a sure thing."

"That was pretty foolish."

"So now you think the whole deal's off?" Marshall felt panic grip him like a clamp.

"That depends."

"On what?" he asked eagerly.

"On how you handle things from now on. But we shouldn't talk here. I've got a private room upstairs."

Jack led the way to a bedroom at the back of the building, unlocked the door, locked it behind him, pocketed the key. The window overlooked a wharf. A single shutter, propped up like a giant eyelid, kept out the fierce heat of the sun. A salty smell from rotting conch-shells drifted up from the quay, where old women squatted behind stalls of starfish and pink coral and fossilized seaweed. Jack opened his briefcase and handed a sheet of paper to Marshall.

"Read that," he said. "It's Sub-section ten of Section 257 of the Penal Code."

"What's it to do with me?"

"A lot. Maybe everything."

Marshall began to read the closely typed phrases, frowning at the unfamiliar legal wording:

It shall be lawful for the Governor in Council to exempt any person, club, or charitable organisation from the provisions of this section and to issue a certificate to any such person, club, or charitable organisation certifying that exemption has been granted as aforesaid.

Any such certificate shall be issued for such period and upon such terms and conditions as the Governor in Council shall deem fit and shall after issue be liable to cancellation by the Governor in Council at any time in the event of breach of any such terms and conditions or otherwise in the discretion of the Governor in Council.

"But what does all that mean?" Marshall asked.

"It means that a rich and smart young lawyer here, Stafford Sands, had just about the same idea as the Outfit, but back in 1939. As legal adviser to the House of Assembly, he discovered that two little casinos operating in the Bahamas — one on Cat Cay, which had just started, and the Bahamian Club, which had been going since 1920 — were both acting illegally. This clause made them legal — and, much more important — also could make others legal *if the Governor agrees.*"

"So how can we make him agree?"

"We can't ourselves, but the Executive Council can, if it wants to. ExCo, as it's called here, has three paid officials — the Colonial Secretary, the Attorney General, and the Treasurer — and six unofficial members, usually Bay Street Boys. Lean on enough of them and you can get your permission. I've checked, and no Governor has ever rebuffed the Council under this sub-section."

"What about leaning on this guy Sands?"

"He's big, he's fat, and he's greedy. His family owns a lot of grocery stores in the Bahamas. He was only a kid when Prohibition started, but he saw the money being made, and he wanted some of the same. He boasts his family's been here for three hundred and fifty years, so they knew all about wreckers, pirates, gun-running, you name it. He wouldn't let the family down. He'd want his share."

"He could have it."

"Don't start giving away what you haven't got," advised Jack.

"But this must be good news."

"All depends on how you use it. Now read these." Jack took a folder from his briefcase. "They've just arrived from Miami. The courier goes back this afternoon, so I can't let you keep them, but look at them now. They're dynamite."

Marshall opened the folder, picked up the copy of a letter dated January 23, 1940, and headed "U.S. Government, Department of State, Foreign Activities Correlation," addressed to Senator John A. Hastings, in New York. Across the top was written, "Read, tear up, and do not trouble to acknowledge."

This Wenner-Gren business gets more and more like an Oppenheim novel. First, Harold Christie, of Nassau, meets me at a party and begs me to assure Washington officials that Wenner-Gren is a fine, upstanding fellow and 100% anti-totalitarian ...

If Mr. Wenner-Gren felt the need of clearing himself of anything, the simple way would be to come to Washington, present himself before the State Department, the Department of Justice or the F.B.I., and put his cards on the table. Between us, there is a queer smell to the whole affair ...

"Christie I know, and Wenner-Gren I've heard of," said Marshall. "Who's this guy Hastings?"

"A political go-between. Let's just say he knows a lot of people we know. He was the youngest guy ever to be elected to the state Senate — then he got mixed up with bad company. There was an enquiry into how the Mayor was running things, and Hastings refused to testify. It got so much publicity, he lost his seat."

Marshall picked up the second letter, headed "Headquarters, Panama Canal Department, Office of the Assistant Chief of Staff for Military Intelligence," and marked "Confidential." It was addressed to Sumner Welles, Under-Secretary of State, and Adolf Berle, Assistant Secretary of State.

The Southern Cross yacht, belonging to one AXEL L. WENNER-GREN *arrived Cristobal from Miami, Fla. (and allegedly touching at a Mexican port en route), on July 4, 1940, and transited the Canal the same day... Information is that this yacht will stop at a Mexican port en route Los Angeles, though she cleared for Los Angeles direct.*

On board were Wenner-Gren, his wife, Marguerita, and his secretary, Gene Cauda Liggett. These were the only passengers.

The yacht operated under Panamanian registry from 1934-36 when she was here before. In 1938 she had changed to Swedish. This trip she has again changed to Panamanian ... She had aboard samples of machine guns, small arms, etc. Wenner-Gren invited certain individuals to come aboard, and demonstrated his guns to them.

Wenner-Gren is described as personally a polecat — officially, a bear cat... He is known to be a close friend of Goering. It was he, according to reports, who negotiated the terms with Goering which have permitted Sweden to remain neutral. The last time Wenner-Gren came through here, Paine and Warlaw [Englishmen] were his agents. This time Hans Elliot, whose activities here are definitely questionable, to put it mildly, was his agent.

The next paper was headed "Department of State, Division of Foreign Service Administration," and dated November 20, 1940, again marked for Adolf Berle, Assistant Secretary of State. It was the report of an agent, again about Wenner-Gren.

Axel Wenner-Gren has since November 1, 1939, been constantly steaming in and out of Nassau Harbor on his yacht, equipped with high-powered radio antennae. This yacht is manned by ex-Swedish navy officers all of whom... are definitely and professedly pro-Nazi...

Marshall picked up the fourth sheet of paper, again headed "Department of State, Washington," dated December 23, 1940, and signed "G. V. Hemett, Special Agent."

... The writer, with Captain Melchen of the Miami Police Department and others, boarded the 55 Southern Cross on arrival at Miami, Florida, 8 A.M., December 10, 1940, and met His Royal Highness the Duke of Windsor and Her Grace the Duchess of Windsor...

Marshall shuffled through several more copies of documents and letters, picked up several from the U.S. Consulate in Nassau and the

State Department in Washington, in the autumn of 1940. The Duchess of Windsor requested the State Department to contact the American Embassy in Paris, and then inform her whether her maid was still in that city. She wanted her to come to Nassau as soon as possible.

The reply stated that the maid had already left Paris for San Sebastian, and from there she would go to Lisbon, presumably on her way to the Bahamas.

The State Department pointed out that since the maid had left German-held territory, any responsibility of the U.S. government in their capacity of custodian of British interests had ended.

"Strictly speaking," a letter from the British Embassy in Washington added, "... it would be for His Royal Highness to pursue the matter of expediting the maid's going to Lisbon through the official channels in London, assuming always that His Majesty's Government felt able to intervene on behalf of a French national, which we understand the maid to be."

A third letter marked "Strictly Confidential" declared that the Duke of Windsor was "quite put out" by what he considered the "unfriendly" tone of this correspondence. However, the French maid finally arrived in Nassau in November, and a handwritten note, attached to these letters on paper headed "Department of State, Division of European Affairs," suggested that "Nassau might be instructed to have the Windsors send their own wires direct hereafter."

The next memo was addressed to Sumner Welles, stamped April 15, 1941, and was about involvement in Mexico. The writer confirmed that he had written to Mr. John A. Hastings, who, while declining to comment upon the merits of the proposed activities of the group or upon the Department's views respecting Mr. Wenner-Gren, stating that the group might desire to consider whether it was advisable to have others than Americans involved in its activities [had explained that] he had long known Mr. Harold Christie of the Bahamas, and that last July he saw Mr. Christie and Sir Harry Oakes in Mexico. He went on to say that Sir Harry was very much interested in the Mexican possibilities and had interested Mr. Wenner-Gren in that country. He also said that following this, Mr. Wenner-Gren came to New York bearing a letter of introduction to him from either Sir Harry or Mr. Christie and, further, that they again discussed Mexico in Nassau at the time of the recent visit of General Maximino Avila Camacho.

The next sheet was marked "Strictly Confidental" and came from the Under-Secretary of the Department of State to Mr. Berle, dated April 16, 1941.

The President told me this morning that he felt strongly that greater energy should be shown by the appropriate government agencies in covering the activities and connections of Mr. Axel Wenner-Gren ...

The President further said that he thought that it was easily possible that the Wenner-Gren yacht might have evidences of suspicious activities on board. He suggested that you talk over with Mr. Hoover the possibility of getting an agent on board, ostensibly as a member of the crew.

Against the last paragraph, Berle had written, in his own hand, "I have done this."

On July 18 a message came in from the U.S. Ambassador in Mexico. At the top was the terse instruction "This telegram must be closely paraphrased before being communicated to anyone."

Secretary of State, Washington. 320, July 16, 5 P.M. Banco Continental now being established in Mexico City ... Sir Harry Oakes now seems to include Wenner-Gren. We understand that Wenner-Gren's influence in such an institution may not be for the best interest of the United States ...

Marshall picked up a memorandum, dated June 2, 1942, from an American agent in Mexico City, giving details of Wenner-Gren's bank accounts, blocked in various countries. In Britain he had the equivalent of $50 million, with $32 million in the United States, $2 million in Mexico, $32 million in Norway, and $2.5 million in the Bahamas.

It is understood that deposits of $2,500,000 in the Bahamas were made at the express request and in part for the benefit of the Duke of Windsor, who until the outbreak of war (United States vs. Germany et al.), was on very friendly terms with A.W. and his wife. It may or may not be known that A.W. had sailed from Mexico in his yacht on December 4,1941, to pick up the Duke and Duchess of Windsor and bring them back to Mexico, but while en route to the Bahamas, war was declared by the United States, and A.W. felt it expedient to return to Mexico without completing his trip to the Bahamas.

Before A.W.'s funds were frozen worldwide, he had negotiated through Senator Hastings of New York, who uses the title of "Senator" in Mexico and who is seemingly a protege of Maximino Camacho, (brother of the President), and Secretary of Communications, and with this tie-up Camacho, Hastings, and A.W. proceeded to make various contracts throughout Mexico, involving the construction of roads, the development of mines, investments in oil and real estate, and opening of the Banco de Continental of Mexico. (It is my understanding A.W.'s money made possible the establishment of this bank, etc.)...

American capital, as represented by big investors and banks planning to invest in Mexico, were apprehensive concerning the investment and the control of over $100,000,000 by one individual in Mexico. With this sum of money aggregating roughly 500,000,000 pesos, A.W. could ... have secured control of almost all Mexico and every phase of its economic life, for he would have been able to retire through purchase of its outstanding loans and driven out of the country for many years to come any reasonable possibility of foreign development such as might emanate from the United States.

Just before his blacklisting in Mexico, Wenner-Gren had formed twenty-two separate corporations, involving almost every phase of Mexican life.

A.W. has done a great deal of entertaining on his yacht and his bosom companions in Mexico have been Maximino Camacho and the so-called Senator Hastings. He is also and has been for many years a close friend of the Duke of Windsor. A.W. attributes his present plight to his former close friendship and relationship with Hermann Goering who was in turn a close friend of the Duke of Windsor...

A.W. has given his yacht and title thereto to Mrs. Maximino Camacho, the furnishing of this very luxurious yacht going to the Camacho home in Cuernavaca...

He also arranged for the purchase of the Hotel Chula Vista. This deal he was unable to complete before his Mexican funds were frozen. It might be mentioned that the Chula Vista Hotel, which is an impressive structure of approximately one hundred rooms and suites, is rather remotely removed from the town of Cuernavaca. It is built in the mountains and ideally situated from the standpoint of protection for any group of people who might seek to congregate there ... Comments on A.W.'s activities as well as comments on Senator

Hastings, Camacho, and A.W. combined are reserved for personal discussion in Washington...

The final paper Marshall read was from the Department of State, dated June 9,1942.

Wenner-Gren had a lot of money in the Mobilia Corporation in Panama, at least $300,000. Since July, 1941, he had run the account down to almost nothing. It appears quite possible that he had been distributing his assets in such a way as to get them under cover or out of reach. It is interesting to note how early he began.

It is also interesting to note that $10,000 went to Empresa Agricola Chincama, Ltda., which turns out to be a Gildemeister subsidiary. The Department has received one report that this corporation is "managed and directed by men high in the Nazi Party..." The tie-up between Wenner-Gren and Gildemeisters is interesting.

The question always remains whether Wenner-Gren is moving funds which are strictly his own.

"I've got the answer to that," said Jack bluntly, reading over Marshall's shoulder. "They're not. Sir Harry Oakes has been salting away a lot. So has Harold Christie. The Duke of Windsor is also somehow involved."

"Why? What could he want out of it?"

"Dollars. He and the Duchess need them for their visits to the States. They're hard to get, because of the currency regulations."

"Doesn't the Governor have an allowance for such trips?"

"No. Not in the Bahamas. And even if he did, dollar restrictions still apply. And what kind of allowance would cover *their* sort of expenses? On one visit they took a whole floor of the Waldorf-Astoria in New York. They had so much luggage, it needed a whole railway truck to move the stuff. On the way back, the Miami Biltmore was shut for the winter, but the manager flew down from New York to open it — just for them. They took the fifteenth floor for themselves, and the one below for their staff.

"That kind of thing needs funding. A lot of other rich guys here have been pushing out money illegally, though that's tailed off, now America's in the war. Until then, they weren't so sure who was going to win. They wanted to be safe, either way."

"Anything else about Wenner-Gren?"

"As far as our government's concerned, he's supposed to be trying to get support to topple the Swedish government — and put in a more pro-Nazi bunch — as well as doing all he can to help Germany to find more oil. And if he could get a tight enough grip on Mexico, the whole of South America might swing against the Allies."

"Where do you get all this stuff from?"

"Friends in Washington. Incidentally, United States censors in Miami have been opening Christie's letters and examining them for secret writing. He's been on their watch list."

"But how does all this tie in with our set-up?"

"It gives you a lever against the three most powerful men on the island. You know the government here threatened to deport Alfred de Marigny — Harry Oakes's son-in-law — because they said his divorced wife had broken currency regulations?"

Marshall nodded. Jack had mentioned this to him at an earlier meeting, but he had not really understood its significance.

"If they'd do that over a relatively small amount of money, think of the uproar if anyone thought that the Governor and the island's two top citizens were involved in any way with a multi-million-dollar deal in Mexico with a man blacklisted by Britain and the United States.

"Would the former King of England really like the world to think that while his country was fighting for its life, he could conceivably be financially involved with a known Nazi sympathiser?

"What would people say if these letters about the Duchess's maid were made public? There are millions of refugees all over the world, and here's the Duchess, wasting the time of over-worked, hard-pressed American embassies just so she can have a French maid here in Nassau. What's so wrong with a Bahamian maid?

"Christie wouldn't enjoy having all this brought out, either. Nor would Sir Harry. Incidentally, you've got to hand it to him. He's not really interested in moving money around. He prefers gold."

"How is that moved?"

"It used to be dumped on one of the Out Islands, usually Great Exuma, for a tender from Wenner-Gren's yacht to collect. Now a courier carries it. There's a fellow here, John Anderson, who's been a go-between. There's another memo on that. The British know about his visits to Mexico City and have warned him privately that if he contacts Wenner-Gren there, he does so at his own risk. I think he's got the message."

Marshall nodded, assimilating all this information, yet not sure how he could use it; maybe those drinks in the heat of the sun had not been a good idea. In the past, he had always held Jack in contempt, as the smaller, weaker man. Now, he felt inferior, because he needed Jack's expertise.

"How do you think I should handle this stuff?" he asked humbly.

Jack paused, as though considering the matter. He had, of course, already studied it carefully from everyone's point of view, most of all from his own. This plump worried goon opposite him would never suspect that the courier from Miami had advised him to let the deal about the casino coast for the time being. For some reason, it was no longer so important. But he did not tell Marshall, because he wanted to destroy him, or, rather, to let him destroy himself.

Jack knew about Marshall's affair with Carole years ago and suspected he was probably still interested in her. She might still even care for him. This thought filled him with bitterness so strong that he had to look away over Marshall's shoulder towards Hog Island, trembling in its noonday haze of heat, in case the other man saw naked hatred in his eyes.

"A difficult question," he said slowly. "But, first, what's *your* answer?"

"I think I should see the Duke of Windsor and put it directly to him that, as you say, he wouldn't enjoy having all this published."

"And where would that get you — if he even saw you, which I doubt?"

"Well, I'd also see Harry Oakes and Harold Christie. Tell them I had proof."

Jack shook his head. "You're too direct," he explained disapprovingly. "You're rushing into things. If I were you, I'd be very careful how I played this one.

"So what do you suggest?"

"This." Jack began to speak quietly, almost in a whisper. Marshall listened, at first resentfully, and then with growing admiration. Jack's plan was simple, yet it contained an answer for every conceivable objection.

"It looks foolproof," said Marshall admiringly.

"It is. If you play things *exactly* like I tell you."

Jack smiled at him, savouring the full enjoyment of having Marshall at last within his power. The man was so unbelievably stupid, he accepted the proposal at its face value; no questions, no doubts. He did not seem to realise that it could have two faces. If the plan failed, then

Marshall would take the blame. If it succeeded, Jack would claim credit — because he would tell the Outfit that it was his idea. What the hell could Carole see in a dumb guy like this?

Marshall was also thinking about Jack's plan, and one small point puzzled him. Why hadn't the courier from Miami come to see *him* with these papers? Was this because, in the Outfit's eyes, Jack was still senior to him?

"An old friend asked me to help," Jack explained. "I was glad to."

Marshall nodded uneasily. Did this also mean that the "old friend" was dissatisfied with his performance?

"By the way," Jack continued casually, "the Outfit knows that you've spent fifty thousand dollars of their money. I thought I should tell you."

"Of course they know. I told them. I said I gave it to various people to smooth things along."

"Sure. That's what I heard you'd told them. But if those people don't deliver, they won't like it."

"I could pay it back."

"Eventually, yes. But right now I've promised it, with a hundred thousand of my own, to another three pilots off to Accra. Diamonds."

He glanced out the window as a squadron of aircraft trailed white vapour trails across the unbroken blue of the sky.

"Maybe that's them now," he said dreamily. "They'll be back as soon as they can. Couple of weeks, maybe three."

"Is that soon enough?"

Jack shrugged. "The Outfit always wants quick results. You know that. And this deal's been dragging on for over a year. That's why I think my proposal could help you. Meanwhile, I'll speak to a few people know. Put a bit more money around on your account. Remember, everyone's voice is equally important when it comes to voting. Poor as well as rich."

"I have no more money," said Marshall flatly.

"But you have," replied Jack sweetly. "I'll use the twenty thousand profit I made for you."

In the warm darkness, lights outside Government House lent to the building an ethereal appearance denied by the harsher light of day. The Union Jack had been lowered at dusk, for such was the size of the British Empire that as the sun went down on one possession, it rose above another; the sun must never be allowed to set on the flag. Beyond and beneath, the lights of Nassau glowed and glittered, and beyond them again, the sea stretched, moonlit to infinity.

The Duke of Windsor stood in an upper room, a glass of Martell in his hand, watching the cars arrive, careful to keep back from the tall windows so that none of the guests should see him; it was not seemly for the host to look down on those he had invited.

The Duke had little stomach for the evening. He would have to show pleasure at receiving men who once would scarcely have been allowed into Buckingham Palace through the tradesmen's entrance, but were rich enough to allow their wives the expense of having hairdressers flown in from Miami to set their hair. The Duchess did the same, of course, but it was different for her. Everything was different as far as she was concerned. He always made excuses for her extravagance, as for her bitter outbursts against his family and this exile in the sun.

He glanced at his watch. The Duchess was apparently still not ready. She would arrive in her own time, wearing a gown by Schiaparelli or Mainbocher, hair ablaze with jewels, and then move from one guest to another, her makeup masking her thoughts as totally as her face.

He walked down the stairs. By the time he reached the ground floor, his own face was set in the Peter Pan way that had so endeared him to his father's world-wide subjects when he was Prince of Wales. Now the boyishness seemed cruelly misplaced: the stature of a youth with the eyes of experience.

At the far end of the ballroom, on a raised dais, under a Royal red canopy, an orchestra played soft music. Not the steel beat of the islands, the goombay drums that had travelled with the slaves from Africa, the music of hot nights and strong rum, but an anaemic transplant from London tea dances of the 1930's. Fan blades beat the stuffy air. On each side of the room six windows opened on to wide verandahs. Beyond them, the garden straggled through lawns dotted with palms and cotton trees and tamarinds.

Faces shone with perspiration and gin and expectation as the Duke circulated with an aide at his elbow, ready with a name should His Royal Highness forget. A pleasant word here, a smile there, his glass raised slightly as though in a mutual and private toast.

"David."

He heard the familiar voice of the Duchess and turned towards her with his fixed and famous smile.

"What is it, darling?"

"Someone who would like to meet you. Mr. Marshall. Plans something that could help the island."

"Anything that helps the Bahamas helps me," said the Duke. He shook hands. The Duchess moved away.

"Honoured to meet you, sir," said Marshall earnestly. "As a matter of fact, I've been trying to have an interview literally for months."

"Really?"

An expression of slight pain crossed the Duke's smiling face, like a tiny cloud before the sun. Of course, he had mentioned this man to the Duchess, months before, but at that time she had not been interested in hearing about him. She must have forgotten. Things he told her never seemed to be quite so important as the things she told him.

Well, neither Christie nor Harry Oakes seemed enthusiastic about Marshall's proposition, so he had seen no point in meeting him after all. Now the fellow was here in front of him.

"Your aides kept putting me off, sir. Said I should submit my ideas in writing. But what I really wanted was a chance to talk to *you,* sir. Personally."

"This is hardly the place," said the Duke. Like all short men, he did not like standing close to someone so much taller, and he moved slightly to one side, looking across the room, hoping to see a face he recognised to give him an excuse to move away. Something about this overpowering American with the hard eyes disturbed him. He felt strangely uneasy, almost threatened. He took a pace towards a retired South African banker whose face he knew but whose name he had forgotten.

Marshall followed him. "I know that, sir. But if I could make an appointment?"

"You must see Gray Phillips. He looks after those things for me," said the Duke. Really, the man was becoming impossible.

"It's about a hotel, sir. With a casino. I represent an American consortium."

"Christie has already mentioned this to me, and I spoke to Harry Oakes about it. They are not enthusiastic, I fear."

"So I believe, sir. But if I may have only a moment of your time?"

"I really cannot discuss such matters now. Impossible. You must realise that."

Major Gray Phillips, the Duke's aide-de-camp, appeared, glass in hand, horn-rimmed glasses firmly on his face.

"This is the man you should see," said the Duke with great relief. "Be so good as to make any arrangements through him."

Marshall turned, and the Duke moved away to be by Wallis's side. Here he felt secure. She might scold him, even humiliate him, but she would protect him.

By half-past eight, the party was all but over. A few determined drinkers or social pilot fish still lingered, hoping for a private word with the Duke or Duchess, for this might elevate their own social position. But the Duke and Duchess had already withdrawn to their separate rooms. They always dined at nine, the hour at which he used to eat in the palace in that far-off happy time when he was prince and King.

A butler tapped discreetly on his door, waited for a moment, opened it, and announced Mr. Harold Christie. The Duke was sitting by the open window. Taxi horns brayed like distant bugles. On the buoys that marked the harbour entrance, lights winked at each other. The night was very warm. Both men's shirts felt damp on their flesh.

"You wanted to see me, sir?" began Christie.

"Take a seat," said the Duke.

He indicated an easy chair, and the brandy and glasses. On the table nearby was the red leather memo pad with the Royal cipher tooled in gold. Next to it were two polished wooden cigar boxes. He passed one towards Christie.

Christie shook his head. "I would prefer a cigarette, if I may, sir."

The Duke nodded thoughtfully and pulled the second box towards him. This contained half-used cigar stubs. The Duke felt several for firmness, then selected one, clipped off the blackened end with cigar cutters, and lit it. He did not like waste.

"I wanted a word about this American, what's his name, Frank Marshall," the Duke said. He drew on his cigar, blew out the match. Christie waited.

"Know much about him, do you?"

"I first met him years ago," Christie replied as casually as he could, not wishing to be drawn into too much detail about his early dealings with Marshall. "Must have been early in 'thirty-one."

"I was in South America then," said the Duke reminiscently. "In Lima, Peru. They were actually on the eve of a revolution and postponed it for my visit. Imagine. We had dinner at the British Legation, I remember. The Acting President, one Sanchez Cerro, sat on my right, with an empty seat on my left for his Vice-President.

" 'Don't wait dinner for him,' Cerro told me. 'I happen to know he is plotting to have me shot. What *he* doesn't know is I am planning to have him shot.' "

"So what happened?" asked Christie.

The Duke shrugged. "Can't remember exactly. Don't think anyone actually *was* shot. But when I next heard of Cerro, he was sailing into exile in the same cabin aboard the same ship in which I had arrived in his country."

"The wheel of fortune," said Christie philosophically. "Like the world, it keeps on turning."

"Anyhow," said the Duke quickly, not wishing to pursue this line of thought, "this fellow Marshall was here tonight. Buttonholed me about his hotel and casino. I told him you weren't for it."

"Some people, of course, wouldn't mind a new *hotel*. That would mean more work, more business. But gambling, they are not keen on."

"What do you feel about it, Christie?"

"I'm a bit dubious, sir. One does not really know who's behind the venture."

"What exactly do you mean?"

"You've probably never come across this situation, sir, but gambling can open the door for gangsters. They can then get rid of hot money without any questions asked — and win it all back. The roulette wheel makes dirty money clean."

"Really?" said the Duke, genuinely surprised. "I had no idea."

"A number of the islanders had brushes with these people during Prohibition and are not anxious to become involved again. They are very ruthless men, sir. When they set their minds on something, they don't take no for an answer. Ever."

"You mean, as in American films, if they don't get their way, they might kill people?"

"I mean just that, sir."

"But surely a hotel and casino here would be of enormous value in the tourist industry when it starts up again after the war?"

"It might be even more valuable to them."

"So you are really against it, Christie?"

"I am naturally in favour of anything that promotes the islands. After all, my business is real estate, and the future here lies with tourists from Europe, Canada, the States. Anywhere and everywhere. But I'm uneasy over the possible identity of Marshall's backers."

"After you told me about Marshall's proposals, I mentioned the plan to Harry Oakes. He's no more enthusiastic than you."

"Probably for different reasons," said Christie. "I wouldn't think he's ever had any involvement with the Outfit, as we used to call them. Oakes likes privacy. He came here to get away from people as much as taxes. I doubt that he would relish the idea of more cruise ships and more aircraft bringing hundreds of holiday-makers every week. It would ruin what he feels the Bahamas should be."

"You're pretty close to Oakes?" asked the Duke.

"I should be," said Christie. "I was working out the other day that he's bought six times as much property from me as any other single purchaser. He's a good friend, too."

"So, if you are both against the proposition, you won't find many to approve it?"

"I think that's a fair assessment, sir."

"Then no useful purpose would be served if I met Marshall again. I suggest you convey the gist of our conversation to him. In a pleasant and friendly way, of course."

"Of course," Christie agreed. "I would not wish to make an enemy of him — or his backers."

Marshall waited to the right of the front door, beyond the sentry and the white floodlit pillars, standing on the edge of darkness, where he could see without being seen. When Christie came out, Marshall moved into the light.

"I want a talk," he said shortly.

"I'm dining out tonight," Christie replied. "It's rather difficult."

"I'll ride with you in the car."

"There's the driver."

"Send him home. If you can't drive, I will."

Christie hesitated for a moment. Then he walked to the car and spoke to the chauffeur, who held open the front door for him and stood watching them drive away. When they were clear of Government House, Marshall said, "I saw the Duke tonight, and I've asked one of his staff to try to fix up a meeting with him for next week. It's not definite, of course, but I'm hopeful."

"You'll be very lucky if you do see him," said Christie, not mentioning that he had just talked to the Duke. "He's a busy man. And he and the Duchess are just back from Miami, so he's a lot to catch up with."

"I gather they spend quite a lot of time off the island?"

"Well, they've been away for eight weeks. The Duchess has poor health."

"I understand that when she had a tooth seen to in Miami, Axel Wenner-Gren took her there in his yacht."

"He won't be doing that again for a while, I dare say. He's in Mexico."

"In any case, he's given his yacht to the President's sister-in-law. Her husband, Maximino Camacho, was staying here, too, I understand. In the British Colonial. Sir Harry Oakes's hotel."

"What of that? He's a rich man. This is a rich man's town."

"The richer some men are, the more they have to lose."

Christie stopped his car, switched off his engine. Across the road, between two cannons and an anchor, Woodes Rogers, the eighteenth-century Governor who had driven out the pirates — Morgan, Blackbeard, Teach, and the rest — watched them with bronze eyes. Beneath his statue was engraved his laconic report on this success, which had become the colony's motto: "Pirates Expelled, Commerce Restored."

"Tell me exactly what you're hinting at," Christie asked Marshall. "I'd like to hear it straight, whatever you have to say."

"My principals would like a quick answer. In the affirmative, if possible, obviously."

"That's quite impossible to give in a hurry. Right now, the feeling is strongly against gambling. As, I think, you know. Most people here did business in the twenties and thirties with the men I assume are backing this consortium, but things have changed now. They can't call the tune here, you know."

"I wouldn't be so sure of that," said Marshall. "I understand there have been some serious irregularities over money leaving the Bahamas. I've been told that you, Sir Harry, even the Duke himself, are involved. The sums are considerable."

"I don't know what you mean," said Christie curtly, but he sounded unconvincing, even to himself. A chill finger of foreboding moved down his spine.

"I don't know, either," replied Marshall frankly. "But I've seen copies of letters and reports about it. Here. In Nassau."

"What sort of letters? From whom?"

"Notes, memos, reports from United States government departments and embassies. Camacho and this guy Wenner-Gren are both mentioned. So's the Governor. Anyway, it's really nothing to do with me. I'm just telling you — in case you feel it could influence you. Or anyone else. It's not the sort of thing some people would like to see made public."

"I simply don't know what you're getting at. Can you imagine Sir Harry Oakes or the Duke being party to anything illegal — and in wartime?"

"I've got a poor imagination," said Marshall drily. "But no doubt lots of people would be only too happy to imagine just that. If you throw enough mud, it sticks. So let's not get into a mud-throwing situation."

"When exactly do you need a decision?"

"No fixed time limit — yet. But I can tell you the pressure's on me as much as on you. I'd say it's a matter of days rather than weeks."

"I'll do what I can, but I've really nothing more to say than this: *Dum spiro, spew.*"

"What do you mean? What language is that?"

"Latin, Mr. Marshall. The motto of that man over there. Woodes Rogers. The most successful Governor the Bahamas ever had. He would know how to deal with you."

"What does it mean?"

"While I breathe," said Christie, "I hope."

8

Special Delivery to a Back Door

THE SEAPLANE'S FLOATS CARVED two white grooves in the emerald ocean, and the Duke, looking out through the round window as the aircraft turned, saw them curve like giant sword blades. The sight instantly took his mind back to Royal salutes, a thousand sabres flashing in the Indian sun on his first Empire tour as Prince. He smelled once more the scented dust of India as his vast entourage travelled by train across seemingly endless baking plains. He had so many advisers, aides, companions, and servants on that tour, with State landaus and horses for a ceremonial entry into each city, and even twenty-five polo ponies generously provided by Indian princes. Three special trains were needed to transport them all. It was so important, and so well-publicised a visit, that his address was simply "The Prince of Wales's Camp, India."

Then, abruptly, he was back in the cramped metal cabin rocking in the wash, shirt stuck with sweat to his back, his companions, a rough-tongued gold miner who had struck a rich seam, and a chain-smoking Bahamian eager to sell plots of land to anyone rich enough to buy. The contrast between memory and reality — or maybe simply the sun striking too brightly off the water — momentarily filled the Duke's pale blue eyes with tears.

Harry Oakes shook his head, finger in his right ear.

"I hate these damn things," he said crossly, as the pilot raced his engine to coast in towards the shore.

"Her Royal Highness refuses to fly."

"Who?" Oakes could not hear very well against the crackle of exhaust.

"The Duchess. My wife. After France fell, my government, I mean *the* government, sent over two flying boats to Lisbon to bring us back to Britain. She said she would rather risk capture by the Nazis than risk flying."

"Not everyone was given the same opportunity," replied Oakes gruffly.

The pilot cut his engine, threw a line to a fisherman who had rowed out to ferry them ashore. Locals appeared, as they always did when Christie visited the island; he was a popular and generous man.

"No restaurants here," he explained, "but I've arranged for a light lunch to be served under the trees."

They walked across white sands towards the welcome shade of the palms. The Duke took off his straw hat, fanned his face, sat down in the shade on a fallen trunk.

"Why exactly *are* we here?" he asked petulantly. "I thought there was something to inspect, something you wanted to show me."

There was nothing within sight on this island, except a cluster of shacks and several fishing boats drawn up on the sand. Children, sucking thumbs, gathered to stare at them, wide-eyed and silent. The heat was intense. There was no wind, and flies settled on their lips and nostrils.

"I wanted to talk to you where there was no chance of being overheard," Christie explained. The pilot was still with the seaplane, standing on one float, checking the engine.

"Why the secrecy?"

"Because it's about the hotel that this American consortium wants to build. The casino."

"But that's nothing to do with me. We discussed that the other night. I'm for any idea in principle that will help the Bahamas. But you pointed out the public feeling against gambling and other factors against it. That's all there is to it."

"I only wish it were. Have you considered what could happen if the House of Assembly turned down the proposal, even if the Executive Council approved it? Or vice versa?"

"No. Why should I? It wouldn't be the first time."

"This is different, sir."

"Is it?" The Duke's voice hardened. "The House of Assembly is supposed to be re-elected every seven years. So what did they do? They deliberately passed a resolution, extending their period of office just to block reforms I wanted that could have helped the poor people enormously.

"I asked for a defence fund.of seven thousand pounds. *Nothing.* Less than your income *every day>* Harry. But they turned that down. Too expensive.

"I could have stopped those terrible riots last year before they ever started, but the House wouldn't listen to me. I do know what I'm talking about, you know. I have been King, not just Governor. Why should I concern myself about what happens to members of the House of Assembly? It doesn't seem to me they've ever bothered much about the people they're supposed to be elected to serve."

"You're missing the point, sir," Christie replied. "We're not worried what happens to them or what doesn't happen to them. It's what can happen to *us* that concerns me."

"I don't understand you. What do you mean, exactly?"

"Let me spell it out, sir. This American, Marshall, knows about Wenner-Gren."

"Well, what about Wenner-Gren? He's stuck in Mexico on the

blacklist of

TOP
Nancy Oakes de Marigny *(Wide World Photos)*
BOTTOM
Left: Sir Harry Oakes *(United Press International)*
Right: Alfred de Marigny *(United Press International)*

Charles "Lucky" Luciano *(Wide World Photos)*

The *Normandie* burning at her dock on the Hudson in New York City, February 9, 1942. Fireboats are pouring water on the burning liner and she has begun to list to port. *(Wide World Photos)*

Westbourne, Sir Harry Oakes's mansion near Nassau, the Bahamas. His bedroom was just above the right-hand end of the veranda. *(Wide World Photos)*

The plan of Westbourne's second floor. Oakes's body was found in the master bedroom. Harold Christie slept in the East Room. *(Wide World Photos)*

The famous fingerprint found on the screen in Sir Harry's bedroom *(United Press International)*

OPPOSITE

Top: The master bedroom with Sir Harry's partially burned body on the bed. The much-discussed Chinese screen is at the left of his bed. *(United Press International)*

Bottom: Inside the door of Sir Harry's bedroom. The carpet is charred and there are scorch marks on the door panels which may have been made by a blowtorch, according to Raymond Schindler. *(United Press International)*

The crowd in front of the Nassau courthouse, waiting for the Marigny trial *(United Press International)*

The trial in progress. Sir Oscar Bedford Daly, M.B.E. presides. Reginald de Glanville, Assistant Attorney General is the man in front of the bench, second from the left. *(United Press International)*

The investigators. Major Herbert Pemberton stands at the left. Seated at the microscope is Captain James O. Barker and at the right is Captain Edward W Melchen. *(United Press International)*

The Marigny defense. At left, Ernest Callendar; the Honorable Godfrey Higgs, center; and Raymond Schindler, right. *(United Press International)*

Harold G. Christie *(Wide World Photos)*

The Marquis Georges de Visdelou, his friend Betty Roberts, and Grisou, Marigny's cat. (The cat's name means "firedamp," an explosive gas.) *(United Press International)* my government — rather, my brother's government — and of the United States government. That's that."

"It isn't, sir. That's only part of it. Marshall tells me he's seen American Intelligence reports — not only on Wenner-Gren, but on us."

"Us?" retorted the Duke in amazement. "What have they got to say about us?"

"A lot. I saw Marshall after your party, sir. He told me a few things. Then he rang me at my office yesterday and told me some more. Do you know that, on President Roosevelt's personal order, the United States put an agent aboard *Southern Cross?* Marshall knows all about the money moved to Mexico. He knows about your gold, Harry."

"What if he does?" Oakes asked belligerently. "I spent years searching for gold. I've not robbed anyone for it, or sold anyone short. I dug it out of the earth. I found it, and it's mine. Don't you or him try to tell me what I can or can't do with my own property."

"I'm not telling you anything," said Christie. "I'm just pointing out facts."

"Your father was a preacher, wasn't he?" replied Oakes.

"Yes. Off and on."

"No doubt he knew the parable in Matthew twenty — about the labourers who agreed to work in a vineyard for pay of a penny a day, and then complained because late arrivals were getting the same amount? The owner of the vineyard asked them: 'Is it not lawful for me to do what I will with mine own?' I say it is."

"Maybe you do. And to a certain extent I agree with you. But we're in the middle of a war, Harry. Here's a text my father used in many a sermon, also from Matthew. Chapter twenty-two this time, verse twenty-one. 'Render therefore unto Caesar the things which are Caesar's.' And in wartime, Harry, all our wealth is legally Caesar's — the government's."

"Just what are you trying to do, Harold? Convert me — or warn me?"

"The latter. Can't you see what this man Marshall can do if he wants to? He can ruin us."

"Why the hell should he want to?"

"Because he's one of the Outfit."

"What is the Outfit?" asked the Duke tetchily. "Explain yourself, Harold. All these texts and riddles."

"It's a corporate name for the gangsters I mentioned the other night. The fellows who made fortunes through Prohibition."

"Prohibition." The Duke repeated the word slowly. It had unexpectedly unlocked another half-forgotten memory.

"I remember I was in Washington during Prohibition. Had to visit the Naval Academy at Annapolis, with a motorcycle escort — my first, actually. Great fellows on the way there. But on the way back — you know what? They were all drunk."

"Drunk?" repeated Christie. "How — during Prohibition?"

"Apparently they met some revenue agents who had just seized a warehouse full of bootleg liquor. So they all sampled it."

"Did they lose their jobs?" Oakes asked him.

"They were going to," admitted the Duke, "but I spoke up for them. And do you know what? All those fellows came individually to thank me."

"You won't get gratitude like that now," said Christie shortly. "And not from the men behind Marshall. They're a hard-nosed crowd. They were making at least a thousand, maybe two thousand per cent profit on all the drink they sold. They invested a lot of this money legally, so now they're straight up-and-down businessmen. But they're still working so many other rackets, they simply have to keep finding new ventures for more investment. What better than hotels, which they can pack with tourists who'll spend money in their casinos? There's millions at stake here. More. And no tax on their takings. They're already in Havana. Now they want in here — and one day they'll be here, all right. They'll get permission for their casinos sooner or later. You can be absolutely sure of that."

"And if they don't get it now?"

"They'll threaten to ruin us. Maybe they'll do more than threaten, so others who've anything to hide — and everyone has *some* secret in their past — will get the warning. They've contacts everywhere, in radio, the Press, government. Never underestimate what they could do, sir, if we don't play along with them."

"But that's blackmail," protested the Duke.

"It's also a fact."

"If they did what you say," said Oakes, "it could be embarrassing, O.K. I agree with that. But they can't *prove* anything. It's only their word against ours."

"I could stop anything derogatory being printed here," said the Duke brightly. "Say it was against the national interest. I have the power."

"They'd simply print it in the States, sir. Give it to one of the columnists. Walter Winchell would love that. He's already had a good crack at Wenner-Gren in his column. Said he built a harbour on Hog Island big enough to take a U-boat."

"I happen to know that it was simply to take his yacht in bad weather," said the Duke stiffly. "Wenner-Gren told me so himself."

"But where Wenner-Gren is now doesn't put him in any position to explain that to WinchelPs readers from coast to coast, does it? They could put out the poison about us, bit by bit. Some every week, maybe every day. Marshall has a lot of ammunition. Not stories we could laugh off."

He paused, and then added softly, "Think what the Duchess would say."

The Duke pursed his lips as he thought. This would be a further failure to add to the list. In time, earlier misjudgements might be forgotten, by the public, if not by her. But not this; never this. It would come too close on the heels of the Bedaux fiasco.

After the Duke's abdication, when he was still in France, he had become very friendly with Charles Bedaux, a French-born American who had invented a system of time-and-motion study that made him a fortune. Bedaux lent his chateau to the Duke and Duchess and arranged for them to make a special visit to Germany. There, they had both met Hitler and other Nazi leaders, and spent two weeks as their honoured guests. This trip aroused so much criticism that the Duke had been forced to cancel a visit to the United States that Bedaux had also organised for them.

After the fall of France, Bedaux collaborated wholeheartedly with the Nazis, and only a few months earlier had been in Algiers, completing plans to build a two-thousand mile pipeline in North Africa, with a railway alongside it. When the Americans landed, the Free French arrested Bedaux and handed him over to the United States authorities, because he held an American passport. At that moment, he was being held in a military prison outside Algiers.

Sir Harry's nasal voice rasped into the Duke's thoughts. "The hell with what the Duchess would say," he growled. "This is a democracy. Everyone can vote as he will, and I'm voting against this proposal. If it's carried through by others, fair enough. I'll stand by that, but I'm not going to help it along. Not in any way whatever."

"But can't you see the good it could do for the Bahamas?" Christie asked him.

"Good?" repeated Oakes in amazement. "How can you possibly say that? You would prostitute the islands. Fill them with tourists, every week of the year. One hotel with a casino is only the start. Before you know where you are, you'll have more. Take my word for it."

"We're talking only about one now."

"Now you are, agreed. But once they're in, they'll agitate for more. Piss in a bucket of water, and you contaminate only what's in that bucket. But piss down a well, and you can poison a whole village. If you let these people in, it's the end of the Bahamas as we know them."

"They've had a pretty rough history so far," said the Duke nervously. "Slave traders. Pirates. Wreckers."

"That's in the past," retorted Oakes. "This would poison their whole future. Before you know it, they'll be running drugs in here from Haiti and Colombia and out again to the States."

"That's going on already," said Christie.

"Can't the customs stop it, or the police?" asked the Duke.

"There's too much money involved. You realise what the Commissioner of Police's salary is here, sir? Seven hundred pounds a year. And he's top man. So think what the ordinary policeman gets. Think what customs officers receive. And remember, one of them has only to look the other way for a second, or wave to a friend while someone comes through with a suitcase — and there's a bribe worth a year's income in his back pocket."

"I never thought of it like that."

"You're lucky you've never had to," said Oakes. He turned to Christie. "When you first persuaded me to come here, you quoted Columbus's description of the Bahamas, 'the isles of June.' No income tax. No inheritance tax. Marvellous climate. Friendly people — and not too many of them.

"This island is only eighty square miles. If you pack it with thousands of tourists, here primarily to gamble, what kind of folks are they going to be? Croupiers? Crowds of idiots who think they can beat the system, turning day into night?"

"It won't be like that at all," said Christie. "You're being unreasonable."

"The hell I am," retorted Oakes. "I've thought it through, and it's a lousy idea."

"He could make things especially embarrassing for me," Christie went on. "Remember, I was appointed a member of the Board of the Commissioners of Currency here just after the war started."

"You should have thought of that before."

"You don't understand'..." Christie began.

"I understand perfectly," Oakes interrupted. "You're scared. Now, understand me. I spent years searching for gold. Now I've got it, I'll do what I damn like with it. Do I make that clear?"

"Perfectly. But you must see how important it is that we don't turn down this request out of hand. Later, perhaps, but not immediately."

"If you're so worried about Marshall, buy him off."

"Impossible," Christie replied. "He's only the messenger. We can't buy off the men who've sent the message."

"That's as may be. But you've heard my last word on the subject," said Oakes. "I don't care what Marshall or anyone else says about Wenner-Gren and Mexico. I've a damn good mind to move all my money there, in any case. The investment climate there looks pretty attractive. To hell with Marshall and all the rest. He can't *prove* a damn thing, and if he tries to, so what? I was reading the other day something that Sir Montagu Norman, the former Governor of the Bank of England, said about criticism: 'The dogs bark, but the caravan moves on.' Those are my views entirely."

"You don't know what you're saying," said Christie earnestly.

"I damn' well do," retorted Oakes. "If it's so important to you, persuade the others. But you won't ever persuade me, so don't waste your time."

"The others will follow your lead, Harry. You know that."

"Then it's time they stopped. Why should I agree to some underworld gangsters building a casino here that I don't want? There's nothing in it for the Bahamas. Not in their best interests. There may be some commission for you, Harold, but there's nothing for anyone else. And I tell you this: the day people come in here with gambling schemes — I move out."

Marigny climbed out of bed, rubbed sleep from his eyes, and looked from his bedroom window at Hog Island, wreathed in mist like a huge grey whale. The sea, the tiled roofs, the houses, all usually so bright, seemed sad and subdued, an out-of-season aquatint. The two carefully unadvertised months of July and August were always humid and often rainy.

It was six-thirty in the morning. He usually was awake at this hour, and often even earlier when his stomach pained him. In New York, before his marriage to Nancy Oakes, a surgeon had removed an internal growth, but sudden persisting pulses of pain brought back memories of Ruth visiting him in the hospital, arguing in her shrill discontented voice. Ruth had been the cause of much of the ill-feeling that had developed between him and Nancy's parents; he was certain of that. Their reservations about him as a son-in-law might have died down if she had accepted the situation more calmly.

Once, she wrote to Lady Oakes claiming that Marigny owed her $40,000. She made the same allegation in a letter to Walter Foskett, the Oakes's family lawyer, as Marigny discovered when he visited Foskett while in Palm Beach for Nancy's operation. He asked Foskett to use his influence to heal the breach between the Oakes and himself, for he felt that he would get on as well with Nancy's parents as he did with her brothers and sisters, if only they would accept him for what he was, and not the rogue Ruth claimed he was. But to Marigny's disappointment Foskett was in no mood to act as mediator.

Marigny had heard that Foskett owed his own independence to Sir Harry Oakes and had never forgotten this. Apparently, Oakes had once called to see his lawyers in Palm Beach, and the partner he usually dealt with was unable to see him. Foskett, as a relatively junior employee, was told to talk to Oakes until the partner was free. Oakes was impressed by the young man.

"Do you like working here?" he had asked Foskett bluntly.

"Well..." began Foskett hesitantly.

"Right," said Oakes. "Quit now and I'll set you up in your own office — and you can have all my business."

Foskett's loyalties were therefore quite understandably towards Sir Harry.

"I think it's a disgrace that you married Nancy in the first place," Foskett told Marigny bluntly. "You've been married twice already *and* twice divorced. Also, you're thirty-three and she's a lovely young girl."

"I'm sorry about those divorces," agreed Marigny. "But since you raise that subject, your own daughter's marriage lasted less than two years before she was divorced."

"That's none of your business."

"I suppose you know that Lady Oakes's brother has also been divorced?"

"That has nothing whatever to do with this case," Foskett retorted. "I cannot mediate in any way. To be frank, I don't like you. I don't trust you. I have received a letter from your ex-wife in which she makes some very serious allegations. She says you stole forty thousand dollars from her."

"In fact, she owed me exactly that amount when we separated. What else did she say?"

"That at the time you married Nancy, not only did you have to marry her because she was pregnant — but your ex-wife was also pregnant by you! That seems to me to be a pretty disgusting state of affairs. I have passed on the contents of this letter to Sir Harry and Lady Oakes."

"Then I consider that to be even more disgusting. As a lawyer, don't you think it would have been prudent to check these totally false allegations before you passed them on?"

"I think you are just a gigolo, Marigny. A man who lives off rich women."

Before Marigny could reply, Foskett walked out of his office, slamming the door. The incident might have ended there, but of course, it did not; incidents like this are rarely conclusive, but signposts on a journey to disaster.

Nancy went into hospital shortly after this for the operation on her mouth, and her father ordered Marigny to leave the nearby room that he had booked for his own operation. Marigny was used to Harry Oakes's sudden outbursts. To outsiders, they appeared more serious than they were: he was like a boiler blowing steam, all noise and fury, but causing little lasting damage. Indeed, within a short time Sir Harry invited Marigny and Newell Kelly to watch a polo match with him. They all lunched together and later played billiards in the evening — and not once did Harry Oakes mention the earlier incident.

Nancy did not recover quickly after the operation. These sudden scenes and accusations, added to her mother's obvious dislike of her husband, did not make for a happy atmosphere in which to convalesce, and Marigny took her to Eleuthera for a few days to recuperate. When they returned to Nassau, there was another shouting match over why they had not accepted an invitation to the Duke of Windsor's cocktail party at Government House.

"I just don't want to go," Marigny explained. "These aren't my type of people. I have nothing against them. But I don't want to stand in line and kow-tow to a man like that."

"You don't like him?" asked Oakes ominously.

"I don't admire him," Marigny replied.

"He was our King."

"Yes, but he isn't now. And he is not my favourite ex-King."

Oakes laughed at that. He admired a quick answer, but the thought rankled that Marigny had somehow insulted the Duke. He might have his own reservations about Windsor, but that was different, he was older — and richer. Who was this lanky, bearded newcomer who could so casually ignore an invitation from the former King of England? This led to more arguments as the Oakeses said good-bye outside Marigny's house.

The worst disagreement Marigny could remember was when Sydney, Sir Harry's eldest son, decided to stay the night with Nancy and him after a party.

Oakes was so incensed that he arrived in the early hours and threatened to break down the front door if Marigny did not open it so that he could take his son home. Marigny had not seen him since then, but this was not significant; he would be seeing him again soon, for an American in Nassau, Freddie Cerretta, working for the construction company on Sir Harry's airfield, had told him that firm contracts for gravel and sand had still not yet been signed. Cerretta suggested that Marigny put in a bid.

Marigny had worked out some figures on the details Cerretta gave him, and planned to get in touch with Sir Harry and say he was going to tender for the contract. Better not rush things, though; give him a chance to cool off. Then, no doubt, Sir Harry would greet him like an old friend and offer him an iced beer. It was quite likely that he would have forgotten all about the last shouting match.

Just one tiny shadow darkened Marigny's optimism for the future. The previous day, he had heard that the government were probably going to refuse him permission to transfer ownership of land he had bought to enlarge his farm. With the demand for chickens and eggs, he needed to expand, and with his greater overheads, he could not make the farm pay if he had to move back to his original, smaller site. Was this a move inspired by people envious of him and his success, to emphasise that as a stranger, an interloper, he must be kept in his place?

Because Marigny was not Bahamian, he had registered the business in his wife's name, since she was a Bahamian citizen. He realised the prejudice against him and thought that this would side-step it. Surely the Executive Council would not veto the request of the daughter of the colony's greatest benefactor? But, almost unbelievably, they had. His lawyer, Godfrey Higgs, assured him that this setback would easily be overcome.

"You want to have a word with Harold Christie," he said confidently. "He's a member of the Council. He'll speak up for you."

The heavy overcast sky seemed somehow symbolic of Marigny's feelings. Only yesterday, on a sunny day, he had seen a small cloud grow darker and larger until it had gradually obscured the sun. A Bible story from boyhood, about a cloud no bigger than a man's hand over the sea that foretold a time of suffering, came to mind. This unexpected refusal to allow him to continue farming on his new site could be like that cloud. For as one success led on inexorably to greater successes, so did one failure — when it was not overcome.

His stomach was paining him. He poured a glass of water, stirred in a spoonful of Maclean's Stomach Powder, drank it. As he dressed, the pain eased and Marigny's spirits lightened. He was never melancholy for long. Life, in his view, was meant for work and enjoyment, not for retrospection and doubt and dwelling on what might have been. You had to accept that it was like a one-way street. You could only go on; you could never go back.

For a few moments after Frank Marshall left her house, Carole stood in the open doorway, listening to the sound of his hired car dwindle and die. Another visitor from the States had called earlier in the week, but Carole was out, and Jack mentioned it to her only afterwards. She guessed that he must have something to do with Frank, but Frank had also not said anything to her about that visitor, so she had kept silent. He either did not know or chose not to mention the matter. Either way, she did not want to become involved.

Frank always telephoned her when he arrived from Miami, because after his first visit he stayed at a hotel. They had a code between them to indicate when Jack was out and what time he was expected home.

This afternoon, Frank had arrived quite unexpectedly, his bags packed, to tell her he was leaving Nassau suddenly for Miami on the afternoon plane. They had made love quickly, not, as usual, in her bed, since the maids were still in the room, but with the swift urgency of animals on a settee in her husband's study overlooking the sea.

"I thought you weren't leaving until next Tuesday," she said afterwards.

"I wasn't. But there's been a sudden change of plans. Something Jack suggested. A very good idea. He's helping me."

"He's helping himself," retorted Carole.

"Not in this instance. Maybe you misunderstand him."

"Jack's never misunderstood. He's just disliked."

"If this comes off," said Marshall dreamily, running a finger down her spine, "I'll be rich, really rich."

"You told me that years ago," Carole reminded him. "Remember? Everyone else *did* get rich. Even Jack."

"I made a lot of money, too," Marshall replied defensively.

'And you spent it just as quickly," said Carole, almost sadly. "They kept it. That's the difference."

"If I keep it this time, will you come away with me?"

"What about your wife and son?"

"I'd see to it that they were all right, of course."

"Of course," she said, not meaning to sound ironic. "But what if it *doesn't* come off? There are so many ifs."

"We always got on in the old days," he said stubbornly.

"Yes," she agreed. But would they get on now? He kept harping back to what had happened in the past, in the old days. But really, what had they shared then except a fierce, brief, passionate affair?

They made love again, and then, while he dressed, she shook out the cushions, glanced around the room to make sure he had left no clue. Men were so careless. She should know; she had entertained many lovers in this room, and they had forgotten keys, a comb, once even a wallet with visiting cards inside it. Jack was no more observant than other trusting husbands, but even he could hardly fail to notice such evidence of callers she did not mention to him. Odd how she invariably prefixed any thought or remark about her husband with that derogatory word "even." Maybe he really was as bright and smart as he thought. Maybe he noticed lots of things — like her visitors, her drinking — which for reasons unknown to her he did not choose to mention.

Thinking about this possibility now, as she stood in the doorway, Carole felt suddenly that she was becoming as foolish as Marshall, dwelling in the past. The thought made her shiver; or maybe it was only because heat had already left the day. Shadows, so small at noon, seemed to grow longer and darker as she watched, like her vague unease about the future. Soon it would be cool and dusk, and then Jack would be home and they would have their ritual drinks on the patio overlooking the sea. Small talk, as always, for she deliberately avoided controversial subjects, feeling the slight concern that troubled her after Frank's visits. Had he left a clue she'd missed? Of course, in such a situation she could explain — as Frank had told her to — that he had just dropped in, hoping to find Jack home, waited for a drink, and then had to rush to catch his plane.

Carole had not expected to see Frank again after he left Nassau more than ten years earlier. He was out of her system, she told herself often enough. But the moment she had seen him, months ago now, she knew that all this time she had been deluding herself. Against Frank, so large, comfortable, easygoing, a man she felt she could steer in any direction she liked, her husband seemed mean-spirited, careful, cautious. But Frank was married, with a son, and not clever with money, whatever he claimed. He could not conceivably keep her in anything like the style to which she had grown accustomed with Jack. It wasn't love she felt, but other emotions almost as strong and even more disturbing: pity, perhaps, and a longing for a different life.

Carole closed the door, crossed the hall, cool as a bodega, with its polished red tiles. She needed a large vodka. This left no taste in the mouth, no scent on her breath. So that Jack would not know she was drinking so much, secretly and always alone, she kept the vodka in a soda-water bottle in the drinks cupboard. Now, she poured four fingers into a glass, drank quickly. The spirits didn't seem so strong as usual, and she had just poured herself another four fingers when the front doorbell rang.

She replaced the bottle and the glass quickly in the cupboard, slid shut the door, waited for a moment, heart beating like a drum. Who could this be?

Again, the bell rang. She crossed the hall again and opened the door. A man was standing under the porch. He was tall, like Frank, but darker-skinned, wearing lightweight blue trousers, blue silk shirt, alligator skin shoes and belt. Suddenly, he moved, and was inside the hall with the door shut behind him before she had even asked his name.

The presumption of his entering her home without permission stunned her into speech. "Who are you?"

"A friend of Jack's," he said easily. "I came to see him a few days ago. You were out."

He was smiling down at her from his superior height. He had an American accent, and she could see hard shoulder muscles ripple beneath the thin silk of his shirt.

"I also know Frank Marshall."

"You've just missed him," she said. "He was here only a moment ago. Dropped by on his way to the airport."

"A long drop," replied the man, raising one eyebrow quizzically. "He was here for exactly one hour and fifty-three minutes. I timed him."

"What do you mean, you timed him?"

"What I say. With my watch. Your husband's not at home?"

"He'll be back around four o'clock."

"Then we haven't got much time, but I think we've got enough."

"What are you talking about? If you want to see Jack, wait until he comes back."

"Maybe I will," he said. "It all depends on you."

"I don't understand," said Carole despairingly. The vodka must have been stronger than she realised. Her mind felt woolly; she could not concentrate on what the stranger was saying, but instinct warned her that it was somehow dangerous.

"Then I'll try to speak more clearly, more simply, if you like. Who else is in the house?"

"No one."

Carole regretted this admission as she spoke, but it was too late to retract.

"At least you're honest about some things," he said approvingly. "I know there's no one else here, but I decided to ask just the same, to see what you'd say. Let me speak bluntly. Does your husband know about you and Frank?"

"There's nothing to know. All three of us have been friends since the thirties."

"Intimate friends, I understand," said the man drily.

He took out a diary and flipped over the pages. "Frank was here yesterday afternoon."

He turned over another page. "And three times last week. On each occasion, he stayed between one and a half and two hours. Once he stayed for three hours."

He smiled at Carole, put his diary back in his pocket. She began to feel faint, almost physically sick. Sweat dampened her back. She leaned weakly against the wall.

"What do you want?" she asked him.

"Your help."

From another pocket he took a small glass test-tube, plugged by a cork. It contained a thick brown liquid, like molasses. She watched a tiny air bubble move very slowly as he turned the tube.

"You also know intimately a houseboy on the staff of Sir Harry Oakes?"

Carole opened her mouth to deny it, but he shook his head slowly, almost sadly, and she knew she was wasting her time.

"If your husband knew about Frank, he might possibly forgive, if not forget. That could be a private thing between three old friends. But if he knew about you and this black Bahamian, he might take a different view. Even if he didn't, your friends would. I want you to give this test-tube to the houseboy."

"Why? What's in it? Poison?"

"Nothing like that at all. Nothing harmful."

"Then why can't you give it to him yourself?"

"Because I'm leaving the island, and I'd like you to be involved."

"Why me?"

"Because no one will associate you with me."

"I don't even know you."

"You won't have to — if you do exactly what I say."

Carole took the phial, still warm from his touch. She looked at it with a mixture of surprise and disgust that she could be persuaded so easily to do something she didn't understand and didn't want to do. Her hand was trembling. She put the phial in the pocket of her dress so that she wouldn't drop it.

"When am I supposed to give it to him?"

"When he telephones."

"Will he ask for it? I'm not here much of the day."

"He'll find you, wherever you are — if he has to. He'll say, 'The weather looks stormy tonight,' and then he'll tell you at which of Sir Harry's houses he'll be, where you can find him."

"He knows about it?"

"Yes. He knows about it. He also has reasons for secrecy."

"What if someone else is in the room when he calls?"

"Say it was a wrong number. If he calls — and I stress //he calls — you'll go to the back door of that particular house. He'll be waiting. Just give him the tube."

"You said *if he* calls?"

"He may not. If he doesn't, then get rid of the tube in the ocean. Not down a drain or in the trash. Open the tube and throw it into the sea."

"How long should I wait?"

"If he doesn't call before the ninth, forget all about this visit. Just get rid of the tube and the contents."

"I'm seeing this man next week."

"I know you are," said the visitor. "But don't mention this to him then if he hasn't called. He'll never raise the subject with you."

"But why should I do this? What's in the tube? It can't be anything good, or there wouldn't be all this secrecy."

"I swear to you that it's not in any way a harmful substance; it can even be considered good, as far as you're both concerned. Because if you do *exactly* as I say, your husband will never know anything about your affairs with Frank or this Bahamian boy or the other gentlemen callers you entertain when you're on your own. Jack may, of course, find out through carelessness on their part — or yours — but not from me."

"He'd never believe it, even if you told him."

"Maybe you're right. Even so, he might believe the evidence of his own eyes."

The man took a photograph the size of a postcard from his inner pocket and handed it to her. Carole recognised the wallpaper in her bedroom, the light with a frilly shade on the bedside table. The sheets were thrown back, and she lay naked, with Frank by her side. Her eyes were closed, as though in ecstasy.

"I think it's pretty good. I've got some more, too. All taken with a telephoto lens from high ground opposite the house. Any other questions?"

Carole shook her head; she felt beyond speech.

"I'm sorry my visit's been so brief," said the man, "but I've got a car waiting down the road, and it's nearly four o'clock."

He let himself out the door. She watched him walk slowly down the drive, not looking back. She listened as his car drove away, then staggered rather than walked to the drinks cupboard, gulped down the glass of vodka, and then another. It could have been soda water, for all the effect it had. She looked again at the photograph, walked into the downstairs cloakroom, folded the photograph in two, and tore it up methodically into small pieces and flushed them in the lavatory. She pulled the handle several times, until she was sure the fragments had disappeared. Then she went back into the room, put away the empty glass, and sat in a chair, trembling.

Her whole life, her whole future, depended on the good-will of a stranger. Vodka pumped through her veins; a pulse beat at the base of her skull. She stood up and swayed, and realised she had drunk too much. Jack must never discover her like this; it would make him suspect she really was a secret drinker, a lush. Somehow, she crawled up the stairs to the bedroom, kicked off her shoes, and lay on the bed.

Her last act before alcohol overcame her was to wrap the phial in a handkerchief and push it under the lining paper of the drawer in her bedside table.

The light was beginning to leave the sky when Marshall gave the order to drop the bow anchor. After the thrum of the two Chrysler marine engines, the cluck and suck of water against the hull of the sixty-foot power boat seemed the sounds of silence.

"How long are we staying here?" the engineer asked him. He was a tall thin man wearing oil-stained jeans, a blue roll-neck sweater, dirty canvas shoes. He was expecting to be drafted into the navy within the week; he did not want to spend his last few days as a civilian moored off an island so small that it looked like a humpback sea-beast. Nassau, with its bars and girls, lay beyond this thin, uninviting strip of land.

"Until we get the signal to move. You certain we're out of sight of the shore here?"

"Positive. But not from the sea, you know."

"Anyone who sees us will think we're fishing," said Marshall confidently.

"Since we're going to be here indefinitely, I might as well fill up with gas."

The engineer called to two crewmen to help manhandle a forty-gallon drum of gasoline from the stern towards the main fuel tank. The drum was heavy and awkward to move. Once, it fell, amid curses, splintering a duckboard. Finally, they held it in position and the engineer unscrewed the cap. This fitted flush with the side of the drum and could not be opened by a spanner, because it was circular, with no flat sides for a spanner's jaws to grip. The engineer used a special metal wrench about eighteen inches long with four short triangular prongs at one end. These slotted neatly into four similarly shaped indentations on the cap's face. The other two men steadied the heavy drum as he poured.

The sun went down, briefly turning the sea to blood, then to a heaving darkness. In the distance, breaking waves on the reef showed as a faint, phosphorescent line. The island was now no more than a shadowy outline ringed by a pale rim of sand.

"I'm going ashore," Marshall explained. "I want one man to come with me.

He nodded to the fourth member of the crew, who was wiping down the port engine with a wad of cotton waste. Marshall took off his shoes and went over the side barefoot into the warm water. The sailor followed him up the sandy beach. They stopped only to put on their canvas shoes before they reached the green luxuriant scrub, where the edge of a fallen leaf could score flesh like a razor. It had been raining heavily, and the island stank of warm, rotting vegetation; leaves the size of soup plates steamed in the twilight. They climbed up the ridge that ran like a spine along the centre of the island. Near the top, they paused.

"Keep off the skyline," warned Marshall. "You watch to the left. I'll take the right-hand side."

"What are we looking for?"

"A light. Morse. Four dots, three dashes."

They lay face down on the undergrowth. Mosquitoes whined around their ears and bit the backs of their hands. Along the coast from Nassau, past the Country Club, car headlights flashed, diminished, and briefly grew brighter on the curving road. Mist thickened over the sea, as evening merged with night.

Marshall could make out the long low roof of Westbourne. A jetty pointed its long finger towards him from the shore. Lights came on in downstairs rooms of the house. Upstairs, a light shone from a bedroom window, then died as someone pulled the curtains.

Three hours was the time he had agreed to wait, and then he stood up, stiff and cold and disappointed. The sailor glanced at him enquiringly.

"Let's go," said Marshall briefly, and led the way down the incline, across the beach, towards the boat.

Next day they put out to sea and anchored on the Atlantic side of Hog Island, making great play with rods and lines. After dark, they moved back in position again. For a second night, he and the sailor waited, watching the shore. Just after nine o'clock, a light flickered. Four dots, three dashes. H.O., for Harry Oakes. A pause, and the signal was repeated. Marshall and his companion hurried back to the launch.

The day had been hot and humid, the sort of July weather that Carole knew would end with a summer storm. But by early evening the rain had still not arrived, although the sky loomed low, and the sea looked like a lake of lead.

Carole stood at the wide glass doors overlooking the patio and the beach; angry waves had thrown a wide, dark rim of seaweed up on the uninviting sand. Distant thunder boomed, and lightning flickered faintly, like blue fireworks, over Hog Island.

Jack was late, yet he had especially asked for dinner to be early, and she wondered, without much concern, what had delayed him; where he was; whether he also had a secret life. Somehow, she could not imagine him with another woman. He lacked the sexual drive, the overwhelming need essential for such liaisons. More likely, he was drinking in some bar or service mess, working out percentages, pay-offs, profit margins, on the back of an envelope or cigarette packet. Money was not only his god; it was his life.

She drank her third vodka, replaced the soda-water bottle in the cupboard carefully and deliberately, as though to convince herself that her hand did not shake or tremble. She was not drunk, of course, but it would never do to be discovered. Jack would think she had been drinking in secret, which wasn't her style at all; she was just drinking alone, which was altogether different.

The Bahamian butler hovered silently in the doorway, his eyes taking in the scene.

"Serve dinner in ten minutes," she told him. This would give her time for a fourth vodka, and then if Jack had still not returned, she would eat alone. The hell with him. Then she heard the hum of an engine, the click of a car door. Jack came into the room, tore off his tie, threw it and his lightweight jacket onto a chair, nodded a greeting, went to the drinks cupboard, mixed a pina colada. He drank it greedily, wiping his mouth with the back of his hand, a habit she detested but could never bring herself to speak to him about.

"I ordered dinner early, as you asked," she said, speaking slowly so as not to slur the words. "Thought I'd have a drink while I waited."

"I was delayed," Jack explained. "And I may have to go out again."

"Then we'd better eat now."

She rang the bell for the butler. Jack sat down at the head of the table, without even washing his hands. The butler served a conch salad, spiced with lemon and hot peppers.

"What will you be drinking, sir?" he asked.

"We'll have two iced beers," said Jack, without asking Carole.

As they started to eat, Carole, not for the first time, noticed how her husband chewed with his mouth open.

"You're very quiet," he said, tearing a piece of white conch flesh with his fingers. "Anything wrong?"

"Wrong? What could be wrong?"

Her voice sounded tight and high-pitched. Her heart began to flutter as the vodka fumed in her blood and brain. She wished she had not taken that third drink. For a moment, she could not remember whether she had finished it or left the glass on the drinks cupboard. She did not want to glance around the room too obviously, in case Jack asked her what she was looking for.

"Had a pretty heavy day myself," Jack went on.

"Successful, I hope?" she asked dutifully.

The telephone rang before he could reply. Carole was nearest to it. Jack, still chewing, lowered his knife and fork as she picked up the receiver. She could hear breathing and said nervously, "Hello."

The breathing stopped. A Bahamian voice she knew so well, a voice that had whispered endearments to her, whose huskiness still made her heart quicken in spite of her unease, said, "Hello, honey. Westbourne. The weather looks stormy tonight."

Carole stood, staring across the room, through the wide windows at the darkening view. A sudden gust of wind rattled the panes, as though someone outside were trying to open them. Her throat felt tight. She swallowed nervously.

"Who do you want?" she asked.

The telephone went dead, and she replaced the receiver. Now she knew where she had to deliver the phial. But how to leave the house with Jack staring at her? She fought down a mad urge to cry, to scream, to run away.

"You ill or something?" Jack asked her.

"No. Just felt a bit dizzy. Must be the weather."

"Who was on the phone?"

"Wrong number."

He hooked a sliver of conch flesh from between two back teeth with a fingernail, examined it, put it back in his mouth.

"I'm expecting a call myself," he said. "Thought that might be it."

Carole sat down, sipped her cold beer thoughtfully. Then she saw her glass of vodka — right there in front of her. It must have been hidden by the glass of beer. How odd she had not seen it earlier!

"You're sweating," Jack told her, frowning. "Sure you're all right?"

She nodded. "It just seems unusually hot tonight. So humid. I'll open a window."

Carole slid open the big window overlooking the beach. Wind blew in, ruffling the tablecloth, shaking flowers in a silver vase, bringing a strong sharp smell of seaweed. The telephone rang for a second time. Jack stood up, pushed the window shut noisily, picked up the receiver.

Carole could hear a man's voice. She could not make out the words, but she recognised the accent: The American who had given her the phial. He must be back on the island — or perhaps he had never left. If so, how much else had he made up? What did that tube really contain? Could it be poison, as she suspected? Oh, no. Please, God, no.

Jack was saying, "Sure. Right. I'll be there. Of course."

He put down the telephone, went back to his chair.

"That the call you were expecting?" Carole asked him.

"Yes. I've got to go out again, as I thought."

"Now?" It was Carole's turn to simulate surprise, to conceal her relief. Now she would be able to slip round to Westbourne without the need for any explanation.

"Unfortunately, yes. Business."

She glanced at the ormolu clock on the wall. Ten minutes to eleven. Jack pushed away the plate, stood up, put on his jacket.

'■'There's baked Alaska for dessert," she told him.

He shook his head.

"Coffee?"

She did not want Jack to suspect that she wanted him out of the way as soon as possible.

"Sorry. No time. I've got a key, so don't wait up."

"But where are you going?"

"Have to see someone who's just arrived."

"At this hour? But there are no planes in after dark."

"He's come by boat."

Jack gave her a perfunctory kiss on the side of her cheek. Carole followed her husband to the door.

"I'm taking the station wagon," he said. There was no reason why he shouldn't. If the rain came, it was drier than the coupe with the canvas top. But why bother to tell her? Her Austin was smaller and used far less petrol, which was an advantage because of rationing. She watched the twin tail-lights of his Ford V8 turn out of the drive. Something was odd about that, she thought, and then realised what it was. The number-plate light was not lit — and the rear number-plate itself was missing. How strange that she had never noticed it before! She wondered whether her husband knew.

Thoughtfully, Carole went upstairs to the bedroom, opened the drawer of her bedside table, and took out the handkerchief with the phial. She kept it wrapped; that way, she felt at one remove from whatever it contained.

She went downstairs, picked up an empty Lucky Strike cigarette packet her husband had thrown into the waste-paper basket, put the phial in this, partly to conceal it, partly to protect it.

"You going out, ma'am?"

She turned. The butler was standing in the hall.

"Just for a walk."

"Mighty big storm on the way, ma'am."

"I'll be back before then."

Carole had thought of taking her car, but Jack often noted the mileage, and he would wonder where she had been to put only three or four miles on the clock. There was no traffic and no one to see her as she hurried along the rough road.

Behind thick protective hedges she saw faint glimmers of lights from downstairs windows, and once heard a snatch of song from a radio. Tamarind pods rattled, and leathery paw-paw leaves rustled like whispers in the dark. In a lightning flash, she saw a palm tree bend before the wind, fronds like a woman's hair streaming behind her as she ran away.

Carole reached the first entrance of Westbourne and paused for a moment; she had been hurrying and was out of breath. She could arouse suspicion if anyone saw her like this. And what had she to fear? A stranger who had watched her and knew some of her secrets? A phial in a cigarette packet that he had assured her could not harm anyone? Why couldn't she believe him? she asked herself. But if its contents really were harmless, then surely there would be no need of secrecy and threats?

She walked slowly up the curved drive, like a small girl unwilling to arrive too soon, hoping the man she knew so well, and loved so well, would not be waiting for her. Then she could go back home and have another vodka and drift willingly into sleep.

Someone stepped silently from the shadows; someone tall, broad-shouldered, narrow-waisted, as she liked a man to be. He held out his right hand silently, and she put the cigarette packet in it. Without a word, either of greeting or farewell, he turned and was lost in the deeper darkness of the trees.

Light spilled from windows, making bougainvillea glow like bushes of blood. A lamp above a doorway reflected on the shining bonnet of a car parked not in the open, where Sir Harry's guests usually parked their cars, but to one side, under the trees, as though someone else did not want his presence known.

Carole walked back more slowly. The thunder was louder now and closer, and almost constant lightning flashes lit up the road. She had carried out her part of the bargain. She could only hope that the stranger would keep his.

As she reached her front door, the storm broke.

9

Two Parties and a Night of Storm

CHARLES HUBBARD pushed back his chair so sharply that its legs grated on the polished floor. He stood up, a self-satisfied, self-made man, proud of his own handiwork, and glanced pointedly at his companion, Dulcibelle Henneage, a pretty woman in her twenties. She also stood up, smoothing down her pleated tennis skirt. The wicker chair had left its pattern on the backs of her legs.

"There's going to be a storm," Hubbard announced ponderously, as though he had private information. "We'd better be going home."

He had invited Mrs. Henneage to lunch at his house near Westbourne, hoping she would arrive alone, but to his dismay she had brought her two young children and a nurse. What he had hoped would be a quiet tete-a-tete had become an unwelcome crowd.

Harold Christie was spending that afternoon at Westbourne with Sir Harry Oakes, who suddenly decided he would like a game of tennis. Christie telephoned to Hubbard and asked whether he would care to join them. When Hubbard explained that he had a guest, Sir Harry invited them both to join Christie's niece and her friend

Hubbard was not a keen player — he had started too late in life to excel — but at least the invitation gave him an excuse to be rid of the nurse and the children. He did not know Oakes well, but he respected his wealth and his generosity. Hubbard had been inside Westbourne on two previous occasions only, but he was impressed by its size and furnishings, and the fact that this was but one of many houses Sir Harry owned in Nassau, Canada, the United States, and England.

They played a few games of tennis, not too many and not too vigorously, in deference to the two older men, but Oakes had the edge on him. He might be sixty-nine, but he had the stamina of a man thirty years younger.

Afterwards, there were gin fizzes before the girls left.

"I've been planting trees all the morning," Oakes told them.

"I thought you'd rather cut them down," said Hubbard. "Every time I see you on a tractor or a bulldozer — and that's nearly every day — you're tearing trees *down* all over the place."

"I like trees," replied Oakes defensively. "I cut them down only because I need to — for a road or the airfield. And then I'd rather do it myself, because I know it's done cleanly. Strange thing, Hubbard; a tree can take seventy or eighty years to grow — and then a man comes along and hacks it down in minutes."

"Same thing happens to people," Hubbard pointed out.

"Maybe," said Oakes. "Anyway, come and see what I've planted today."

He led the way up a flight of hardwood stairs to the northern verandah, which stretched from one end of the house to the other, overlooking his private beach and the ocean. The new saplings he had planted looked raw and defenceless against massive palm trees and bushy sea-grapes.

"I can't understand why people plant trees," said Mrs. Henneage. She had been rather quiet, not relishing the prospect of any intimate encounter with her ageing escort when they were alone, and not quite sure how she could avoid it tactfully if she wanted other invitations to lunch or tennis. Being an evacuee wife from England, and on her own in an island of the very rich was not always easy.

"I'll tell you *exactly* why I planted them," Oakes explained. "Because they're beautiful. Because they give me a sense of continuity. O.K., I may not live to see them fully grown, but there's an answer to that, too. Other people *will* enjoy them and walk beneath their shade. Those seem pretty good reasons to me."

"Never knew you had a poetic side to you," said Christie, half-bantering. "Like my father."

Oakes shrugged, smiled, and led the way downstairs.

"Will you stay for dinner?" he asked Hubbard and Mrs. Henneage.

"That's very kind of you, but why don't you and Harold be my guests at the Prince George?" Hubbard suggested.

"We haven't booked, and it's so crowded these days. Stay here. Take pot luck."

"Shouldn't we change?" asked Dulcibelle doubtfully.

"It's not worth it," replied Oakes. "You're fine as you are."

"I'm changing," said Christie.

"You do what you like, Harold."

A splendid meal was served by Sir Harry's silent Bahamian servants in their starched white jackets.

"Now," said Oakes brightly. "Chinese chequers."

They sat down at the card table in the drawing room and began to play. By eleven o'clock, the combined effects of unaccustomed exercise, gin fizzes, wine with dinner, and an excellent brandy afterwards began to make Hubbard feel drowsy. Christie had bathed and changed into a suit and appeared fresh, but the others still wore their tennis whites, now rather creased.

"Thank you very much, Harry," Hubbard told his host. "We've really enjoyed ourselves. Next time, the party's on me."

"We'll have to wait a while for that," Oakes replied. "I'm flying up to my family at Bar Harbor tomorrow. I'll be away for several weeks at least."

"You've a date in the morning," Christie reminded him.

"I know that. Those damn sheep I brought from Cuba. They're infected with screw-worm, of all things."

Hubbard shook his head. "Can't even trust sheep these days," he said lugubriously.

"Etienne Dupuch of *The Tribune* and Moseley of *The Guardian* are coming here at eight-thirty. Makes a story for them. There's lots of grass at the Country Club and on the golf course the sheep can eat. No reason why they shouldn't breed and help the food problem here. Then I'm due to play a round of golf with the Governor. And then — away."

"You saw that poem in *The Tribune* today about your sheep on the golf course?" Hubbard asked him.

Oakes nodded. "Sure. Thought it was very good."

Harold Christie picked up a copy of the paper and read what John Hutton, the island's Controller of Petroleum Supplies, had written:

"There seems a lot of grumbling from the golfers by the
sea, Who follow little pillules round the course at Cable B.
They criticise the livestock browsing quietly on the green,
Then, putting, curse the cards they leave, that scarcely can
be seen. The players call them Oakes' Acorns."

"I must drop him a line," said Oakes, as he led the way to Hubbard's car and held open the door for Mrs. Henneage.

"You got your car here?" he asked Christie, as they returned to the house. He had driven Harold Christie out from Nassau earlier that day, and he suddenly wondered how he would get home.

"Yes."

"Oh. I didn't see it outside."

Christie said nothing. Shortly before dinner, when he left to change into a suit from his tennis clothes, he had telephoned to his office and asked his driver to bring his car to Westbourne. He told him to park it beneath the trees; it was completely out of sight of house and road.

"Come in and shut the door," Oakes told him. "Those damn mosquitoes are everywhere."

"It's a very warm night," said Christie, closing the door behind him. "Hubbard was right. Going to be a hell of a storm soon. Hope your plane isn't held up tomorrow."

A houseboy followed them into the room and stood to one side, head bowed respectfully, in case they had any orders for him.

"Like a nightcap?" Oakes asked Christie.

"Thank you. A small brandy."

"I've drunk enough," said Oakes. "Fix me a fruit juice."

The houseboy brought a bottle of Martell and a brandy glass from a side table, put them on a tray by Harold Christie's chair. Then he went out to his pantry and returned with a tall glass of iced pineapple, orange, and lemon juices, coloured pink with grenadine.

"That's all," Oakes told him.

"Good night, Sir Harry. Good night, Mr. Christie, sir."

"Good night to you."

Christie poured himself a brandy, and the two men raised their glasses solemnly to each other.

"To a happy landing and a safe return," said Christie.

"To the future," Oakes replied. "When thousands of passengers land on my airfield — and all want to buy expensive houses from you."

"I'll drink to that."

They did so, then Oakes wrinkled up his face and sniffed at the glass.

"Tastes a bit sweet."

"Maybe too much grenadine," Christie suggested. "I usually add Angostura to take the sweetness away."

He sat down and lit a cigarette.

"I often think this is the best hour of the day," said Oakes ruminatively. "It's a time you can lose — like that business when you cross the Pacific and lose a whole day. It makes me think of other evenings years ago. Up in the Yukon, we'd spend the day digging for gold, then, in the evening, we'd get a fire going — and think about what we'd do when we found the gold. Never *if*— always *when!*"

"Have you done all you thought you'd do, Harry?"

Oakes shrugged. "Some of the things, yes," he admitted. "But your ideas change when you've actually found the stuff. I reckon life's like a relay race. You have a baton and you run with it, and then you hand it on to your family. You give them every chance you can to win. But it's up to them to do better than you did yourself."

"It'd be difficult to do better than you, Harry."

"I hope my boys will try."

"And the girls?"

"Of course. Bit sorry about Nancy's marriage, but Marigny's not really a bad sort of guy. You've got to know these Frenchies. They're touchy. Not like us. And he's got his good points. I can see how a woman would go overboard for him."

"But not Eunice, I fancy?"

"Not Eunice; agreed. But, then, she's Australian. Level-headed."

"I was brought up to believe that money can't buy happiness," said Christie with the air of one who was no longer a convinced believer.

"Sure as hell allows you to be as miserable as you like in comfort," Oakes retorted with a grin.

"I agree," said Christie, and paused.

He knew that when Sir Harry left Nassau on the following day he would not be back until the hot, humid summer was over. For this reason, he had stayed at Westbourne for the past two nights, because he calculated that Marshall must also know that Oakes was going away for a long while, and this could make him anxious to see him before he left. Christie did not want Marshall to find Oakes alone, for Oakes was tough and stubborn and might not take kindly to being pestered. If he was with him, however, perhaps he could help to keep any discussion in a safely low key. Nothing could be gained from a shouting match, but Sir Harry did not always accept this — as Marigny had discovered. Also, if Marshall did try to pressure Oakes, then Christie wanted to know exactly what was said. And if Marshall also became angry, then Christie had his car handy to drive him back to his hotel and try to talk him out of any threat he might make. The matter of Mexico might not be of great importance to Sir Harry, but it could be crucial to him.

"You're very quiet all of a sudden," said Oakes.

"Not really. But I've been thinking about this hotel idea."

"Then forget, it," said Oakes shortly. "You know my views. I'm just not interested. It's a matter for ExCo, not me."

"But what about the Mexico business? Maybe Marshall knows more than he's letting on — and what he's told me already is bad enough."

"You think so? I don't. So you and the Duke use money from Mexico or push out money there. That's your affair. I've moved gold — and that's mine. And I'd have shipped a hell of a lot more if Wenner-Gren hadn't been put on the blacklist."

"It's because he *is* on the blacklist that we could be in such trouble. Dealing with someone who's blacked for helping the enemy in wartime, as well as the Exchange Control factor."

"To hell with that. We're only helping ourselves with what's already ours. We're not defrauding anyone."

"We've gone against the law."

"There are laws of God and laws of man. You frighten too easily, Harold. You know my motto? *'Per Ardua'* — through hard times, if you like. Not with any aim, like *'Per Ardua Ad Astra* the R.A.F. motto — through hard times to the stars. Just surviving. I've been quite good at that up to now, and I don't intend to change."

He took another sip of his drink. "Far too sweet," he complained, wrinkling his nose in distaste. "Wonder if the juice has been standing around in the heat? This weather plays funny tricks."

He put the drink on a side table with a slow, almost exaggerated movement, as though he could not quite relate the bottom of the glass to the table top. Christie looked at him sharply.

"You all right, Harry?" he asked him.

Oakes nodded, deliberately, weightily, not in his usual quick way. "I was just thinking," he said slowly, almost solemnly. "After I struck gold, I started to read what people had said about gold — just for fun. Do you know that Disraeli said in the House of Commons that more men had been ruined by gold than by love?"

"I don't know how he reckoned that."

"I also discovered that for at least six thousand years, men have searched for gold, lied for it, fought for it, killed for it — willingly. You know the King of Spain's advice to his sailors when they set off three hundred years ago to find the New World?"

Christie knew, but shook his head to humour his host.

" 'You may get land,' the King told them. 'But at all hazard — get gold.' I took his advice; I *got* gold. And I didn't harm anyone doing so, either, which is more than the Spaniards could say. So I can move my own gold wherever and whenever I want. Just as I can move *myself* where I want. And maybe I'll go to Mexico, too. I don't have to remind you, a preacher's son, what the Good Book says: 'For where your treasure is, there will your heart be also.'

"Do you know why I've stayed on here these last few days, before going up to Bar Harbor? I'll tell you. Because I had a telephone call. There's a launch coming in. Someone's bringing me a message from Mexico City."

"Are you *certain}"* asked Christie doubtfully. He had heard nothing of this from any of his contacts, and they had never previously let him down. "If he is, he's leaving it pretty late. After all, you're off tomorrow."

"They're not to know *that,* of course."

Thunder boomed like gunfire as Oakes spoke, and a blue blaze of lightning flickered between the half-drawn curtains. The lights in the big room dimmed slightly and then came up more brightly. As though it were part of the storm, both men heard a faint, regular tapping on a windowpane. It could be a branch, a twig, perhaps even a bird's beak, but instinctively they knew that it was none of these things. Then they heard it again, clearly this time.

Oakes started up for the front door.

At the other end of Nassau, in Marigny's house in Victoria Avenue, a dinner party was in full swing. He sat at the head of the table, lit by trembling candle flames, listening to the chatter of his guests. Outside, thunder rumbled and lightning flared across the lowering sky. It was almost the end of a day that had begun smartly at half-past six in the morning and then somehow tailed off into a rather unsatisfactory mixture of work, play, and simply passing time.

For nearly two hours that morning, he and his driver had loaded brown cardboard boxes, punched with airholes, into the back of his truck. These boxes contained nearly four hundred chickens hatched out in an incubator he kept in his garage. He hatched chickens here, because, with the door closed, and on a concrete floor, they were safe from rats or other predators. When the truck was full, Marigny climbed in behind the wheel and drove off to his farm.

On the previous evening, in the bar of the Prince George Hotel, he had seen Freddie Cerretta with two girls.

"Freddie, I want to introduce you to the two prettiest girls in town," Cerretta announced in his flamboyant way.

"I thought I knew them all already," Marigny replied smoothly. "But now I see how wrong I was."

"Jean Ainsley and Dorothy Clarke. Freddie de Marigny. Known to some as Count de Marigny," said Cerretta.

"Pleased to meet you," said Mrs. Clarke.

"The pleasure is mine," Marigny assured her. "But not the title. Not here, at least. Now, to more serious matters. What are you all drinking?"

They told him; he ordered another round.

"The girls are over here from England with their husbands in the RAF," Cerretta explained.

"But they're not here with us now," added one of the women.

"That's a pity," said Marigny gravely. "I was going to ask them to join you all at my house for dinner tomorrow night."

"We'd love to come," said Jean Ainsley, "but we haven't a car, and we live out on Cable Beach."

"He's got a very big car," said Cerretta, *"Enormous"*. Somehow he made the statement sound suggestive. The women looked at each other and giggled into their drinks.

"I think I've seen you in it. A Lincoln, isn't it?"

"That's right. I'll pick you up. That's no problem. Shall we say around seven-thirty?"

"We're at the Hubbard Cottages," said Dorothy Clarke. These were near the beach, some way beyond Westbourne.

Driving out to his farm, Marigny remembered these invitations he had given so casually, on the impulse, without considering who else he should ask. He really must invite a few more people; it would be flat with only five — if he included Georges — around his big dining table. Unfortunately, there wasn't a great deal of choice in Nassau. On every social level the same people tended to meet time after time; only the meeting places changed.

He'd ask Georges's girlfriend, Betty Roberts, and Donald McKinney, who worked in Godfrey Higgs's law office, and Oswald Moseley — no relation of Sir Oswald; they spelled their names differently — whose family owned *The Guardian* and Nassau's bookshop. He also decided to invite Harold Christie. Marigny had still not been able to speak to Christie on the telephone about transferring the land, although he had left messages asking him to ring back. It would be far easier to discuss the problem over drinks before dinner.

He also had to call in at the Central Police Station and tell them that he and his driver had sawn through the body of a car and in its place constructed a wooden platform to carry boxes of chickens or eggs. The vehicle was still registered as a private car, and it should probably be relicensed as a truck.

Out at the farm, two of Marigny's helpers had already lit a fire of dried driftwood. Above the red-hot embers was an old oil drum, cut down the centre to make a bath, and filled with boiling water. Men squatted around this on their haunches, dunked newly killed chickens into the water, and then plucked the feathers from the softened flesh.

Marigny nodded to them all, but he did not join them. He had spent most of the previous day working near that fire, and his eyes still smarted from the smoke. Instead, he went into the office and telephoned to Harold Christie in his office.

"A couple of things," said Marigny. "First, I'm having a bit of trouble about transferring the licence for the farm."

"Don't worry," Christie told him reassuringly. "I'll iron that out for you. Someone's got his lines crossed, that's all."

"Thanks," said Marigny, much relieved. "I thought it might be difficult."

"Nothing is when you know the right people and go about things in the right way. Now what's the other thing?"

"Purely social. I'm giving a little dinner party tonight. On the spur of the moment. I very much hope you can come along."

"I'd love to, but I can't make it tonight. I'm in the Assembly all day, and then I've promised to go and see Harry Oakes and have dinner with him and stay the night at his place. He's off tomorrow, you know, and we've several things to discuss. Another time, perhaps?"

"Of course," said Marigny. "Next time I'll give you more notice."

The boxes of chickens had all been unloaded from the truck by the time he returned, and he drove back into Nassau, parked outside Higgs's office, went in, saw McKinney, and invited him to dinner. The rest of the day was his own.

He lunched at home, then went to the Yacht Club, where races had been arranged for that afternoon. He took part in three races, but, unusually for him, was unplaced. Afterwards he drove back to the farm to check that all the chickens for that day's orders had been dispatched and the young ones he had brought out were doing well. He then went home. He had a leisurely bath, shaved, put on a lightweight brown jacket and trousers, a cream shantung shirt, a dark tie, and brown and white shoes. He did not wear socks; Marigny never wore socks in the summer.

He found that he still had time to kill before he was due to pick up the two young women, so he drove back to the Yacht Club to see whether a notice had been posted about the disqualification of a friend, Basil McKinney, in one race that afternoon. It hadn't. He hung about, hoping that some members might come in and he could have a chat with them, but the bar was empty. He felt oddly lonely, isolated; he wanted cheerful company. Finally, he drove on to Hubbard Cottages, going slowly, because he did not want to arrive too early.

Marigny had intended to have dinner outside by candlelight, but the mosquitoes were troublesome — always a sign of changing weather — so it seemed more sensible to eat inside the house.

His servants had originally laid the table outside, using three large candles with hurricane shades, intended for outdoors, and two candelabra, each of which took six candles. They reset the table in a hurry because of his change of plans, and the candles were now so badly placed that they screened three of the guests from Marigny's view. He made a joke about this as he lit them, using his left hand for candles on the left, his right hand for the others.

"I'm ambidextrous, you see," he said as he finally blew out the wooden taper he had used.

"But not all that quick," retorted Jean Ainsley, for Marigny suddenly pulled back his hand, blowing on his wrist.

"You've burned yourself," said Dorothy Clarke in a concerned tone of voice.

"I was looking at you, not at the candles," Marigny replied with a smile, but he had actually singed his skin, and the burn hurt more than he cared to admit.

"That candle's like Drake," said someone brightly.

"What do you mean?"

"Well, *he* singed the King of Spain's beard, didn't he? And that candle singed a count's."

They all laughed.

"But I burned myself quite painfully," Marigny protested. "It's not a laughing matter."

At that they all laughed even more. He really is a card, the women thought; what a pity he's married.

Christie followed Oakes into the main hall of Westbourne, wondering who could be calling at this late hour and on such a night. Oakes opened the front door, and wind gusted in, shaking the heavy curtains, making tassels tremble on the silk shades of ornamental lamps. The night was warm; the wind felt like escaping steam and brought with it a strong, dank smell of seaweed and rotting vegetation. A bad storm was due any minute, with more rain. In the darkness, unseen beyond the bougainvillea, ocean rollers broke and bellowed on the beach.

An outside lamp was burning, but the drive was empty. Oakes leaned weakly against the door-post, for suddenly he felt dizzy. Sweat shone like varnish on his forehead. Maybe Eunice was right; he should take things more easily. He was getting old, no denying it, and he'd had a hard, tough life. Just how tough no one could ever imagine if he had not endured it. A sweet flavour returned to his tongue; that damn' drink. It *had* tasted odd ...

He heard a slight movement in the bushes outside and tensed, instantly alert, nausea forgotten.

"Anyone there?" he called sharply.

Marshall stepped into the fan of light from the hallway.

"What the hell do *you* want here?" asked Oakes, irritation overcoming relief. "I've told you before. This is private property. Get out!"

Oakes turned to Christie. He wanted to say for the last time, that he would have nothing whatever to do with this man or his project, but somehow he seemed unable to form the words. Perhaps he was ill. He had never felt like this in all his life.

Marshall said, "I've come to tell you, Sir Harry, the launch has arrived off Prince George Wharf."

"The launch? What launch?" asked Christie. For the moment, he forgot what Sir Harry had told him only a few minutes earlier, perhaps because he had not believed him.

"Sir Harry knows about it," said Marshall coolly. He saw no reason to be friendly to Christie; the man hadn't helped him when he needed help.

"There's a message from Mexico."

Oakes found his voice. "From Mexico?" he repeated. This would tie in with his telephone call. "We'd better go and see what it is," he said.

"I have my car here," said Christie.

"I've got one of my own," replied Marshall. "We'll go in that."

"How are you involved with Mexico?" Christie asked him. He did not trust the man, nor did he believe him. He smelled treachery and trouble.

Marshall did not answer; he had heard a car coming along the road, travelling slowly. Such was the tension between the three men that they all paused, listening to its engine. Two red tail-lights dwindled as it passed the gate, and for a second the car's body was silhouetted against its own headlights.

"Who's that?" asked Marshall.

"Charles Hubbard. He was here for dinner."

"Who's he?"

"Retired Englishman. Lives along the road."

Marshall relaxed.

As the three men started to walk up the drive to the west entrance, rain began to fall, softly at first, and then like a cataract. They ran towards the station wagon that Jack had reversed into the gateway. Thunder pealed above their heads. Lightning bathed the palms and bougainvillea in fierce blue light, like giant fuses exploding. They piled inside the wagon; Christie in front with Jack, Marshall and Sir Harry in the back. No one spoke as Jack drove out of the gateway. Spears of rain mushroomed off the shining road, beating on the roof like demented drummers.

Inside Westbourne, the houseboy came silently into the sitting room, removed the two glasses, replaced the brandy on the side table, and turned off the lights.

Sir Harry lay back wearily against the seat. Soon, he seemed to sleep, breathing heavily, as though snoring.

"Is he all right?" Marshall asked anxiously. He wanted Oakes to be alert, willing to listen, not like this.

"He was playing tennis," Christie explained. "Then he had a couple of gin fizzes, a glass of wine, and some fruit juice. I think he's just tired."

Jack drove quickly on dipped headlights, through streaming streets. Water swirled around blocked drains. They passed the British

Colonial Hotel, where Woodes Rogers raised his sword against the storm, then the cathedral, all glistening metal railings and closed shutters. The gold hands on the black-faced clock on the tower pointed towards midnight.

A car suddenly appeared coming towards them, headlights dipped, windscreen wipers working furiously. Captain Sears, the Police Superintendent, was driving.

Christie gave a gasp of horror.

"What's the matter?" Jack asked him.

"Edward Sears. In that car. He recognised me."

"Was he alone?"

"No. Someone was with him, but I couldn't see who."

"Then ten to one he couldn't see you."

"He did. I know he did. Our eyes met."

"He wouldn't recognise the car, though. I've taken the numbers off."

Jack turned down into Church Street, facing the Palladian front of the building that housed the Bahamas Electricity Corporation, once the Vendue House, where slaves were sold. Old buildings leaned out towards each other across Bay Street. Red and white tiles, pink, grey, brown-washed walls, shone with rain, and behind and between them water from broken gutters streamed along narrow alleyways, past metal staircases. Locked and bolted doors, padlocked clasps, chains, and weights and pulleys kept gates closed to strangers. After the riots, shopkeepers were nervous.

Under a flickering sky, Queen Victoria stared stonily through the downpour across Rawson Square, above the simple inscription "Regina et Imperatrix, 1837-1901."

Jack turned left towards the harbour, past Kelly's Lumberyard. White shutters like giant eyelids closed in sleep protected every window. A liquor store, the customs office, a flagpole with rigging, and beyond this, the masts of anchored yachts rocked uneasily in the rough swell. In the distance, through the rain, lay Hog Island, the trees on it thin and sparse, like hair on an old man's scalp. Lights twinkled from marker buoys, the turning beam of the lighthouse cut through the rain, and above everything hung the basic, salty smell of sea.

They stopped on a concrete quay. Stone steps led down to the water and a launch moored alongside, held by ropes through iron rings. Jack could see dim lights behind curtains in cabin windows. A man in his shirt sleeves came out and peered up at them as he heard the car doors open and close.

In the rain, stone flags glistened like glass. Jack and Marshall opened the rear door of the station wagon, helped Sir Harry Oakes to climb out.

"What's happening?" he asked in a blurred voice. Then the rain on his face revived him and he stood upright.

"There's a cup of coffee aboard the launch, sir," said Marshall politely.

Oakes nodded, moving slowly like a man in someone else's dream. Lights on Hog Island winked at him across the rain-pocked sea.

Christie opened the front door to climb out after them.

"You stay here," Marshall told him curtly. "We'll be back in a minute."

"But..." protested Christie.

"Stay here," Marshall repeated. "There's nothing there that affects you."

Oakes allowed Jack and Marshall to help him down the slippery stone stairway. As they stepped on the deck, the launch tipped at the sudden extra weight. They steadied themselves, went below to the saloon. A single shadeless bulb glowed above a bench seat on the port side, reflecting varnished woodwork and polished brass. Oakes sank down thankfully on to blue canvas cushions. The wind and the rain had refreshed him, and the strange sleepy feeling had all but gone. He was trying to think of the right word to describe the torpor that had nearly overcome him. *Drugged.* That was it. Not only had he felt drugged; he had *been* drugged. That mixture of fruit juices, perhaps? Something wrong with it. He'd damn well find out what in the morning.

The engineer brought Sir Harry a cup of black coffee.

"The weather's closing in," he said to Marshall. "Glass is dropping all the time. Is it O.K. if I fill up the starboard reserve tank? Better now than trying to do it in a Force Nine."

Marshall nodded; anything to get him out of the way. He heard footsteps overhead as the engineer and two of the crew loosened the chains that secured their last drum of gasoline amidships.

Sir Harry drank the coffee gratefully, put down the empty cup.

"Now, where's that message?" he asked.

Marshall took a deep breath. This would be the most difficult moment of Jack's plan. Pass it successfully, and he had no worries at all. Above his head he heard the clank of the engineer's wrench against the drum; metal boomed like a giant gong.

"There is no message," said Marshall quietly.

"No message? What the hell do you mean, no message? Is this some sort of joke? What have you got me here for?"

"Because I wanted to talk to you privately. This was the only way."

"You mean you got me here on a goddamn wild goose chase?"

Sir Harry stood up slowly, his face contorted in amazement. Suddenly, the launch dipped sharply to starboard under the dead weight of forty gallons of gasoline, as the three men overhead trundled the drum across the decking. The vessel's unexpected movement caused Sir Harry to pitch forward. For a second, he almost lost his balance, and threw out one hand to steady himself against the bulkhead. Marshall, thinking he was about to fall, gripped him by the wrist.

"Keep your damn' hands off me!" shouted Sir Harry angrily. He tried to shake himself free, and in that moment the floor lifted as the launch righted herself. Now it was Marshall's turn to lose his balance. Still holding the older man's wrist, he staggered, hit the edge of the bench seat with the back of his knees, and sat down heavily. 'His head struck the bulkhead, smashing the electric bulb.

"For God's sake!" shouted Jack warningly in the sudden unexpected darkness. A clattering of feet on wooden steps, and the engineer appeared at the door.

"What's going on?" he asked, and shone his storm torch into the saloon. In its thin beam he saw Marshall, now sprawled on his back on the long bench seat. The blue cushion was half on the floor, and he was still gripping Sir Harry's wrist. The older man was above him, pushing him down with one hand, trying to pull his other wrist free of Marshall's grip. Jack seized the sleeves of both men in a futile attempt to separate them. Everyone seemed to be shouting abuse or advice, or exclaiming in pain as feet and arms and elbows thrashed in the gloom. Oakes was surprisingly strong and forced Marshall's head against the wooden wall.

The engineer lifted his wrench and aimed a blow at Sir Harry's head. He did not mean it to be a heavy blow, simply hard enough to separate the two men and break up the fight, but as he struck, Marshall suddenly arched his back, and Sir Harry jerked up to avoid the punch he threw at him.

The metal prongs on the end of the wrench struck him on the side of his head with far more force than the engineer had intended. Sir Harry collapsed untidily on the floor. Marshall released his grip and sat up, rubbing the back of his head where it had hit the wall.

"That'll cool *him* down a bit," said the engineer. Marshall nodded and glanced across at Oakes.

"My God," he said slowly, and knelt by Sir Harry's side, feeling for his pulse. In the dim light of the engineer's torch, the triangular marks of the four prongs were red and raw in his temple. As Marshall watched, they slowly and ominously filled with blood.

Marshall raced up the stone steps to the quayside. Christie was still in the car, puffing a cigarette. Several stubs lay in the ashtray, and the car seemed full of smoke.

"There's trouble," Marshall told him breathlessly. "Sir Harry's been hurt."

"How do you mean, hurt?"

"An accident."

"What happened?"

"He fell. He hit his head."

There was no need to go into details yet; with luck, he might never need to do so.

"I'll get a doctor," said Christie.

"No," said Marshall. "It's too risky — yet. The launch shouldn't be here. He'll only start asking questions."

"But is Harry badly hurt?"

"He's out. That's all."

"That's all, for God's sake! He's sixty-nine, remember."

Christie jumped out of the car now, threw away his half-smoked cigarette, ran down the slippery steps into the saloon. The engineer had fitted a new bulb into the holder, and Jack had lifted Sir Harry onto one of the benches and was dabbing his face and temples with a damp towel. The engineer knelt by the bench, a mug of whisky in his hand.

"I can't get a drop down his throat," he said.

"What's that mark on his head?" Christie asked him.

"Where he got hit."

"Got hit? By whom? I thought you said he fell?"

"He did," said the engineer. "Hit his head."

"We *must* fetch a doctor," said Christie. "He looks bad."

"We've got to move him out of here first," replied Marshall nervously. "Help me carry him up to the car."

"No way," said Jack. "What if that policeman Sears saw me a second time? It'd be asking for trouble. I've got no plates on the car. He'd stop me."

"You came down here without them," Marshall pointed out.

"That was different," said Jack. "But I'm not going back with him like that."

"We'll take him round in the launch, then," said Marshall. "There's a jetty near his house."

"I'll have a doctor waiting," said Christie.

"No," said Marshall brusquely. "We'll deal with this. We got him here, we'll see he's all right."

"He's my friend."

"All the more reason for letting us handle things."

"What about that message from Mexico? What was that about? Did that upset him or something?"

Marshall did not answer. There was no message; there never had been one. He called to the engineer: "Start your engines, prepare to cast off."

The launch's two engines began to run. The night wind blew acrid exhaust smoke into the cabin. As the vessel trembled under their feet, Sir Harry groaned slightly.

"Wait for me by the jetty," said Marshall.

Jack and Christie went up the steps to the station wagon.

Behind them, through the rain, Marshall was already reversing the launch out into the main channel. She carried no lights. The growl of her engines rose briefly as he opened the throttles. Then the dark shape, rimmed faintly with phosphorescence on a darker sea, turned west and set off towards Cable Beach.

Freddie de Marigny's dinner party was a leisurely affair; only the host had to be up early in the morning — and then simply because he wanted to be. For the rest, their hours were entirely their own. They had servants to do all the chores, and war was several thousand miles away. They smoked cigarettes between courses, played records on the gramophone, held heated or hilarious discussions while dark-skinned Bahamian servants waited patiently for instructions.

They reached the sweet course at around eleven o'clock, when rain began to fall. At first there were the big solitary drops of the tropics, like single tears, then a patter of rain, then a gust, blown like a wind from the sea, and then the mad roar of a torrent on the roof. Water sluiced across tiles, filled gutters already jammed with leaves, and streamed down the walls of the house, hammering on the patio and on the roof of Marigny's car.

Blue lightning flashes lit up palm trees bent against the wind, shaking long feather-duster fronds as long-haired swimmers shake sea-water from their hair. Thunder grumbled in the sky, and the candle flames trembled beneath their pale shades.

The driving, pounding rain suddenly cooled the spirits and atmosphere of the party. There seemed something fierce, elemental, frightening about its strength and intensity that destroyed the intimate ambience of the evening. For the two RAF wives, it was a sudden, unwanted reminder that they were not in the safe homely suburbs of southern England, where rain generally fell gently.

Conversation dwindled. The mood of banter and mild flirtation died. Guests consulted their watches, and about midnight, after coffee and brandy, they began to drift away. The storm appeared to have blown itself out, but so had the party; it was time to leave. Rain was still falling, but the wind had dropped, and the air felt humid, heavy with alien sickly scents from flowers that had no smell at all by day.

Georges de Visdelou had a bad cold. He kept coughing and blowing his nose and whispering to Betty. Finally, they excused themselves and went upstairs together to his apartment. Donald McKinney went home, and Freddie Cerretta and Oswald Moseley and the two RAF wives were left. Marigny suddenly felt tired. The evening had started off as fun, but somehow had become tedious. It was difficult to make up a successful dinner party on the spur of the moment, and the storm had spoiled everything. The two women looked at each other, neither wishing to ask for a lift home, both hoping that their host would offer one. He did.

"I can drop you off too, Freddie, if you care to come along."

"No thanks," replied Cerretta. "Oswald's offered me a lift."

"But it's out of his way to take you back. It's not out of mine."

"I know, but listen to me for a minute. Have you ever thought what would happen if we were seen, the four of us? Two fellows and two girls in your car, and *all* of us married — to different people?"

"Well, what about it?"

"You know damn well what about it," said Cerretta. "Think what the gossips would say."

"They say what say they, let them say."

"Well, that's your view, Freddie, I take the opposite one. Thanks for the offer, but I'll be fine on my own — and safer."

Marigny held open the front door of the car for the two girls. The only sounds as they drove were the click-click of the windscreen wipers and dance music from Miami on the radio; Kay Kyser and his orchestra were playing "Praise the Lord and Pass the Ammunition." In the Lincoln's headlights, the streets of Nassau shone silver and empty, washed clean. Under overhanging roofs shops stood shuttered and silent and secretive. Here and there, in a doorway, a dim light burned. The windows of Lightbourn's Pharmacy at the corner of George Street were more brightly lit than the other shop windows. In their light, Dorothy Clarke glanced at her watch.

"It's late," she said. "Twenty-five past one."

Marigny wore a luminous wrist watch; he looked at it. "You're wrong," he said. "It's only five past."

They were passing the British Colonial Hotel.

"Are you sure?" she asked him.

She held her watch up to her ear, shook her wrist, and listened. Marigny pointed to the illuminated clock on the dashboard.

"Two to one," he said. "Five past."

Mrs. Clarke wound back the hands of her watch.

They reached Hubbard Cottages, and he stopped the car. Through the big windows, the boom of the waves sounded faint and heavy, like the breathing of some asthmatic animal.

"Will you come in for a coffee?" Mrs. Clarke asked him.

"Thank you, but no," replied Marigny. "I've got to be up pretty early in the morning."

"Your chickens?"

"My chickens," he agreed.

He leaned across the seat and opened the front door for them. They climbed out, waved him good-bye. He turned the car and drove slowly past Westbourne. The great house lay in darkness. Beyond it, surf pounded on the beach. He wondered whether his father-in-law was staying there, when he would see him next; he really must work out figures for that sand and gravel contract and give him a ring.

Jack parked off the road down an empty track leading to the beach, next to a warning sign: "Private Property. Keep Out. Bad Dogs."

"What about the doctor?" asked Christie anxiously.

"Wait until we get the old guy into his own house," said Jack soothingly.

They walked down the track towards the sea. Rain had stopped, but the sand was sodden and stuck to their shoes like clay. Waves foamed, white and angry, and the night smelled strongly of seaweed. To their right, a trellised pier stretched into the water.

Frank Marshall and two of the crew were already carrying Sir Harry Oakes along this pier, stumbling on slippery boards, cursing his weight. They went up the beach, through the private gate to the back garden of Westbourne.

The front door was unlocked; Sir Harry never locked doors. They entered the hall. A standard lamp was alight, but the house seemed empty. The only sounds were their breathing and the faint background dynamo hum of mosquitoes.

"Anyone here?" Jack called. There was no answer.

"Up the stairs," ordered Marshall. "And hurry."

They had difficulty carrying Sir Harry around a bend in the staircase, and their feet left sand and mud into the treads as they manoeuvred, fearful of dropping him. Marshall and the engineer helped, putting out their hands to steady themselves. Jack could see their fingermarks clearly from where he stood in the hall. When he followed them up the stairs, he was careful not to touch anything.

"Where's his bedroom?"

Christie pointed to the room that Sir Harry always used when he was on his own.

"Where are you staying tonight?"

"I was staying here. In that room."

"Then go there now."

"But what about the doctor?"

Marshall ignored his question. "What time do you get up when you stay here?"

"Around seven or seven-thirty."

"What do you do then?"

"I walk along the verandah to Sir Harry's room. Usually, he's already awake. We have breakfast together." How friendly and informal that familiar routine sounded; how reassuring to believe he would carry it out again in the morning.

"Do that tomorrow. Just as usual," Marshall told him, relishing the rare opportunity of giving orders to a richer man.

"But what about the doctor?"

"Listen," said Marshall wearily, looking down at Christie from his superior height. "You're supposed to be a clever guy. Well, get this straight, once and for all. If we call a doctor now, when you're hanging around, he's going to ask *you* what happened. That way *you're* involved. *You* have to say why you were down on the quay at midnight on a strange launch. Can't you see what that means?"

Christie swallowed. He realised what this would mean: questions, evasive answers, lies, rumours.

"But if you're safely asleep in your room," Marshall went on, "you don't hear or see a thing. You know what they say in Sicily? 'He who is deaf, blind, and silent, lives a hundred years in peace.' "

Christie nodded. Marshall had made himself plain. He walked slowly along the corridor to his room, like a man old, tired, and beaten before his time.

In Sir Harry's bedroom a maid had placed reading glasses on the bedside table, next to a tumbler of water and a neatly folded copy of that day's *Miami Herald,* because Sir Harry sometimes read for half an hour before going to sleep. She had unfurled his mosquito net over the bed and tucked it in neatly around the mattress. The windows were open, facing the sea. An electric fan stood on the floor, should Sir Harry need it. On humid summer nights spent beneath a close-mesh mosquito net, an air current was often welcome.

Marshall rolled up the net, and then, moving sideways, he and Jack placed Sir Harry on the bed. Streaks of blood stretched down his head towards his nose. His face glistened with rain and sweat. He looked very pale and had a waxy appearance. His eyes were closed.

"What about that doctor?" Jack asked nervously.

Marshall nodded and held his fingers on Sir Harry's pulse. Then he looked down at him more closely and raised one of his eyelids.

"We don't need a doctor. We need a mortician. He's dead."

"Dead? He can't be," protested the engineer. "It was only a light tap."

"With a wrench eighteen inches long on an old man's skull?"

Marshall picked up a hand mirror from the dressing table, held it in front of Sir Harry's nose, desperately hoping for the tiniest patch of condensation that would prove he was still breathing. The mirror stayed bright and clear. Marshall replaced the mirror carefully, wiping its handle with his handkerchief. As far as he knew, he had touched nothing else. If everyone kept quiet, his involvement could still stay secret. If, if, if. Why had that stupid bastard hit him?

Marshall's worry showed on his face. His hair hung damp with rain like rats' tails over his sallow skin. His bulk seemed somehow to have shrunk. He looked old, as he might look in ten years' time, but not then, not at his age. Jack wished Carole could see him now. She may have loved him once, but surely the sight of Marshall, worried at the prospect of explaining how a routine assignment was bungled, with $50,000 missing and the richest man in the Bahamas dead, would end anything between them. Women weren't interested in failure; at least, his wife wasn't.

But she wasn't here to see his discomfiture, and of course she must never know anything about this, for that way lay danger, possibly even death. The British didn't use an electric chair — they used the rope. He slid one hand beneath Sir Harry's pillow, and his fingers closed around the butt of a pistol. He slipped it into his pocket.

"What about these marks on his head?" he asked Marshall.

"I'll show you."

Marshall pulled down the mosquito net, tucked the edge carefully beneath the mattress, turned to the engineer.

"Bring us a gallon of gas from the boat. And hurry!"

The man raced down the stairs and was back within minutes, holding a can. Marshall sprinkled petrol over the bed and the carpet. Picking up a pillow, he ripped it open and scattered the feathers over the corpse. Then he turned the fan towards the bed, switched it on, and walked downstairs, tipping the can every few steps.

The others followed him, trying not to tread on the wet areas. In the hall, Marshall nodded to them, took out a box of matches, held three matches together, lit them, dropped them on the nearest small patch of petrol. With a quick *whoof,* the flames spread rapidly, moving like a lit powder trail. Up the stairs they flared, along the landing, into the bedroom where the dead man lay. Marshall waited for a moment, sniffing the burning carpet and then the unforgettable sickly sweet smell of roasting flesh.

"What about Christie?" Jack asked him.

"He'll be all right!"

"He lives, here, in Nassau."

Marshall looked at him. "So do you," he replied softly.

Jack stared back at him in horror. He remembered the surprise on Captain Sears's face as he recognised Christie when their cars passed. Had Sears also recognised him? If Sears could trace his station wagon without numbers — and there were only forty-seven station wagons registered on the island — what could be his excuse for being out so late with Christie? In such a crisis, would Christie shop him if he felt that this could save himself?

Jack swallowed and said nothing. Marshall nodded to the others. It was time to go.

Carole sensed rather than heard the faint tapping on the windowpane, like a twig or the beak of a lost night bird. She had been asleep, but the noise woke her, because it was so persistent. She sat up, her mouth dry from too much vodka. No birds or branches were near that particular window; someone must be outside, trying to contact her cautiously, secretly.

She glanced at the clock by the bed: ten minutes after midnight. It couldn't be Jack. If he had lost his front door key, he would never tap gently, but would bang on the window imperiously, and if she didn't answer at once, he would shout. Jack never liked to be kept waiting.

Carole lay for a moment, wondering whether to ignore the sound. She was alone in the house, and the possibility of being attacked or robbed surged through her mind. There were so many strangers on the island now; this sort of thing had never happened before the war. Now, it could.

The tapping continued, discreet but insistent. She climbed out of bed, put on her dressing gown, crossed the room. She opened the window and looked out. The rain had stopped some time before, but the wind was still shaking drops of water from branches and leaves. In the distance, the sea roared like a caged beast. Thick clouds obscured the moon, but she could make out the familiar features of the Bahamian to whom she had handed the phial.

"Oh, it's you," she said, relieved. "What's the matter? What do you want?"

"I must talk to you."   i

"But my husband? It's only luck that he's not here now. He'll be back any minute."

"Not just yet. He went off in a car with Sir Harry, Mr. Christie, and another man. I saw them go."

"Where to?"

"Nassau."

"I'll see you tomorrow," she said. "Same place, usual time."

"No," he replied. "Now! It's important."

"Then wait a minute."

Carole closed the window and went to the front door. He was waiting under the porch. She brought him into the hall, closed the door behind him, bolted it, then took him into the big room that overlooked the beach. If her husband arrived unexpectedly, she would say she was afraid on her own; this would give her visitor at least an extra minute to escape through the French windows onto the patio.

"What's the matter?"

"You know what was in that tube, don't you?"

She shook her head.

"A drug for Sir Harry."

"A drug? Why?"

"Your husband and the other American wanted him to agree to something he didn't like. It was to make him fuddled so he wouldn't know what he was doing. He's a very strong-minded man, Sir Harry."

"So I've heard."

"Tomorrow, Sir Harry's leaving for Miami. They wanted to get his agreement tonight — before he left.'

"What was it about?"

"I don't know."

"You haven't come here now just to tell me that?"

"No. Not just that." He paused. "I didn't want to put that stuff in Sir Harry's drink, but they made me."

"Who? My husband and his friend?"

"No. Another American. I don't know his name. I've never even seen him before. But he knew about you and me. He said he'd tell if I didn't do it."

"My God!" Was there no end to this blackmail?

"One good thing though," the Bahamian said, more cheerfully. "I got my hands on gold."

"*Gold?* Here? In Nassau?"

"It *was* here in Nassau," he corrected her. "Sir Harry kept some bars and coins in his house."

"How'd you get it?"

"Just took it. I switched some stones for it in a box."

"Where is it now?"

"Not here on the island. Somewhere else."

"So why tell me now? At this hour?"

"Because I'm not staying here too long. I may not get another chance like this. Why those men want me to drug Sir Harry? He never done me no wrong. I'm going away. I'm good as any white man, but I've never had the chance to prove it. When you're black, no one wants to back you or lend you money. Now I can back myself. I'm starting my own business. Somewhere away from Nassau." He paused. "You've said often enough you like me. Now I'm not poor any more, come away with me."

"What? Now?"

"Not right now. Later. I just want your word now."

"I'll think about it."

Was he speaking the truth — or was she imagining all this? Carole's throat constricted with panic. She must keep calm — and she must get rid of him. Jack could return at any moment.

"Promise," he said in a hoarse, urgent whisper.

"I'll see you," she replied, compromising. "Tomorrow."

He put out his hands, drew her towards him, kissed her briefly. Then he was gone. Carole walked slowly into the sitting room, opened the cupboard, and without even bothering to take out a glass, put the bottle to her lips and drank greedily.

She went back to bed and lay awake until she heard the engine of her husband's car, the click of the front door closing, and his footsteps in the hall. The main bedroom lights came on, but she pretended to be asleep. If he had been drinking and she was awake, he might become amorous, and she could not bear his hands on her body, his breath sweet and heavy with rum.

Jack glanced at her. She was obviously asleep; must have been at the vodka again. He knew how much she drank, because he frequently checked the level in the soda-water bottle. But at least she would not know what time it was, and in her state he could insist he had been home since eleven. That would cover him completely, for with any luck no one had seen him drive on from Westbourne. He had experienced one bad moment, when the car had backfired just after starting, making a noise like a gun going off, but who would hear that so late at night, and in such a place?

Carole watched her husband through half-closed eyes. Jack's jacket was soaked across the shoulders, his hair plastered to his skull with rain. He undressed and threw his wet clothes into the wicker laundry basket that the maid emptied every morning. The door to their bathroom was open, and Carole watched Jack examine his face in the mirror, turning his head from side to side. There were dark smudges on his neck. He washed them off with unusual care, and then put on his pyjamas and climbed carefully into bed so as not to wake her.

She could smell not only sweat and rum, but something else: burning. He must have been very close to a fire. But who would light a fire on a stormy July night in Nassau?

When Marigny reached his house in Victoria Avenue, Georges de Visdelou's Chevrolet was still parked on the lawn, where it had been when he left. Marigny drove slowly past it, into the double garage, then went upstairs to his bedroom. It was nearly a quarter to two. In less than five hours he would be starting

work again. He undressed, climbed thankfully into bed, and lay for a few moments, turning over in his mind the events of the day.

He must have fallen asleep without realising it, because a sudden commotion caused him to sit up in bed, heart pounding. Georges's Maltese cat, Grisou, was in the room, making a lot of noise. He called for Georges to come and collect the animal, but there was no answer. Then he heard the slam of a door and looked out the window. Georges was backing his car out on to the road to take Betty Roberts home. Marigny glanced at his watch. Three o'clock.

A strong wind rattled the palm leaves. He waited until he heard the car return and Georges moving about downstairs; then he called out to him, "Come and get your damn cat out of here."

"Sorry," said Georges apologetically. "Didn't want to disturb you."

He came upstairs and, without putting on the light, opened the bedroom door and called to his cat. Grisou went out willingly enough. With only a small twinge of pain from his stomach, Marigny gratefully went back to sleep.

10

Early Morning Activity in Nassau and Sicily

IN THE GUEST BEDROOM at Westbourne, Christie lay awake, listening to the wind.

The storm had driven mosquitoes into the room, and some had found their way under the net and woken him.

He climbed out of bed, opened the window, and peered through the warm sweating darkness towards Oakes's bedroom. The moon was down, and he could see nothing. The pounding roar of surf on the beach was the only sound. Were the others still there? Had they taken Oakes to the doctor's surgery — or had the doctor visited him here? Christie wanted to see for himself, but something held him back: not Marshall's warning or fear of the consequences so much as fear of what he might find.

He crawled back into bed beneath the mosquito net, tucked it carefully around the mattress, and picked up a copy of *Time* magazine from his bedside table. Individual words in news reports caught his eye and bludgeoned his mind: *killer, murder, death.*

Christie put the magazine to one side and must have dozed, because suddenly he was awake again. He did not wear a watch, so he had no clear idea of the time, but the night was still dark, and the wind was throwing handfuls of rain against the windows. Had this woken him, or had there been some other sound, some other reason? He dozed again, and when he woke next, the sun was up. He lifted the mosquito net and walked out on to the verandah. As he leaned on the rail, already warm in the sunshine, the sea seemed so calm and peaceful that it was difficult to believe it could have appeared so angry only hours earlier.

It was also difficult to accept that then he had seen his best friend and client carried along the jetty and across the beach. How was he now? Christie took a deep breath before he began to walk slowly across the scrubbed floor-boards of the verandah to Harry Oakes's room. As he reached the door with its horizontal slats, he cleared his throat.

"Hi, Harry," he called.

There was no reply. Reluctantly, he opened the door.

Sir Harry lay on his bed under the charred, still smouldering wooden frame of his mosquito screen. The net had almost completely burned away, and Sir Harry's body was blackened and covered with feathers that trembled in the morning breeze. The fluffy white down gave the corpse the grotesque appearance of some giant bird brought down in death.

The reading glasses that Marshall had so carefully placed on his face had cracked. Sir Harry's skin was dark with soot, his pyjama jacket burned away, leaving raw red wounds. Black shining blisters the size of crab-apples had erupted elsewhere on his body beneath the feathers, and wisps of smoke still rose lazily from the bottom of the bed. The carpet and bedside rug were badly charred, and smoke had smudged the wardrobe, the bedroom walls, and the lacquered screen at the side of his bed.

Christie looked down in horror at Sir Harry's dead face. It was one thing to help move an unconscious man on the understanding that a doctor would be called. It was another altogether to imagine the violent and terrible death of someone with whom he had been on such close terms, had genuinely liked and greatly admired. He saw streaks of blood and a deep, small hole in the dead man's temple. Had Sir Harry been shot? Then he saw the other holes he had noticed in the launch. How could Sir Harry have injured his head so severely in a fall aboard a small boat tied up at the quay?

Gradually, Christie's heart slowed to a normal beat. Oakes was now beyond all earthly censure, personal, political, or financial, but he and the Duke were not. He must inform him at once that Sir Harry was dead, and let him decide what to do. After all, he was the Governor.

In an automatic action, Christie beat out a burning patch on the bed with his hands. Then he looked down at his palms in disgust. They were black as Sir Harry's face. He went into the bathroom, washed his hands under the tap, rinsed them several times, dried them with a towel.

There would obviously be an investigation. The police would arrive; Colonel Erskine Lindop and the head of the local C.I.D., Major Herbert Pemberton. As long as he stuck to his story, that he had never left his room, he would be safe, he kept assuring himself. Then he remembered Sears's face through two sets of car windows, blurred by rain and darkness. Sears had recognised him. Well, he would just have to bluff that out. It would only be the word of one man against another, and he was by far the richer and more influential man in an island where money spoke above all other voices.

Through the window, he could see steam rising from the trees; it was going to be a hot day. He suddenly remembered that two night watchmen were always on duty around Westbourne. Where the devil were they? Had they seen anything?

He flung open the window and shouted for them. There was no answer.

He shouted, "Help! Help!" Again, no one replied. The house was empty, the grounds deserted. Christie walked downstairs, feeling calmer now that he was actually doing something, reacting as anyone would who had just found his best friend dead in bed.

He knew that Newell Kelly, Sir Harry's manager, was away, but his wife was in their house in the Country Club grounds. He telephoned her from the hall. Then he rang his brother Frank and asked him to bring a doctor as quickly as possible.

He had just replaced the receiver when it rang. He was not expecting an incoming call, and his heart leaped at the sound. He picked up the receiver; Etienne Dupuch was on the line.

Dupuch was already in his office — the staff of an evening paper begin work early — and he wanted to confirm his appointment that morning with Sir Harry. Dupuch knew from experience how the rich would casually break appointments or make new arrangements without the courtesy of informing those they had agreed to meet, and he wanted to check that Sir Harry was still there and expecting him.

Christie told him that Sir Harry was dead. Then, remembering the deep hole in his friend's head, he added, "He's been shot!"

He lit a cigarette to soothe himself before he made his next two calls, to the Commissioner of Police and the Duke of Windsor.

In Nassau, streets still shone with rain. Gutters were blocked with leaves, and Bay Street was awash with sandy mud. Outside Government House sentries stamped their feet, sloped arms, turned, marched their prescribed six paces in one direction, turned, and marched back. The Union Jack hung damp and limp against the flagstaff. A mist covered the long low shape of Hog Island. The sky was heavy with unshed rain.

The telephone rang by the bedside of Major Gray Phillips, the Duke of Windsor's ADC. Phillips, who had joined the Duke and Duchess as their comptroller when they were in Paris, was a bachelor in his late fifties. He was as tall as Marigny, and shared Marigny's liking for brown and white shoes and lightweight suits of pale gabardine. Phillips was more poetic and artistic than Marigny, however: several visitors to Government House had congratulated him on his gift for flower arranging.

He reached out first for the telephone and then for his glasses. A voice thick with panic and horror spoke urgently in his ear.

"The Duke of Windsor, please."

Phillips recognised Christie. "But it's only half-past seven. He's still asleep."

"You'd better wake him up. It's very important. It's about Sir Harry Oakes. He's dead."

"Dead? How?"

Phillips listened as the voice gabbled an explanation. "I'll tell him at once," he said, and replaced the receiver.

Gray Phillips stood up, all lethargy gone, put on his dressing gown, walked along the wooden verandah towards the Duke's bedroom, tapped gently on the door. The Duke was a late riser, and the Duchess even later. As far as they were concerned, half-past seven in the morning could be the middle of last night. A sleepy male voice called, "Who is it?"

"Phillips, sir. It's important."

Major Phillips waited. The door opened and the Duke appeared, looking absurdly small and slight, with tousled fair hair, his ageing face still crumpled with sleep. He wore a silk dressing gown with the Royal arms embroidered on his breast pocket.

"Well?"

"It's about Sir Harry Oakes, sir."

"What about him?"

The Duchess was stirring, a shadowy form seen dimly through the doorway. Phillips whispered his news. The Duchess heard one word that beat like a pulse in her head: murder.

The Duke repeated the word incredulously. *"Murder?"*

He looked out at the damp, early morning scene, at the sun beginning to burn its way through the clouds. He thought of Lady Oakes and the family, the kindness that she and Sir Harry had shown to him in letting them use Westbourne while Government House was being redecorated.

"For her sake," he said almost thinking aloud, "I do hope it *is* murder. But for the sake of the island, I hope it is suicide."

He stood for a moment, fingering the silk tassel on his dressing gown.

"The police know about this yet, Phillips?"

"I understand they have been informed, sir."

"Sir Harry was a very great benefactor to the Bahamas. This is an immense loss to the colony. We want to keep his death quiet for the moment. Lady Oakes must be informed before the press get on to her. I will put a security ban on all press and radio messages from Nassau about this terrible happening until further notice."

"As from now, sir?" asked Gray Phillips.

"As from now."

Jack's bedside telephone was also ringing. As he picked it up, he glanced across the bed, then at his watch. Carole had gone. It was five minutes to eight in the morning. He heard a faint click on the wire and knew that someone in the house had lifted the extension. Then an American voice spoke urgently in his ear.

Jack replaced the receiver, picked it up again, and asked the operator for Government House. Carole came into the room as he finished speaking. She held a tumbler of colourless liquid. As she sat down shakily on the edge of the bed, some slopped out onto the counterpane. Jack put out a finger, dabbed the damp patch, and licked his finger. Vodka.

"Early for that, isn't it?" he asked her.

She ignored the question. "I picked up the phone," she said tonelessly. "What did that man want?"

"A business matter. It doesn't concern you."

"He was here the other day."

"I know."

"Yes, but not about the second time."

"The second time? You never told me."

"That was a business matter, too. It doesn't concern you, either. But I don't like him."

"You don't have to."

"You're in trouble, Jack. Deep, deep trouble. You came in last night late, and you smelled of burning. The maid has just arrived. She tells me Sir Harry Oakes has been burned to death."

Jack jumped out of bed, started looking for his clothes. Had the fire destroyed the house — and any evidence? He must find out.

"That man who just phoned. He threatened me," Carole went on.

"Threatened you? How? Why?" Jack stared at her in amazement. Was she drunk?

"Over Frank."

"Frank Marshall? But that was years ago."

A terrible thought stabbed Jack's mind like a hot, poisoned lance. "Wasn't it?"

Carole smiled at him enigmatically, put the glass to her lips, and gulped down two mouthfuls. Some vodka ran down her chin, staining her blouse. He pushed the glass roughly from her hand.

"Wasn't it?" he repeated.

Carole's expression changed from amiable vacuity to sudden rage. "No. It wasn't. You think you can leave me here while you go out to your sordid meetings. Don't fool yourself that I don't know about that room in the Prince George. Well, J can have *my* life, too. With a real man. Someone I admire."

"You mean that bastard Frank Marshall? That no-good son-of-a-bitch?"

"That's all you can do, Jack — shout at him, abuse him. But I love him."

"Well, since you told me, there's not much you can be blackmailed about now, is there?"

"That's only a part of it. The unimportant part."

"What's the other part?"

Suddenly, through the fog of alcohol that clouded her mind, Carole realised her own danger. She was saying far too much. She sat, staring at her husband, her lips tight as the mouth of a metal-topped purse. He must never know about the Bahamian and the others. She must never reveal their names, or about the gold. Never.

Jack hit her across the face with the back of his hand. She clawed and spat at him. He hit her again and again and again.

The Duke of Windsor came downstairs to his office, through the glass door engraved with the insignia of the Order of the Garter, and the motto, *Honi soit qui mal y pense* — Evil to him who evil thinks.

The room overlooked the rear garden of Government House, and the lawn was littered with fallen palm fronds. Power lines would be down, palm trees uprooted, families homeless after the storm, he thought. During a hurricane in 1866, waves higher than the lighthouse had surged over Hog Island and hit Nassau Harbour with such ferocity that of two hundred vessels at anchor, only one was left afloat. The flood then poured on through the cemetery and propelled bones and skulls through the streets. Six hundred and one houses had been totally destroyed and as many badly damaged. Mercifully, the previous night's storm would not produce a catastrophe on that scale. But what had happened at Westbourne during the storm could have infinitely more serious repercussions for him.

He sat down at his desk, with its huge photograph of the Duchess, the much smaller and uncomplimentary one of his mother, Queen Mary, which the Duchess insisted was the best that could be found. He rearranged his leather-backed folder, stamped "E" with a crown, and an ashtray engraved *Edwardus Rex* prepared for a coronation that had never taken place. Here, he felt secure, surrounded by symbols of his past: a row of pipes in a rack, a midshipman's dirk, a field marshal's baton. He had held both ranks in his lifetime, as Prince and King. Gray Phillips tapped respectfully on the door. The Duke looked up at him, frowning, as though he were busy and could not afford any interruption.

"The Commissioner of Police is at Westbourne, sir. And I have just had a telephone call about the investigation."

"From him?"

"No, sir. The caller did not give his name, and rang off before I could ask him, as a matter of fact. But he had a slight American accent. Said that it would be advisable — I quote the exact word he used, sir — if United States police carried out the investigation."

"What's wrong with our own people?"

"Nothing at all, sir. But he said the head of the Miami Police Department would be sympathetic to any request you might make. He actually named two officers from the Miami Police Department. Captain Edward Melchen and Captain James Barker. Apparently, Melchen met you on one of your trips to the States. He came aboard Mr. Wenner-Gren's yacht, *Southern Cross.* "

"Oh, yes. I remember him."

The police in Miami had always been very civil. They kept back the crowds, shouldered him to his aircraft or his car, made him feel important, Royal again, not an unhappy exile with a discontented wife, in a crumbling third-rate outpost of his younger brother's Empire. After all, it might be wise to call in the Americans. They would have modern equipment, which the local police force probably did not possess. That would mean a quick solution — and the longer enquiries lasted, the greater the risk that other matters might be brought to light.

"Telephone the Chief of Police in Miami, then," the Duke instructed Phillips. "I'll speak to him myself. And draft a cable about this for London."

"Very good, sir. And one other thing. I am sorry to have to tell you that the ban on news getting out was too late. Etienne Dupuch of *The Tribune* was to see Sir Harry this morning. Going to write a story about his sheep."

"Well?"

"Dupuch telephoned Westbourne to check that there had been no change in the arrangements, and Christie — who'd spent the night there — told him what had happened. The telegraph office says he has already sent telegrams to *The Daily Express* in London and to the Associated Press."

The Duke pursed his lips. This was unfortunate, but he could do nothing about it now; he could still be prudent, however.

"When you get through to Miami, say I want to speak to Captain Melchen personally," he told Phillips. "Explain that it is an investigation to confirm the death of a prominent citizen who has died this morning in, shall we say, extraordinary circumstances."

Within minutes, Melchen was on the line, more surprised at his caller than at the nature of the call. Neither man realised that his conversation was being monitored by United States government security officers.

"I should like you to fly down here immediately," said the Duke.

"That will be difficult, sir," replied Melchen. "I haven't got a passport."

"Come without one," said the Duke. "I'll speak to the immigration people here."

"The only plane from here today is the twelve o'clock Pan American flight from Miami, sir."

"I'll see that it is held for you," said the Duke.

"It's that important, sir?"

"It's that important," replied the Duke. "The investigation *must* be done today."

Within the hour, an "Immediate" coded cable went from Government House to the Secretary of State for the Colonies in London.

Deeply regret to report that Sir Harry Oakes has met violent death under circumstances which are not yet known. Hope to obtain expert advice of Chief of Miami Detectives immediately, to assist local police. Will telegraph further.

By then, Marigny had been awake for some time. His stomach was paining him again; he really should not drink black coffee and brandy late at night. He climbed out of bed, poured a stomach powder into half a glass of water, swirled it around, and drank the milky mixture. Then he washed, shaved, dressed, and went downstairs to make his breakfast: Ovaltine and dry toast, with a boiled egg. He did not have a toaster, so he lit the gas oven and put two slices of bread on the rack.

After breakfast he checked a ledger in which he kept a record of all eggs hatching in the incubator, and the dates. He was a methodical worker; each egg had its own number. More chicks were ready to be moved, and he put these into cardboard boxes and drove out to the farm in his truck. His helpers were already scalding and plucking chickens for delivery later that day.

At a quarter to nine Marigny drove back into Nassau, happened to see Basil McKinney in the street, and asked him how he felt about being disqualified in the races the previous day. McKinney shrugged his shoulders; these things happened. Oswald Moseley was going into his bookshop, and he paused to say how much he had enjoyed dinner the previous evening. They both jokingly commiserated with McKinney, and then Marigny remembered that he should see the police about re-registering his truck. Since he was only a few yards from the Central Police Station, he went in and asked the duty constable whether it was necessary for a police officer to examine this vehicle, which he had converted from a car. Apparently, it was.

Marigny then drove back to the farm to check on the day's orders. It was still early, not ten o'clock. His farm manager wanted some cheese-cloth, and with nothing much else to do, Marigny said that he would collect it for him in Nassau. In fact, he did not do so, for as he drove past the Pan American office, he saw John Anderson driving towards him. Anderson blew his car horn excitedly and stopped, waving his hand to attract Marigny's attention.

"What's the matter?" Marigny asked him.

"Haven't you heard the news about Sir Harry?"

"What about him?"

"He's dead."

"Dead? How? Did he have a stroke or something?"

"I don't know. All I know is, he's dead."

"Well, where did he die?"

"Don't know that, either."

Marigny drove home, with Anderson following him, to tell Georges.

"Let's go and find out what's happened," said Georges, his cold forgotten for the moment. They were not sure in which of Sir Harry's several houses he had spent the night, but as they passed Westbourne, they saw several cars parked in the drive.

"It must be here," said Anderson. "Let's go in."

Mrs. Kelly came out of the house to meet them as they reached the front porch.

"What's happened?" Marigny asked her.

"Sir Harry has been murdered."

"Murdered?" Marigny repeated in amazement. This was infinitely worse than he had anticipated. "I'd better call Lady Oakes."

He could telephone her house in Bar Harbor easily enough.

"That's already been done. Someone has also rung Mr. Foskett. He'll be here as soon as possible."

"I must cable Nancy." She could not be reached by telephone in Vermont without many connections and long delays.

"You won't be allowed to."

"What do you mean, won't be allowed to?"

"The Governor's given orders that no messages mentioning Sir Harry's death are to leave the island. Everything about it has been censored."

"Censored? But why?"

"You'd better ask the Duke."

Marigny's breakfast lay uneasily in his stomach. He felt shocked, almost overwhelmed, by the news of his father-in-law's murder, and put one hand against the wall to steady himself. For a moment, he thought he was going to be physically sick. He swallowed hard, for he could feel chill sweat on his back, his forehead.

' Mrs. Kelly regarded him with distaste. This long, thin foreigner with his strange accent and goatee beard was not a man she found it easy to admire. Her feelings showed in her voice.

"Get a hold of yourself, Freddie," she said shortly.

Marigny walked past her into the house, as though he had not heard. Frank Christie was there with Harold.

"What's happened?" Marigny asked him.

"Harold rang me this morning in a terrible state. Told me to get a doctor and come down here myself at once. He was so shocked, he even forgot to say where he was ringing from. Luckily, we tried Westbourne first."

"I was here all night," added Harold. "In the next bedroom."

"What exactly happened?"

"I've no idea. All I know is that I went in at about half-past seven this morning. We were going to have breakfast together. And there he was. Dead. He'd been hit on the head and the room had been set on fire."

"Did you hear anything odd in the night?"

"Nothing at all. There was a storm."

Marigny remembered the howling wind, the thrum of rain, waving palm trees, and the flickering candle flames in their hurricane shades. The telephone rang. Frank Christie answered it, spoke briefly.

"Foskett's office," he explained to the others. "He'll be here on the afternoon plane with Lady Oakes."

Marigny went upstairs. The smell of burning flesh and feathers hung acridly in the air, reminding him of the open fire at his farm, the steaming drum with labourers squatting around it, plucking damp chicken carcases. He went into Oakes's bedroom.

The mosquito screen over the bed had been totally burned away, and there were sodden, charred areas on the carpet near the window. The body of Sir Harry Oakes was still uncovered, and the feathers that were stuck to gross blisters on his flesh trembled like moths' wings in the morning breeze from the sea. He looked much smaller in death than in life. A second wave of nausea swept over Marigny at the sight. Again, he put out a hand to steady himself. He was farther away from the wall than he imagined, and his fingers touched the Chinese screen that his father-in-law used to deflect any draught from the open window. Colonel Erskine Lindop came into the room and nodded a greeting.

"Terrible business," he said briefly.

Marigny nodded. "Awful," he agreed. "Have you any clues?"

"Oh, we'll find the fellow who did it, all right."

"I certainly hope so. But it won't bring back Sir Harry."

He walked downstairs; Anderson was waiting for him in the hall.

"I'm going back to town," Marigny told him. There was nothing useful he could do here; the police were obviously in control. "Give you a lift?"

"Thanks."

They climbed into his car.

"Where's Newell Kelly?" Marigny asked him as they drove off.

"Madeline tells me he's on Abaco, on a fishing trip. Lucky for him."

"What do you mean, lucky for him?"

"Well, he's one man on the island who has a cast-iron alibi."

"What exactly do you mean by that?"

"Just what I say."

Something in Anderson's tone of voice disturbed Marigny: he had a sudden presentiment of danger. But why? The feeling was totally irrational, yet it persisted. Well, he had as good an alibi as Newell Kelly; he'd been host at his own dinner party all evening, until quite late. Again, he saw Lightbourn's Pharmacy in his car's headlights, heard Mrs. Clarke prattling on about her watch being fast.

"Where are you having lunch today?" he asked Anderson.

"No plans."

"Then join me at the Prince George."

"Delighted. I'll feel better with a stiff drink inside me."

"Who do you think did it?" Marigny asked him.

"How the hell do I know?" retorted Anderson. "He must have had a lot of enemies, a man like him. You don't make millions without treading on other people's faces."

"I don't think he did much of that. He dug his fortune out of the earth. That's why he prospected for gold. He wanted to be rich, but not at anyone else's expense."

"He must have been unique, then, as a millionaire," said Anderson drily.

Marigny looked at him sharply. "He was. And not only as a millionaire. As a man."

After lunch, Marigny usually went out to the farm, but today was different. It seemed impossible to settle down to a normal routine. He walked to the telegraph office and wrote out a telegram for his wife, explaining that her father had died, not that he had been murdered. Censorship must be lifted sometime, and it was his duty to inform her as soon as possible. Then he drove back to Westbourne. He might not be a member of the Oakes family by blood, but he was by marriage; he felt he should be available to help in any way he could.

Cars were now parked bumper to bumper along the road and down the drive. A crowd of sightseers had gathered on the lawn and stood, staring up at the house. Marigny knew several of them. They nodded a greeting to him and murmured subdued condolences.

Two strange men were in the hall. One was tall, wearing a well-cut suit. He had greying hair and looked like an actor playing the part of a senior diplomat or a successful surgeon. The second was short and muscular. He wore round, steel-rimmed spectacles, and his hair was cut very close to his head.

"Who are those two?" Marigny asked Anderson.

"Two American detectives. The big one's Captain Barker. The other's Captain Melchen. Apparently the Duke of Windsor telephoned the Miami Police Department and asked for them *by name"*

"But why? Erskine Lindop is the head of the police here. And Pemberton is in charge of the C.I.D. There aren't many crimes they haven't solved since I've been here. And how did the Duke *know* their names?"

"You'd better ask him that, hadn't you?"

At that moment, everyone stopped talking. People who had been sitting on the grass or lolling against cars all stood up respectfully. The crunch of heavy tyres on the gravel announced the arrival of the Duke of Windsor's Buick. The Duke nodded in the direction of the crowd as the Bahamian policemen saluted smartly. He wore a lightweight suit, with a buttonhole, his tie loosely tied in the Windsor knot, brown and white shoes. He looked vaguely theatrical, like an ageing matinee idol at a garden party: pleasant face, pink cheeks, but old about the eyes.

The two American detectives stepped forward briskly.

"I remember you," said the Duke, shaking hands with Melchen.

"Yes, Your Royal Highness. I was detailed to look after you aboard Mr. Wenner-Gren's yacht, *Southern Cross,* when you visited Miami."

"Of course. Of course."

"I am Captain Barker, sir," said his companion.

"Ah, yes. We've not met before, I think. Have you anything to report?"

As he spoke, the Duke looked briefly past the two detectives to where Marigny was standing. Then he turned back towards Barker as the officer began to speak.

"Perhaps you could tell me upstairs?" suggested the Duke tactfully.

"Very good, Your Royal Highness."

As soon as the Duke was inside the house, everyone relaxed, began talking again, lit cigarettes.

Harold Christie turned to Marigny. "Foskett's coming in on the five o'clock plane," he explained. "I know you had a bit of an argument with him, Freddie, but you *are* the son-in-law, and I think it would be a gesture if you drove out to the airfield to meet him."

But Foskett was not on the aircraft, and Marigny drove home thoughtfully. Georges had gone to bed in an attempt to cure his cold, and Marigny did not feel like eating alone. He wanted company, people he knew. On the impulse, he drove to the Prince George Hotel. Anderson was already in the bar, and they had dinner together.

Whereas before, at lunch, their conversation had been casual, now, inexplicably to Marigny, both men seemed ill at ease.

He saw that people at other tables were looking across at them, and sensed they were talking about him. But why?

"I've eaten here once or twice most weeks since I've been in Nassau," he said to Anderson, "and no one has ever looked at me before as everyone seems to be doing tonight. What's the reason? Am I suddenly a celebrity?"

"Getting that way. Haven't you heard the talk?"

"No. What about?"

"About you. People are saying you're the only person who *could* have done it. Because you have the most to gain."

"By killing my own father-in-law? Are you serious? He never gave me any favours when he was alive — and I never asked him to. So why should I gain a penny from his death? Is this your idea of a joke?"

"I'm deadly serious," Anderson replied.

The word deadly jarred in Marigny's mind. He turned and deliberately stared back at a man at the next table who was staring at him. The man coloured and looked away, embarrassed.

"If I were you," said Anderson slowly, "I'd call my lawyer, just in case anything unexpected happens. You're pretty friendly with Godfrey Higgs, aren't you?"

"He's in New York."

"Then call Stafford Sands. He acts for me. Ask him what you should do. He knows everything that goes on here."

Marigny telephoned Sands as soon as he reached home.

"I wouldn't worry about rumours," the lawyer told him jovially. "People have to talk about something, and this must be the biggest thing that's happened in the Bahamas since Columbus landed."

"What if the police accuse me of murder?"

"Are they likely to?"

"Not so far as I know. But someone must have started these rumours. It could be them."

"Then don't talk to the police on your own. Make sure your lawyer's present."

"But Godfrey's out of the country."

"So he is. Then I suggest you contact him as soon as he comes back. If he won't act for you, then I will."

As soon as Marigny replaced the receiver, Lieutenant Johnnie Douglas, a police officer he had known since his arrival in the colony, telephoned to say that he was coming to see him. Douglas had been born in Britain, where he was an amateur athlete of almost Olympic standard. Then, after he came out to the Bahamas, heat and general inertia had softened him. He was now fat and overweight, soured by the nagging feeling that promotion — like life — was passing him by. He drank to assure himself that this was not so.

"Erskine Lindop wants to see you out at Westbourne," Douglas announced when he arrived.

"Right now? But it's late."

"He's asked me to drive you over there. Just in case."

"In case of what?"

Douglas laughed, but did not meet Marigny's eyes.

Out at Westbourne, the crowds had gone. A Bahamian policeman stood on duty outside the front door. The colonel was in a downstairs room. He introduced Marigny to the two Americans. "I'm sure you won't mind if they ask you a few questions?"

"Of course," said Marigny — and then remembered Sands's advice. Well, he must help these people all he could, and it was easier to agree than to stand on his dignity. After all, what had he to fear?

Captain Barker examined Marigny's arms for any traces of burning, then asked him to take off his shirt. Through a magnifying glass he looked at the hair on Marigny's chest, at his eyebrows, his beard.

"You are aware that the murderer of Sir Harry Oakes — your father-in-law — set fire to the bedroom, Mr. Marigny? How do you account for your singed hair?"

"I never thought of having to account for it," Marigny replied jocularly. "I smoke a number of cigars a day, and at this time of the year, when it's so damp, they frequently go out and then I have to relight them."

"That could account for your moustache and beard," agreed Barker. "But what about your hair? Do you have it singed at the barber's?"

"I have done — say a couple of haircuts back. I also do a bit of cooking, and make toast for breakfast in the oven every day."

"And your forearms?"

"I really don't know. Out at the farm we haven't a machine to pluck the chickens, so my men dip them in a tank of boiling water over an open fire. When there's a rush on, I help them."

"I see. We'd like to come back to your house, if you don't mind."

"Of course."

Again, he recalled Stafford Sands' advice. But the Americans appeared friendly and had accepted his explanations without any hesitation. Once they had inspected his house, he'd be in the clear, and all the rumours would stop. But what could they be looking for in his house? He soon discovered.

"Where's the suit you wore last night?" Barker asked him.

"Here," said Marigny. He lifted down a hanger from his wardrobe.

"But this suit is pressed. If you'd worn it, there would be creases in it."

"Not in Nassau," corrected Marigny. "My clothes are pressed every morning by my butler."

"Oh. I didn't understand that. And your shirt?"

Marigny lifted the lid from a wicker basket that contained handkerchiefs, shirts, underpants, to be washed. He picked out two cream shirts.

"I wore one like that," he said.

"But not that one?"

"I can't say. I have a dozen in that colour. It may already have been washed."

"I see. Well, thank you for your co-operation."

Marigny saw them to the door. Colonel Erskine Lindop was the last to leave. He paused while Barker and Melchen went ahead to the car.

"I hope you won't mind if Douglas stays here with you. And we'd like to see you at Westbourne at nine 'o'clock tomorrow morning."

"I'll be there."

Marigny closed the door. Douglas looked at him.

"You son-of-a-bitch," he said, only half-humorously. "This is my night off. Now I have to spend it here with you."

"I've a few bottles in the house," Marigny assured him. Douglas brightened up.

"Lead me to them," he said.

"I'll say good night," said Marigny after he had set out a bottle of rum, a jug of fresh lime juice, ice cubes, and one glass.

"My orders are that I have to stay with you," Douglas informed him. "The police station is going to telephone me every hour, just to check everything's O.K. Since your phone is in the living room, you'd better doss down on the couch here."

Marigny shrugged. He had co-operated so far; he might as well continue.

Next morning, he was up as usual at half-past six, mixing his stomach powder, warming milk for his Ovaltine, making toast. Both men had spent an uneasy night, being jerked into wakefulness every hour by the telephone. Douglas had poured himself another drink every time this happened. Now his face was puffy, his eyes red. Marigny drove him out to the farm with more chicks from the incubator, and then they went on to Westbourne.

"You weren't on very good terms with Oakes, were you?" remarked Douglas, as they passed the British Colonial.

Marigny shrugged. "My ex-wife wrote some pretty horrible letters to Lady Oakes, you know. That didn't help."

"Women," said Douglas disparagingly. "That guy, Sir Harry, the old bastard, should have been killed anyway. What boils me is that if it was some poor coloured fellow in Grant's Town who'd been killed. I'd just have gone and taken down a few statements, and that's all there'd be to it."

"That's the difference between dying rich and dying poor," said Marigny philosophically.

"There's no difference when you're dead," retorted Douglas. "You know what Stafford Sands says? 'When you're dead, you're dead.' "

Again, Marigny remembered Sands's advice. Why was he ignoring it for so long? Douglas looked out at the white beach and the sea. The waves looked bright, inviting as a young girl's smile.

"You're dead a long time," he said slowly.

"Forever."

They drove on in silence. Then, to make conversation, Marigny remarked, "Someone else was burned to death last year on the island. Can't remember much about the case, but how did they catch whoever did it?"

"Circumstantial evidence. No one actually *saw* him do it. But they got him just the same."

"I know they can convict on circumstantial evidence under French law," replied Marigny, "but I didn't know they did so under English law. Say someone was shot, and they couldn't find the gun. Could a suspect still go down?"

"I believe so."

"Sir Harry had a pistol. Have you found that?"

"Is it missing?" Douglas asked him sharply.

"I have no idea. I was thinking, it could have been used to hit Sir Harry about the head. Or have they found that weapon?"

"I don't think so."

Marigny parked the car. They had a few minutes left before nine o'clock, and the sunshine seemed so pleasant that they walked along the beach, breathing the .salty air. Then sandflies began to pester them, and clouds obscured the sun. Suddenly, the beach lost its attraction, and they turned back towards the house.

In the downstairs study, the two American detectives were waiting with Colonel Lindop and Major Pemberton. In another room, Dulcibelle Henneage waited with Jean Ainsley and Dorothy Clarke. Georges de Visdelou arrived, his nose red from his cold. Douglas and Marigny sat down with the others. They discussed the weather, the state of the war, anything but the subject that really occupied their thoughts. Barker and Melchen called out the visitors one by one and interviewed them in the study. Finally, Marigny was on his own.

"Please come upstairs," Melchen said to him, "I'd like to ask you a few questions on your own."

Why upstairs? thought Marigny. Everyone else had been interviewed downstairs. Was there something specially significant about the questions Melchen wanted to ask him? He followed him up the stairs and into a small room facing the sea.

"Are you willing to help us?" Melchen asked him bluntly.

"Of course. That's why I'm here."

They sat down on wicker chairs, with a glass-topped table between them. On the table stood a carafe of water and two polished glasses. Melchen asked Marigny whether he knew anyone who might have a grudge against Sir Harry. Marigny said that he could think of no one. Melchen then asked him what he knew about Harold Christie. Marigny replied that Christie was probably Oakes's closest friend, and he had certainly been a good friend to him. Melchen nodded, as though this was what he had heard from others. He sat for a moment, apparently thinking about the case, then took a packet of Lucky Strike cigarettes from his pocket and casually threw it across the table. The packet was new, still wrapped in a sealed cellophane cover.

"Have one," he said.

"Thanks."

Marigny lit a cigarette, handed back the packet. Melchen did not pick it up.

"You know that Sir Harry's car was seen outside your house on Victoria Avenue on the day he died?" he asked casually.

"Sir Harry owned several cars," Marigny explained. "That car, which is often parked near my house, *used* to be his, but then he sold it to a neighbour of mine. I haven't seen Sir Harry since the thirtieth of March."

"You had a fight?"

"An argument. He was up and down, you know."

"You know you were seen here on the night of the murder?"

"I defy you or anybody in Nassau to say any such thing."

Melchen nodded again, as though the matter was really of no importance, an absurd rumour that did not concern either of them as two men of the world in a backward, isolated island community.

"Would you mind pouring me a glass of water?" he asked.

"Of course not."

"Have one yourself."

"Thanks. I will."

The cigarette had made Marigny's mouth dry. He preferred cigars, but he had none with him, and did not wish to appear churlish, since the detective was obviously doing his best to be friendly and to put him at ease. As Marigny poured out two glasses of water and handed one to Melchen, the door opened. Barker put his head around the door and looked at Melchen enquiringly.

"Everything all right?' he asked him.

"O.K." replied Melchen. He stood up.

"That's about all," he told Marigny. "Let's join the others."

Downstairs, Colonel Erskine Lindop nodded to him in a friendly way.

"I think that's about everything," he said.

"In that case, gentlemen, I'll leave. I have things to attend to."

"I wonder if you could give Johnnie Douglas a lift back to Nassau. And perhaps you could bring him back here in the afternoon, say around four o'clock?"

As Marigny drove home, he wondered why he had agreed to return. He had answered every question honestly and fully. He had allowed his hands, arms, chest, his beard, and his hair to be examined for evidence of burned hair. Melchen and Barker had visited his home. What could they want with him at four o'clock?

That afternoon, the Duke of Windsor paid a second visit to Westbourne, and was leaving as Marigny arrived. As the Duke climbed into his car he paused, turned and glanced at Marigny. Then the door shut, and he was driven away. To anyone else, the glance meant nothing at all; to Marigny, it seemed to have the significance of the look a witness at an identification parade gives to the man he feels is guilty.

Colonel Erskine Lindop was waiting in the hall. "I wonder if you would just come in here?" he said to Marigny, and opened the door into a living room. The Attorney General and Major Pemberton were already there, with Barker and Melchen. The colonel closed the door. For a moment, the others stared at Marigny in silence. Eric Hallinan was the first to speak.

"Alfred de Marigny," he said quietly, "you are under arrest for the murder of Sir Harry Oakes."

In Government House, high on the hill, another "Immediate" telegram from the Duke was being encoded for the Colonial Secretary in London.

Alfred de Marigny, British subject from Mauritius and son-in-law of Sir Harry Oakes, arrested and charged with his murder ...

After the concurrence of the Commissioner of Police, whose local police force lacks detective with the requisite experience and equipment for investigating the death of a person possessing such widespread international business interests, I was fortunate in securing the services of Capt. E. W. Melchen, head of Homicide Bureau, Miami, and Capt. James Barker, identification expert of the Miami Police Department, who arrived by aeroplane afternoon of 8th July, within twelve hours of Sir Harry's death.

Capt. Melchen, who has been known to me for three years, and his assistant, have rendered most valuable service by their relentless investigations, which have in a large measure resulted in the arrest of the accused.

Every official telegram arriving at the Colonial Office in London had a minute sheet attached to it for comments by anyone concerned with its contents. Several days later, on July 14, an official noted:

The Governor is at some pains to explain why he took the rather unusual step of calling in men from outside, which I must confess I don't very much like. But, in the circumstances, I would not question his judgement.

The following day another official added his comment:

The time to question it was when [the cable] arrived. We can hardly do so now. Put that by.

As Marigny faced his first night in cell number two of the Nassau jail, 160,000 Americans, Britons, Canadians, and Frenchmen of his generation were preparing for a more martial ordeal: the assault on Sicily.

This was the Second World War's first full-scale amphibious attack on Axis-held territory, in Churchill's assessment, "The greatest amphibious operation so far attempted in history."

Sicily, a rocky, triangular mountainous island, with an area of ten thousand miles, and ringed by six hundred miles of coast, lay like a giant stepping-stone between Italy and North Africa. The Axis considered it so important as an obstacle to any Allied invasion of Italy or Southern Europe that they had packed it with 405,000 troops: nine Italian divisions with 315,000 men, and four German divisions with another 90,000. They could also call on 1,850 aircraft based on the island and in Sardinia, southern France, and Italy.

The Italians, with a complex defence system of heavy concrete pill-boxes, barbed-wire entanglements, and hidden artillery positions, were largely to the south and west of the island, while German forces were in position in the east. To attack what was virtually a gigantic fortress, the U.S. Seventh Army committed six divisions, one of them airborne. The British Eighth Army comprised seven divisions, with the Canadian 1st Division and part of the 1st Airborne Division. These two huge Allied armies brought with them fourteen thousand vehicles with eighteen hundred mobile guns and six hundred tanks aboard three thousand ships.

On July 9, while Sir Harry Oakes's body was being flown from Nassau to Miami, the Allied forces, some from North Africa, and others sailing directly from British and United States ports, converged at a rendezvous south of Malta. The armada, made up of ships of almost every size and type, from cruisers to infantry landing craft, then set course for Sicily — and almost at once ran into a fierce and totally unseasonable gale. It was too late to turn back; the only way lay ahead. Flashes of lightning lit up the vast flotilla as vessels struggled on through mountainous seas against a cannonade of thunder. Towards dawn, when the ships were in sight of Sicily, the storm eased, but the swell and surf were still heavy on the western beaches, where the Americans were to land.

At the hour when a jailer was waking Marigny to begin his first full day in prison, Allied troops were already wading through the waves to the beaches.

Deception plans had led the enemy to expect that any attack was most likely to be on the west coast. Instead, the Americans landed in the south and south-west, between Pozzallo, Gela and Licata, and the British and Canadians in the east and south-east, north of Pachino.

The Americans faced what appeared to be the more difficult task. They had to cross a harsh landscape of rocks and mountains to reach their objective, Palermo, on the northern coast. This was Sicily's capital and the island's second most important port. The British and Canadians meanwhile would advance up the east coast, capturing the ports of Syracuse and Catania, aiming for Messina, Sicily's largest port, only two miles from the toe of Italy, across the Strait of Messina.

They met fierce opposition from German defenders. Pilots of American aircraft, towing gliders with airborne troops aboard, cast them off too soon, and the gliders came down in the sea. Soldiers already ashore toiled painfully up barren rocks, along tracks too narrow for any tank to pass, under a constant hail of fire from the Hermann Goering Division. Casualties were heavy, progress was slow, and this was only the beginning. A series of bitter battles lay ahead.

In contrast, the landing of the American forces to the south-west met with unexpectedly muted resistance. Once ashore, they paused unexpectedly. They could advance along either of two main roads that led from the coast, through the interior of the island, to Palermo. Both routes passed near to the small towns of Villalba and Mussomeli, and then the roads linked up through a narrow pass between the mountains at Mount Cammarata.

This was an obvious site for an Italian ambush, which could delay the American advance indefinitely, as indeed similar ambushes here had held back foreign invaders since Roman times.

High in the hills, deep caves, linked by underground passages with several entrances, overlooked this defile. Behind camouflaged rock emplacements around the pass, a brigade of Italian motorised artillery were dug into positions that offered the greatest fire power with the smallest target. This brigade, under the able and energetic command of Colonel Salemi, a regular officer, had anti-aircraft guns, which could be swung down to bear on the roads, and 88mm anti-tank guns arranged around the mouth of the pass. Machine-gun nests in the mountain slopes were not only inaccessible to any direct attack, but virtually invisible, because the gunners had been issued with smokeless cartridges, which gave no tell-tale muzzle flash of flame.

This combination of a narrow, high-sided pass with concentrated and sophisticated fire power could provide a formidable obstacle to any attack. Eventually, no doubt, the United States divisions would force their way through by sheer weight of numbers and overwhelming air superiority, but their casualties in such a rash advance could be extremely heavy; even one tank put out of action could block the narrow pass indefinitely.

So the Italians waited for the Americans — and the Americans appeared to be waiting for something else, for instead of advancing to the north, they consolidated their beachhead, a task that stretched to four days. On the fourth day, a small United States plane flew so low above the houses in Villalba that the black shadow of its wings moved like a travelling cross over the cobbled streets. The white star of the Allies was painted on the underside of each wing as well as on the fuselage, and the pilot deliberately wiggled the plane's wings so that this could be clearly seen and recognised.

From the cockpit trailed a yellow pennant, twelve feet long. On it was stencilled in black a single letter, L.

The aircraft circled twice over the house of the local priest, Monsignor Giovanni Vizzini, then the pilot cut his engine and threw a small bag over the side of his cockpit. While the bag was falling, he opened his throttle, rapidly gained height, and disappeared.

Some watchers thought that the bag must be a bomb of some kind, and screamed in terror; others, more knowledgeable, reassured them. A member of the local carabinieri picked up the bag and opened it. Inside was a large silk handkerchief, the same yellow colour as the pennant, also stamped with the initial L.

Next morning, at exactly the same time, the plane returned and the pilot threw out a second bag in front of the priest's house. Two words were printed on the outside of this bag, Zu Calo — Uncle Calo, the name by which Don Calogero Vizzini, the priest's brother, was known to his intimates. Don Calo was chief of the Sicilian Mafia, and he lived in Villalba. Inside the bag was another folded yellow handkerchief, also marked with a black L.

That evening, a horseman galloped from Villalba towards Mussomeli. Sewn into his jacket was a pencilled letter from Zu Calo addressed to Zu Peppi, the familiar name of Genco Russo, the Mafia leader in Mussomeli. The rider was under strict orders not to let this note fall into Axis hands. If this seemed at all likely, he was to swallow it. Yet the message appeared innocuous and apparently dealt with local farming matters:

Turi, the farm bailiff, will go to the fair at Cerda with the calves on Thursday 20th. I'll leave on the same day with the cows, cart-oxen, and the bull. Get the faggots ready for making the cheese, and provide folds for the sheep. Tell the other bailiffs to get ready. I'll see to the rennet.

In fact, this communication had a deeper meaning. It informed Russo that Signor Turi, a Mafia member of distinction, with considerable New York connections, would travel with an American motorised column as far as Cerda, a small town within a few miles of Palermo.

Don Calo himself would meanwhile be moving north with the main United States force (the cows), the tanks (the cart-oxen), and the Army commander (the bull).

Faggots, generally used to light fires, referred to civil uprisings in favour of the Allies. These would be prepared in advance so that, if required, they could erupt quickly and with apparent spontaneity. The reference to folds for the sheep meant that the advancing American troops were to be given every help. Next morning, at dawn, the rider returned with a reply confirming that the bailiff had prepared the faggots as requested.

Now the American troops began to advance. When they were still about thirty miles away from Villalba, a United States Jeep arrived ahead of them, with a yellow pennant, bearing the black L, flying from its radio antenna.

The roads were badly signposted, and the driver mistook one turning for another and came under fire from an Italian patrol. One American soldier was killed. His body fell out onto the road as the Jeep reversed at speed and raced away. Villagers waited until the Italians also withdrew, and then went out cautiously to examine the dead man. One knelt down beside him and removed a small pouch from his belt. It was addressed to Zu Calo.

That afternoon, three American armoured cars rumbled into Villalba, still in advance of the main force. Their bulk virtually filled the narrow streets, and as they turned, their sides scuffed the walls of houses, removing chunks of masonry. From the radio antenna on the turret of the leading vehicle flew the familiar yellow flag with the black L.

An American officer with the dark face of a Sicilian asked a lounger in a doorway to inform Don Calogero Vizzini of their arrival. The officer spoke in the dialect of the area and used the Mafia leader's full name, a sign of respect, to admit publicly that he readily acknowledged the Don's importance.

Don Calo now came ambling along the road towards the car, keeping out of the sun, as befitted a man of the shadows. He was plump, in shirtsleeves and braces, with a large stomach. He had pouched eyes and wore thick-lensed glasses that made his eyes seem larger than they were. They lacked all expression and warmth and appeared as impersonal as two camera lenses. They also missed as little.

Don Calo carried his jacket over one arm and puffed at a cigar. No heads turned as he pushed his way through the crowd that had gathered to gaze at the armoured vehicles. Etiquette (and prudence) decreed that it was not seemly to stare at such an important man.

As though to emphasise the great gulf in terms of status between a *Capo di Capi* and an ordinary serving army officer, Don Calo did not shake the officer's hand. No word passed between them, but as a sign of recognition and introduction, Don Calo pulled from his pocket one of the yellow silk handkerchiefs that had been delivered to him. At the sight of this, the officer deferentially helped him up into the armoured car. Behind Don Calo was his nephew, Damiano Lumia, one of several men who had recently arrived from the States in an American submarine.

The drivers started their engines, and the vehicles lumbered out of town, back to the main body of U.S. troops.

Shortly before dawn, Colonel Salemi, who had been listening to American radio traffic, much of which was, surprisingly, *en clair,* alerted his brigade that an American attack was imminent. He did not realise that the messages were deliberately sent uncoded to give him the opportunity of reading them more easily. Now, his subordinate commanders reported an extraordinary state of affairs; two-thirds of their men had disappeared, taking their rifles with them.

None of Colonel Salemi's officers could account for this mass desertion. They did not know that members of the Mafia had secretly approached each outpost on the previous evening. They talked their way past sentries and, in the reasonable way of men expounding a simple mathematical theorem, told the Italians what most were ready to believe. They might indeed prevail for days against the advancing American forces, but, in the end, the Allied combination of fire power, air strikes, and sheer force of numbers could have only one result.

Instead of accepting such defeat, with death or wounding very likely and the humiliation of capture certain if they survived, how much wiser it would be to accept from the locals suits of civilian clothes — and, if they so wished, help to return to their families on the Italian mainland.

To Italian soldiers who argued that this was against their oath of allegiance, it was pointed out firmly that other locals might then be forced to act on their own against them in order to save unnecessary suffering. This message was equally unambiguous, and so, by roll-call the following morning, two thirds of Colonel Salemi's brigade had simply disappeared. He immediately sent an urgent request for reinforcements to be rushed to the position.

Colonel Salemi was a doughty fighter, but if he were suddenly removed from command, it was possible that the defenders, even if reinforced, would lose heart, and many more would desert. Equally, if the local Mafia members failed to neutralise his force, they would lose respect with the Americans, which was unthinkable.

To prevent such a catastrophe, the military telephone line was tapped and an Italian deserter brought in to speak to the colonel. He explained that he was ADC to the commander of the Aosta Division, who wished Colonel Salemi to report to him at once. Divisional headquarters was slightly to the north; the only road the colonel could take lay through Mussomeli. As his car approached the town centre, an old man ran out, his hands in the air. "Stop! I beg you to stop!" he cried in anguish.

The driver swerved and stopped the car, believing that he was being warned of danger ahead. In that instant, other men rushed from houses and wrenched open the car doors. Colonel Salemi was bundled out and marched away to the town hall, to be held prisoner for the next twenty-four hours.

Now the American advance began to accelerate. A column of Moroccan troops, under the French General Juin, halted outside the village of Raffi at nine-thirty that morning, apparently for a brief rest. In fact, they waited for so long that local people brought out flagons of wine to share with them. At four o'clock in the afternoon, a Mafia messenger arrived from Mussomeli to explain that the way ahead was clear. The officers ordered the men to fall in, and off they marched.

Thus, while the British and Canadians toiled up the east coast to reach Messina, fighting hard battles and taking five weeks, at the cost of thousands dead and wounded, the Americans in the west fared quite differently in their drive for Palermo.

They had faced what initially seemed to be the far more hazardous task of crossing mountains that had held back conquerors through the centuries, and of encountering nearly four times as many defenders. But, in the event, they advanced so quickly that their journey took exactly one week and was accomplished with relatively few casualties.

The End of Some Matters — and the Beginning of Others

AT TWENTY MINUTES PAST SEVEN on the evening of November 12 — one hour and fifty-five minutes after the Chief Justice summed up — the jury brought in their verdict in the case of Rex *versus* Marie Alfred Fouquereaux de Marigny.

Hundreds of sightseers in the square around the court pressed forward against rows of policemen, who tried to hold them back as the twelve jurymen filed back into the court. A chill November wind blew in from the sea, ruffling Nancy Marigny's hair as she walked, head down to avoid photographers, from the police station to the court. Marigny, teeth set, doing his utmost to appear unconcerned, came in with a police guard. The Court Registrar walked towards the jury benches.

"Gentlemen," he asked the foreman, "are you agreed on a verdict?"

The foreman, James Sands, replied, "Yes. We are."

This was the moment that could mean life or death for Marigny; the moment he had awaited since July, lived through a thousand times, waking and in dreams. He clenched his fists and stared at the clock on the north wall of the court. Before its minute hand could move, he would know whether he was to live or die. Like a man in a nightmare, he heard the Registrar ask the last two questions of his trial.

"How say you ? Is the prisoner guilty or not guilty of the offence of which he is charged?"

"Not guilty."

It was a nine-to-three majority verdict, and Marigny allowed his face muscles to relax in a smile. He glanced towards his wife. She closed her eyes and seemed to sway in her chair. Now, all over the public gallery, people began to cheer. They waved at him, shouting congratulations and good wishes — the same men and women who, at his arrest, four months earlier, would have happily seen him lynched.

Policemen on duty in the court tried frantically to restore order, threatening to clear all spectators if the commotion continued. But it did continue, and reached a crescendo when the Chief Justice discharged the prisoner.

As Marigny walked down the steps from the prisoner's dock, a free man, people he did not know, had never even met, might never see again, fought to shake his hand, to pat him on the back in euphoric delight at the verdict. News of his acquittal had already reached the crowd outside, and they cheered and shouted and stamped their feet as though celebrating a victory. Whose? he wondered. His — or that of the murderer, who had gone free?

The noise inside and outside the court was by now so great that Mr. Sands could barely be heard as he addressed the Chief Justice on behalf of the jury; and, by then, Marigny and his wife were out in the square and could hear nothing but cheers all around them. Photographers' flash bulbs exploded as policemen with truncheons forced a way for them through the crowd. Someone had provided a car, and they drove to Godfrey Higgs's home to spend their first night together in many months.

As their car accelerated along Bay Street, the shouting and cheering fell away behind them. In the relative silence of an almost empty court, the foreman was expressing the jury's regret that Colonel Erskine Lindop had been allowed to leave the colony without being able to give evidence in the case. He added a rider: "We wish to recommend the immediate deportation of Mr. de Marigny and the Marquis de Visdelou Guimbeau."

The Chief Justice was surprised at this.

"This court has no jurisdiction over such a decision," he pointed out. "But no doubt the proper authorities will take cognisance of your recommendation."

Mr. Sands then thanked Sir Oscar for the kindness and consideration that the court had shown to the jury, and the Chief Justice in turn thanked them for reaching a verdict so swiftly, and discharged them from further jury service for the next eight years.

By this time, Marigny was enjoying a celebration drink with Godfrey Higgs, and neither he nor his wife knew of this extraordinary rider. The crowds thinned in the square and gathered outside the house to cheer when Marigny and his wife left to go to the Church of St. Francis Xavier. The priest, Father Bonaventure, was saying Mass elsewhere, but they knelt together in front of the altar and gave thanks for deliverance. Next morning, although Mrs. Marigny was not a Catholic, they both attended Mass in the same church.

That night, Mr. Sands, the jury foreman, personally took his dog for a walk for the first time in twenty-five days. Other jurors, who had been held incommunicado while the case unfolded, were free now to go as they pleased. Some visited the cinema; others held their own private celebrations in bars and houses around the island. Their toast was simple: Freedom.

This was also the toast at a dinner party Marigny gave in his home. He deliberately lit every candle himself, including those with hurricane shades that had caused him to singe his wrists in July. Raymond Schindler and Leonarde Keeler were among the guests, and after dinner, over brandy and coffee, everyone urged Marigny to undergo tests with Professor Keeler's lie detector. The jury had acquitted him; would the machine do the same?

Professor Keeler asked his first question.

"When you took the guests home from your last dinner party on July seventh, did you come straight home yourself?"

"Yes."

"Did you enter Westbourne?"

"No."

"Did you kill Sir Harry Oakes?"

"No."

"Were you in the room when someone else killed Sir Harry Oakes?"

"No."

"Do you know who killed Sir Harry Oakes?"

"No."

"Did you put your hand on the Chinese screen between the time of the murder and the discovery of the body?"

"No."

As Marigny answered, everyone watched the tell-tale needle on its white dial. If Marigny were lying, it would jump from side to side.

The needle did not move.

In Government House, Leslie Heape, as Acting Governor, was drafting an "Immediate" coded telegram to the Colonial Office to give the result of the case. He added:

Am strongly of the opinion that deportation order should be made to ensure that de Marigny leaves and can never be permitted to return ...

American consul who advised me unofficially that if deportation order is made against de Marigny, he will not be permitted to enter the United States in any circumstances, and further that if de Marigny endeavours to leave of his volition before an order has been made, it is

extremely unlikely that he will be permitted to enter the United States
...

Because of attitude of American authorities in regard to undesirable persons generally, Pan American Airways is unlikely to agree to carry de Marigny, and there is no other method of transportation from this Colony.

Could you persuade Air-Officer Commanding R.A.F. Transport Command, London, to permit de Marigny to be conveyed by military aircraft to Accra and thence onwards to Mauritius?

If special arrangements can be made, presume it may be necessary to consult American authorities controlling bases at which R.A.F. Transport Command calls, plus the Governments of the countries over which Transport Command passes.

Shall be grateful for your assistance in this difficult matter as considerable feeling has been aroused over this case.

He felt that this cable could benefit by being amplified and therefore sent an explanatory letter to the Colonial Office.

"The general opinion," he declared unequivocally is:

(1) Marigny is guilty of the murder but the Chief Justice could only sum up in his favour on the evidence produced in court.

(2) Melchen and Barker, the two American detectives, ruined the case for the prosecution.

(3) The local police stood back when the Americans came in and no one knew what the other was doing. A typical example of too many cooks.

The police will be savagely attacked when the House meets. My own view is that they only did badly because they didn't know what the Americans were doing, and also that a murder of this complexity would be beyond the capacity of any small police establishment such as we have here ...

Nothing matters if we can get Marigny and de Guimbeau out of the Colony and I sincerely trust that by the time you get this the R.A.F. Transport Command have taken both these beauties back to Mauritius.

Officials who studied this letter were able to compare its second paragraph with the eulogistic telegram that the Duke had sent on July 10, referring to the "most valuable service" and "relentless investigations" of the two American detectives.

On the morning after his acquittal, Marigny walked through Nassau, enjoying the November sunshine. Again, men and women came up to shake his hand or pat him on the back. Overnight, the outsider had become a local celebrity. He reached the harbour and strolled along the quay near Prince George Wharf.

Roland T. Symonette, the Bahamian who had bought JMarigny's three houses and 101 acres of land at Governor's Harbour during the trial, was busy near his yacht, with a coil of rope. Marigny saw with surprise that this was of a type and quality not available since before the war.

"Where did you get that from?" he asked him.

Symonette laughed.

"You take it," he said. "In a way, it's really yours, Freddie. At least, it was meant for you."

"How do you work that out?"

"It was ordered to hang you by."

Jack walked quietly into the big room overlooking the sea, paused for a moment to make sure his wife was still talking to the cook in the kitchen, then crossed to the cupboard. He opened the door carefully, lifted out the soda-water bottle, which the previous evening he had marked with a single pencilled dot on the label. He unscrewed the cap, sniffed, examined how far the level had dropped. As he replaced the bottle, the telephone rang; someone was calling him, person-to-person, from Miami. He recognised the codeword and replied with his own identifying response.

The caller in Miami said, "A lot of rumours up here about a launch calling on the night things happened."

"I've heard them, too. I don't think they're very important," said Jack reassuringly.

"I'm not asking you what *you* think, buster. I'm telling you what others think. Find out who's telling those stories. Deal with them any way you think best. Finally."

"It's a little difficult right now," Jack replied cautiously. "Lots of reporters still on the island, all looking for a new angle, now that the suspect's been cleared. They might just get wind of something. I say we should let this one die a natural death."

"Who cares what you say, buster? What I say is that if you want to die a natural death, do as I say. Now."

Jack replaced the receiver slowly. Why the hell were they worrying over ridiculous rumours about a launch? The trial was over, finished, dead. Sure, there were lots of rumours around. That Sir Harry had been killed by voodoo. He had cuckolded a native, which could explain the deliberate humiliation of his corpse with fire and feathers. An unknown intruder had found him on his knees counting gold bars he kept under the bed and struck him down. The hell with all that. The more crazy the theories, the less chance that anyone would guess the truth. On the other hand, he had been given an order, not a request. He was halfway across the front hall when Carole called him from the kitchen.

"Going somewhere interesting?" she asked him, almost accusingly.

"Not really."

"Then take me. It's boring, being stuck here in the house all day. Nassau is so crowded. All these tourists and rubbernecks here for the trial. I don't like to go into town any more."

"I'm only going beyond Adelaide."

This was a village in the centre of the island, founded in the early nineteenth century to provide homes for Negroes freed from slave ships captured at sea.

"I'll come with you. Anything to get out for even half an hour, see some new faces."

It was eleven o'clock in the morning, but Jack noticed that Carole's voice was slurred.

"All right," he said grudgingly. "But don't complain if you don't like it."

"Do I ever complain?" she asked him belligerently.

He did not answer. They drove south in silence.

"What are you coming here for?" she asked him once.

"To see a man. A business matter."

"Business. That's all you care for. Business."

Trees and bushes had been tamed near the north coast, where the rich had their homes; here, they grew wild. Pines, casuarinas, palms with coconuts or red berries stood so close together that trunk rasped against trunk. Heat made the road ahead shimmer like molten metal. On the other side of Adelaide, a few huts, crudely painted in vivid blues and purples and bright greens, crouched beneath sheltering palms. Some were without windows, and their primitive front doors, made from packing-case panels or enamelled metal advertisements, were tightly closed.

Jack stopped the car, climbed out.

"Will you be long?" Carole asked.

"No longer than I have to be. If it's too hot in the car for you, take a walk around."

"Not here," she said and shuddered. "It's spooky."

Jack knocked at the door of a corrugated iron shack. An old man opened the red front door on its crude leather hinges. A gust of hot, fetid air from the unventilated interior made Jack turn away. The old man's shirt was open to his waist, and skin hung on his chest in loose wrinkles and folds, as though intended originally for someone much larger. There was grey stubble on his chin, and flecks of yellow matter at the corners of eyes that stared blankly past Jack as though at some far-distant scene. He puffed a cigarette made from a dried leaf. Jack sniffed ganja. The old man's eyes narrowed as he tried to focus them.

"I wasn't expecting you," he said at last, recognising his caller.

"I'm not staying," said Jack. "I only want some information."

He took a five-pound note from his pocket, folded it, and held it between his thumb and forefinger. The old man heard the welcome crackle of currency and forced himself to be more alert.

"What about?" he asked.

"People say a launch was seen off Lyford Cay or in Nassau Harbour on the night the rich man died."

"Maybe they say it was one place — because it really was at the other," said the old man. "I pay no attention to talk like that. Someone else could get killed if they stuck their nose in."

"Meaning you?"

"You get it, boss. Meaning me."

"But who keeps spreading this story? And why?"

"I know nothing, boss."

"Tell me. You know you'll be all right. No one will hurt you. I'll see to that."

The old man looked cautiously at the other windowless houses. Why had this American come here? Jack had never visited him before. Whenever he wanted information, they would meet casually on a wharf or in a side alley. He might pretend to be a beggar and Jack would give him a coin, and they would exchange a few words. He didn't like Jack calling on him openly, in daylight. Safest thing was to get him out of the way as quickly as possible.

"There was a boy in the rich man's house," he said sullenly.

"What's his name?"

"I don't know. He's a big fellow. He's about."

"How will I recognise him?"

The old man shrugged. Then, glancing beyond Jack towards the car, he saw Carole. "Ask the lady. *She* knows him."

"Yes? And where is he now?"

"He's got a boat near South Beach. He likes working on it. Makes long trips when he has the gas."

"How long?"

"Abaco. Great Exuma. Grand Bahama."

"Where on South Beach?"

"You'll see a track. He keeps his boat up under the trees."

"Why does he keep it there, of all places?"

The old man shrugged; he had said enough. He held out his hand. Jack shook it. The folded five-pound note passed expertly from one palm to the other. The old man closed the door. Jack walked back to the car.

"We going home now?" asked Carole hopefully.

"No. On to South Beach."

"I don't like it there," Carole complained.

The car felt like an oven, and the vodka was making her drowsy.

"We're going to see an old friend of yours."

"I don't know anyone who lives on South Beach."

Jack did not answer, and again they drove in silence. Now and then she looked at her husband resentfully. There were few houses on this side of the island; it was unfashionable, too far from Nassau, and lonely. Jack cruised slowly until he saw the track the old man had mentioned, between high trees. He pulled in, reversed his car, parked it in their shade.

"Come with me," he ordered Carole. She could identify this man.

He began to walk between trees that grew like tall green walls on either side. Their feet made no sound on dried grass and a soft carpet of last year's pine needles. Carole's shoes had high heels and were unsuitable for a long walk. She opened her mouth to complain again, but something in her husband's face made her think better of it. She struggled on a few paces behind him. Soon, they saw sea glitter through a lattice of branches and heard the noise of someone tapping metal on metal. A few more quiet steps and they were on the beach, white as bleached bone, soft as flour.

A small wooden boat was drawn up, prow facing the sea. A black man was working on the outboard engine, his back to them. The motor had been lowered, and he had scraped a hollow in the sand beneath the propeller and rudder fin so that he could make adjustments. He heard the soft shuffle of feet in sand, and turned and stood up with the grace and speed of a wild animal.

He was very tall, and broad in proportion. His blue sweat shirt might have been painted on his bulging biceps. Jack saw him glance from his face to Carole's, the sudden wary look of surprise and recognition in his eyes. The old man in the hut had been right. Carole *did* know this fellow. That, in his mind, meant only one thing: she had been having it off with the bastard.

"This is a private beach," said the man insolently, not the tone of voice in which a black man usually addressed a white man in Nassau. "You want something?"

"Yes," said Jack. "I believe you can tell me something about a boat seen in Nassau or Lyford Cay on the night the rich man died."

The Bahamian smiled. "I reckon you could tell me more, boss. Considering you were in that boat."

"I want to know what *you* can tell me."

"I can't add nothing to your story, boss. What I hear is only second-hand. *You* can tell at first-hand."

He smiled at Carole over Jack's head. Jack looked at his wife with cold and hostile eyes. Her face was pale, and her forehead shone with the sweat of fear and discovery.

"You know this man, don't you?" Jack asked her in a dangerously calm voice.

She said nothing.

"Answer me."

"Don't talk like that to her, boss."

"You tell me how to talk to my own wife?" said Jack.

"I can tell you lots of things about your own wife you don't even begin to know. Is that all you wanted to see me about? If so, forget it. I got work >to do."

He turned his back on them with calculated rudeness.

"Just why do you keep a boat here?" asked Jack. "No fishing down here."

"It's quieter down here."

The man went on tapping a spanner with his hammer; a nut had jammed and he needed to free it.

"There are other rumours, too," said Jack, watching him. "Like Sir Harry Oakes kept gold in his house."

"That will never be found," replied the man. "If it even existed."

"Why so sure?"

The Bahamian laughed.

Something in his confidence, so different from the usual subservience with which men of his type would talk to someone as rich as Jack, made Jack say: "You know where that gold is, don't you? You probably stole it."

The man turned now, not easily, languidly, but like a lion at bay.

"You got a big mouth," he said. "I don't like whiteys with big mouths."

He leaped at Jack, spanner in his hand. Carole had no idea then — or ever — whether he meant to hit her husband, to kill him, or simply jumped to frighten him.

Jack fired through his jacket pocket. At the whipcrack of the shot, birds flew out, cawing, towards the sea. They whirled over the bright water, then glided back cautiously, parentheses in the sky, ready for instant retreat if any further danger threatened.

The black man lay where he had fallen. The top of his head was missing. Bone and brain lay splattered over the beach like pieces of bloodied sponge. Ants were already crawling towards the body; flies buzzed greedily around his terrible wound. Jack threw Sir Harry Oakes's pistol into the bottom of the boat.

"You've killed him! You bastard!" cried Carole.

"That's one lover you won't have again, you whore."

"You don't know what you're talking about! He *did* know where the gold is. *He took it"*

Jack looked at her in astonishment. "What do you mean?" he asked hoarsely.

"What I say. He was the only one who knew where the gold was. Can't you see? I was stringing him along. Now no one will ever know."

Carole knelt down beside the dead man and began to cry. Her tears dropped on his dead black face. Suddenly, she stood up, and, hair streaming behind her, she began to run towards the track. Jack caught up with her in three paces and pulled her round by her wrist. She swung her handbag at his head. He gripped her other wrist roughly.

"Where do you think you're going?" he asked her.

"The police. I've had enough of you. I could live with a gangster. But not a murderer."

"And what exactly are you going to tell them, Carole?"

"That you killed a man. Shot him dead. I saw you."

"All right," he said, releasing her. "You go and tell them that. Here are the keys."

He threw the car keys at her. She caught them. They still felt warm from his pocket. She paused, wondering why he was doing this. There must be a reason. Jack never did anything without one.

"Go on," he said gently.

"They'll arrest you."

"They won't."

"You mean, you've fixed them?"

"No."

"But you're a murderer."

"And you're the only witness."

"That's enough, isn't it?"

"No. Not here, it isn't."

"What do you mean?"

"Hold out your left hand."

Her wedding ring glowed dull gold in the sun.

"You're married to me. That's what I mean. You're my wife. This is a British colony, not the United States. Under British law a wife can't testify against her husband."

"But he's *dead.*"

"And we're alive. Now come here and give me a hand. We're going to put the body into his boat and start the engine on half a tank of juice. Then I'll kick a hole in the side. If they find the pistol, that'll only add to the mystery.

"By the time the fish have finished with him, no one will ever know what happened. Except you and me together. And that will be our secret, won't it, darling?"

During Marigny's time in jail, he had been visited by Anglican and Catholic priests. One said to him, "My boy, when you are acquitted of this murder charge — that is when your real trial will begin."

For two days after his acquittal Marigny enjoyed the illusion of freedom — and then was suddenly made to realise how true this forecast was. The Governor in Council, with Leslie Heape, the Colonial Secretary, in the chair because of the Duke of Windsor's continued absence from Nassau, decreed that Marigny and Georges de Visdelou should be "invited" to leave the Bahamas. If the two men did not accept this invitation, then they would be deported.

Godfrey Higgs, who was present, argued strongly against this proposal. His client had been acquitted after a fair trial. Why should he now be victimised in this way? But his was a minority view, and he was over-ruled. The others were well aware of the Duke's antipathy towards Marigny, and this was a matter on which they could let him have his way.

Heape cabled the news to the Colonial Office, with a copy to the British Ambassador in Washington, "For the information of His Royal Highness, the Duke of Windsor."

Deportation Order made by Governor in Council against De Marigny and his friend Guimbeau, who also comes from Mauritius.

Question of De Marigny had been prepared for consideration of the Executive Council before the murder, as De Marigny undoubtedly a most undesirable person. His friend is equally undesirable. If you are successful in making arrangements to transport De Marigny, grateful if Guimbeau can be sent with him.

The United States Consul, as Heape had predicted, would not grant Marigny a visa to enter the United States; *ergo,* Pan American Airways would not accept him as a passenger. RAF Transport Command had infinitely more important duties than to ferry across the world, from one flying base to another, a man who had been acquitted in a court case and his companion. So how could Marigny travel — and where? Civilian passages by sea and air were at a premium as the war entered its fifth year, so could the deportation order be executed? A farcical Flying Dutchman situation seemed possible. Mr. Heape acquainted the Duke in New York with this unhappy situation. The Duke reacted strongly and at once with a cable to the Colonial Office:

I am convinced that failure to deport them would constitute a deplorable evidence of the impotence of the local government and have a very serious effect on the reputation of the Colony throughout the world.

This appeal produced no immediate response. What might seem important to the Duke of Windsor on prolonged leave in New York was not necessarily considered so important in London. And was it the colony's reputation he was so concerned about — or his own?

Earlier that year, before the trial, the Duke had written a letter to the Colonial Secretary, about Sir Harry's murder, in which he claimed that "the whole circumstances of the case are sordid beyond description." He did not go into these circumstances, but added that he intended to leave Nassau before the trial started.

To this proposal, the Colonial Secretary replied, "I am sure that in view of the sordid circumstances ... you are wise in arranging to be away from the Colony at the time when the accused, if committed for trial, will appear before the Supreme Court."

The Duke had also previously described Marigny to the Colonial Secretary as

"a despicable character [who] has the worst possible record, morally and financially, since his adolescence, has insidiously bought his way with his ex- wife's money into the leadership of a quite influential, fast, and depraved set of the younger generation, born of bootlegging days, and for whom they have an admiration bordering on hero worship ..."

Why did the Duke of Windsor dislike so intensely a man he barely knew? Surely Marigny's description of him as "not my favourite ex-King" was insufficient reason for such animosity? Some wondered whether at least part of the Duke's abhorrence might be due to an almost chemical reaction; the basic dislike of a man of insignificant physique, accustomed to nearly half a century of public adulation now all but removed, towards someone younger, taller, and infinitely more confident and, in the eyes of many, more physically attractive.

The Duke and Duchess returned to Nassau, expecting that Marigny would already be on his way. To their surprise, he was still in town.

The Duke was infuriated at London's continued lack of response, and cabled again, playing his ultimate card.

Although I would be loath to worry the PM at this time, I feel so strongly on this question that I would not hesitate, as a last resort, to approach him direct, because I am convinced that unless the Bahamas Government is armed with the power to move both deportees, the British colonial administration will be subject to derision in the United States, and the relations of the Government with the local people strained to breaking point.

To add emphasis, he then cabled:

Reasons for deportation as follows:

(a) De Marigny. His matrimonial history shows him to be an unscrupulous adventurer. Twice divorced and three times married since 1937. Despoiled second wife of £25,000 and then married daughter of millionaire. Has evil reputation for immoral conduct with young girls. Is gambler and spendthrift. Suspected drug addict. Suspected of being concerned in the unnatural death of his godfather Ernest Bronard. Evaded Finance Control Regulations by obtaining divorce from second wife. Convicted of offences of being in unlawful possession of stolen gasolene and of gasolene rationing orders. Engaged in two business enterprises in violation of Immigrants Act. Jury upon acquitting De Marigny on charge of murdering his millionaire father-in-law unanimously recommended immediate deportation.

(b) Guimbeau. Has evil reputation for immoral conduct with young girls. Convicted of offences of being in unlawful possession of stolen gasolene and gasolene rationing orders. Believed to be financially dependent on De Marigny.

Marigny knew nothing of these extraordinary allegations and had no idea of the depth of the Duke's dislike for him. But hardly had he learned that he was to be deported than he was arrested for a second time, and was back in jail, awaiting trial in the Magistrates' Court, with Georges de Visdelou, on charges that four drums of gasolene bearing RAF marks, had been illegally in their possession. These were the drums about which Marigny had sought John Anderson's advice on the day he heard of his father-in-law's murder. Both men were found guilty and fined £100 each. The magistrate added that if they were not due to be deported, he would have sent them both to prison.

Marigny believed that since he was a British subject, he could not be deported. Godfrey Higgs, while agreeing with the first point, corrected him on the second. Because of the law passed in Prohibition days, when some residents feared that American gangsters might remain in Nassau, the Executive Council could deport anyone without charge, trial, or any right of appeal. So Marigny had won — and he had lost.

He sold his chicken farm to his farm foreman, his car to Ernest Callender. John Anderson, who owed him $6,000 in gambling debts, realised how short of money Marigny must be, and offered him $800 in cash in total settlement. Marigny accepted his offer.

It was said that Marigny and his wife would be married in a Roman Catholic ceremony at St. Francis Xavier, and a date and time for the service were set, but at the last moment the wedding was cancelled, without any reason being given.

Finally, an Under-Secretary of State in Cuba, whom Marigny had met yachting, invited Mr. and Mrs. Marigny to Havana. They accepted gratefully — and then another snag arose. The only way to reach Havana from Nassau by scheduled airline or aboard a passenger ship was by way of the United States, and although Marigny had lived and worked in New York, and visited the States on twenty-three occasions, the authorities would not issue him a transit visa.

After the Nassau Yacht Club gave a dinner in his honour, and presented him with the trophies he had won during the racing season, Marigny hired a small fishing boat with a crew and, with his wife, sailed direct for Cuba on December 6, 1943.

A week later, the Cuban Under-Secretary denied that he had ever really *invited* Marigny to Cuba; it was all a misunderstanding, he said. Even so, Mr. and Mrs. Marigny would be allowed to stay in the country for several months. Ernest Hemingway, whom Marigny had met when he travelled to New York aboard *Normandie* before the war, was at that time living in San Francisco de Paula, fifteen miles out of Havana. He heard of their plight and offered them hospitality.

Georges de Visdelou also left Nassau; Haiti was his immediate destination. He invited his friend Betty Roberts to accompany him. She did not accept his invitation, nor did he stay long in Port-au-Prince.

On January 21, 1944, the Governor of Jamaica cabled to the Colonial Office:

Visdelou Guimbeau, British subject born in Mauritius, witness for defence in trial for murder of De Marigny in Nassau in November, who is at present in Jamaica, has been granted an exit permit for the U.K. I am informed by the Governor of the Bahamas that person named was deported under Section 26 of Chapter 258 of Bahamas Laws on the grounds that he had an evil reputation for immoral conduct with young girls and was convicted of the offence of being in unlawful possession of stolen gasolene rationing orders. Governor of the Bahamas adds person named is believed to be financially dependent on de Marigny.

Visdelou went to Britain and joined the army. After his discharge, he was reported to be living in London and then in Paris.

For Nancy de Marigny, the climate of Cuba proved even more humid and trying than Nassau, and she moved to Vermont, where she entered a hospital for an operation. Alfred de Marigny was still refused a visa to enter the United States, but he was determined to see his wife. With the help of the British Consul in Havana, he signed on as third officer aboard a merchant ship sailing for Halifax, in the hope that they could meet in Canada. Canadian immigration officials initially refused to allow him to land, but then the ship unexpectedly went into dry dock for repairs, and he was given permission to stay in Canada for thirty days. He travelled to Montreal to meet his wife. Here, he learned that his journey had been in vain; their marriage was at an end.

Marigny, homeless and without funds, applied to join the Canadian army and enlisted as a private soldier. He was later discharged and eventually returned to Cuba. Several years later, he was given permission to enter the United States, where he still lives.

From time to time in the years since then, whenever the murder of Sir Harry Oakes was mentioned in a newspaper, he was sought out and interviewed. After one such experience, in 1950, he wrote bitterly to Cholly Knickerbocker, whose column was syndicated across the United States. Knickerbocker printed the letter.

A few days ago [Marigny wrote] a man was arrested after having made a statement in a bar that he knew the name of the murderer of Sir Harry Oakes. I was interviewed by the press about the incident. Unfortunately, as usual, comments were passed on my accent, my clothes, and my being broke. But nothing about my statement was printed.

I stated that neither the Government of the Bahamas nor the Oakes family have the slightest desire to have the party involved in the murder of Sir Harry Oakes made public.

Had they so desired, it would have been an easy matter at the time. Mr. Raymond Schindler, to whom I owe my life, endeavored to clear me by showing to the Nassau Police who was the party. An aide-de-camp of His Royal Highness, Edward, Duke of Windsor, then Governor of the Bahamas, informed Schindler in the name of the Government that his action was an insult to the crown ...

Raymond Schindler returned to the United States and on June 26, 1944, wrote to the Duke of Windsor, offering his services free, with those of his colleague, Professor Keeler, if the Duke, as Governor, would allow them facilities to reopen the case. The Duke's secretary acknowledged the letter, but no further action was taken.

Schindler, from time to time, would imply in articles, and in interviews on radio and TV, that he would solve the mystery of who killed Sir Harry Oakes. It remained his belief that evidence had been suppressed and that the Governor and officials were shielding someone he described as a prominent local person.

On May 19,1959, the House of Assembly in Nassau passed a resolution asking the Governor to reopen the case and to call in Scotland Yard to carry out a full and independent investigation. Mr. Schindler was also asked to submit any new evidence that he might have, but he suffered a heart attack and died six weeks later in New York without doing so.

On August 31 of that year, the Governor gave the House of Assembly a formal reply to their request.

Since no conviction has ever been made, the case remains open and will be pursued in case fresh information becomes available which would justify so doing...

The case was referred in 1947 to the Criminal Investigation Department, New Scodand Yard, where the evidence in the case was subjected to a detailed analysis. The Department spared no pains in their examination and came to the conclusion that there were no grounds for a reinvestigation at that time.

Recent correspondence bearing on the case has also been referred to New Scotland Yard but nothing has come to light which would in their opinion justify any variation of the conclusion reached in 1947.

Epilogue

The Subsequent Years
WHEN CAPTAIN JAMES BARKER returned to Miami after the case, the International Association of Fingerprinting, in Detroit, asked him to submit a report on the fingerprint work he had undertaken in Nassau. His performance had done nothing to increase public confidence in this part of police procedure.

Barker was then sent on indefinite sick leave. He became heavily addicted to drugs, and left home. After a time he returned to his wife and son, giving them his assurance that he was cured.

On Christmas Day, 1952, his son, also a policeman, returned home to find his father beating his mother. James Barker's son knocked him unconscious.

Early on the following morning, Barker called out to his son, and when the young man came into his bedroom, Barker pointed his .38 police revolver at him. In a struggle to seize this, a single round was fired. Captain Barker died instantly. The verdict was "justifiable homicide." After his death, it was revealed that Captain Barker had been in the pay of the Outfit for a number of years.

For the rest of the war, Axel Wenner-Gren, in Mexico, wrote at regular intervals to President Roosevelt, asking him to remove his name from the United States blacklist. Despite these appeals, which carried Wenner-Gren's word "as a gentleman", and strenuous efforts by powerful friends in the Senate and House of Representatives, his request was not granted. Wenner-Gren accepted the situation and bought property and founded factories in Mexico. After the war, he invested heavily in British Columbia and Andros, in the Bahamas.

As Wenner-Gren grew older, his interests turned more to charity and good deeds; perhaps these had always been close to his heart. He subsidised the Wenner-Gren Fund in Sweden, to help scientific research and to develop cultural links and understanding among Scandinavian countries. He founded the Wenner-Gren Cardio-Vascular Research Laboratory, and the Wenner-Gren Centre for Integration of Scientific Research. In New York, he was responsible for the Wenner-Gren Foundation for Anthropological Research.

He had no children; all these generous benefactions bore his name. When he died of cancer, in 1961, aged 80 in Stockholm, it was said he had given as much as $50,000,000 to such institutions out of a fortune estimated at $1,000,000,000.

Etienne Dupuch, who first reported the news of Sir Harry Oakes's murder, is now 83, and still writes from three to six columns every day for *The Tribune*. He started working for this newspaper, which was founded by his father, when he was five years old, selling copies at street corners. He was its editor-publisher for 53 years; a world record for any editor.

For many years, Dupuch was a member of the House of Assembly and the Legislative Council, now the Senate, and for his services to the community he was knighted in 1965.

As publisher, editor and contributor, he has seen *The Tribune's* influence and stature grow with his own. Under its masthead, "Being bound to swear to the dogmas of no master," he has tirelessly campaigned against corruption, nepotism, blindness in high places and all barriers of class and colour. He still does.

Mrs. Eileen Dupuch Carron, his daughter, has been publisher-editor for the past ten years, and continues her family's great tradition.

Jack did not repay the $50,000 that Frank Marshall had entrusted to him, nor the $20,000 profit it had earned. He had a good excuse, for he had no address for Marshall. Neither, it seemed, had others who wished to find him.

Shortly after Marshall returned to Miami and reported what had happened in Nassau, he flew on to New York, where others wished to question him more closely about the night of Sir Harry Oakes's death. There were many questions demanding urgent answers, but Marshall did not keep his appointment. With his wife and son, he left his apartment and when several callers arrived shortly afterwards, they learned that the family had not given a forwarding address.

Marshall, who was unfit for military service, moved to Crescent City, Oregon, under another name and worked in various hotels and motels. After the war, his wife left him, and Marshall took casual jobs in bars in southern Spain and Portugal, always moving on at the end of each season.

Jack and Carole lived on at Cable Beach, but Carole's drinking grew less secret and more embarrassing. Jack did nothing to stop her; in fact, at parties he always seemed quick to refill her glass. She died in hospital of cirrhosis of the liver.

Jack moved to Geneva and set up as a financial consultant. It is said that he helped to provide financial backing for casino, hotel and residential developments in various parts of the world, including the Bahamas.

Seven years after the death of Sir Harry Oakes, several Bahamians on the island of Great Exuma, about 100 miles south east of Nassau, began to live in a more expensive style than their small seasonal earnings would appear to support. United States sailors at the naval base on this island also began to boast that they could buy gold coins at much below their true value. These coins were dated between 1853 and 1907, so they could not have belonged to pirates.

Police found that locals had discovered a box of gold bars and coins hidden inside a cave on a remote part of the island. No satisfactory explanation has been given as to how this might have come to be there — or whose it was.

Nancy de Marigny returned to Nassau after her marriage failed, and it was reported that she was to marry a Dutch airman, but he was killed in an accident. She married Baron Ernst-Lyssandt von Hoyningen-Huene, a member of a distinguished German family. This marriage also ended in divorce. She subsequently married for a third time.

Her brother, Sydney, who inherited the baronetcy, died in a motor accident.

William Pitt, a second brother, also died young.

Her sister, Shirley, was seriously injured in another motor accident, and was for months in a Florida hospital.

In June, 1982, Baroness von Hoyningen-Huene was involved in litigation with her surviving brother, Harry P. Oakes, over two paintings by Turner from the art collection of their late father and mother. The value of these pictures, "Going to the Ball" and "Returning from the Ball" was estimated at £1,650,000.

Of Sir Harry's murder, the Duchess of Windsor wrote in her memoirs, "The sense of shock and terror sent through the community by this crime, and the mystery of its perpetrator, were never quite dispelled during the remaining time we were there".

It was usual for a Governor of the Bahamas to serve for five years, so the Duke could have stayed until August, 1945. But, five months earlier, he gave notice of his resignation.

The Duke had previously petitioned Mr. Churchill, and Lord Beaverbrook, who came to Nassau, about the possibility of a more important appointment, but was offered only what he considered to be another island exile, as Governor of Bermuda. He declined it.

The Duke apparently felt that to serve his full term in the Bahamas, and then to leave without any new and more significant appointment being announced, might be more embarrassing than to resign earlier. He therefore chose this second course, and on April 30, the day Hitler committed suicide in Berlin, he formally ended his period as Governor. He and the Duchess left for the United States, and several months later, when sea passages became available, they sailed for France.

The House of Assembly in Nassau had given him a special Address of Appreciation, and the Colonial Secretary in London was warm in praise of the Duke's administration. There was, however, no offer of any higher official appointment, and the Duchess did not receive any official recognition whatever for her years of work on behalf of many good causes in the colony.

After the war, the Duke spent much time golfing, gardening, and entertaining. He and the Duchess travelled regularly to New York, down to Palm Beach, on to Paris and the Riviera. Their peregrinations were described in much detail by gossip columnists, and they were frequently photographed at fancy dress parties, masked balls, and the like, always on the move. It appeared that in motion lay the illusion of progress, for never again did the Duke figure in serious world affairs.

General George Patton, who commanded the American forces in Sicily, later described the extraordinarily swift advance through difficult terrain as "the fastest blitzkrieg in history." The Mafia's influence advanced with equal speed.

In the 1920's and 1930's, Mussolini's prefect had nearly stamped out the Mafia's authority in Sicily. In 1943, with what appeared to be tacit approval from the United States government, its influence was not only restored but increased.

Once the German and Italian armies had been defeated on the island, an American Army officer, Colonel Charles Poletti, became Military Governor of Sicily and, later, of Rome. Poletti, who had been Lieutenant Governor of New York under Thomas Dewey's predecessor, had parachuted in before the invasion and had been concealed by a Sicilian family. In Luciano's careful description, he was "one of our good friends."

Even before the Allied forces arrived, Colonel Poletti had arranged for about 85 per cent of the towns and villages to form councils or committees to organise each community under the coming occupation. The representatives were, overwhelmingly, Mafia nominees. The British were astonished at the speed at which these local assemblies had been formed, but of course they had neither experience of the Mafia nor knowledge of the crucial part the Mafia played in island matters. Lord Poole, the liaison officer, was surprised when, in his description, men "with black moustaches and American military uniforms, who hardly spoke any English," attended so many of their meetings with American staff officers.

Under the authority and direction of such councils, food and other supplies unloaded at the docks for troops and civilians were immediately removed, often in stolen army trucks, to be sold on the black market.

As a mark of gratitude, the American authorities presented Don Calo Vizzini, with two Fiat 621 trucks and a Palese tractor found in an Italian stores compound. The trucks immediately joined the fleet of other stolen or borrowed trucks transporting supplies of black market food and drink. The tractor was broken up for spares to be sold at inflated prices.

Don Calo was commissioned as an honorary colonel in the United States Army for his part in the successful invasion of Sicily, and became mayor of Villalba. Genco Russo was appointed Mayor of Mussomeli. Convoys of trucks packed with flour, olive oil, and cereals would unload in a mill he owned there. When Italian policemen discovered a railway wagon in Villalba full of stolen salt, beans, and lentils, they were posted elsewhere before they could proceed with any investigation.

An American security sergeant, Orange C. Dickey, investigating similar black market deals in Italy, discovered that Vito Genovese was behind many of these activities. Genovese had become Colonel Poletti's associate and had presented the colonel with a white Packard to mark his appreciation at this appointment.

Genovese offered Dickey a bribe of $250,000 to call off his investigations. Dickey refused, but was surprised when he could not persuade any senior officer to support his request to arrest Genovese. Colonel Poletti, by then in Rome as chief of the United States sector of the Allied Military Government of Occupied Territories, would not even discuss the subject. Everyone else spoke most highly of Genovese, who had always worked hard, refused to accept any payment, and was totally loyal.

Dickey was not easily dissuaded from what he believed was his course of duty, and sent a signal to friends in the F.B.I, in the United States to ask whether they knew of any other crime that could call for the return of Vito Genovese. They did — an old murder charge that had faced him ten years earlier, for they now had a single witness, one Peter La Tampa, prepared to testify against him.

Genovese was shipped back to New York to face a charge of murder. He did not seem in any way alarmed at this prospect. So important to the Prosecution was their key witness La Tampa that, at his request, he was housed in a police cell for his own safety.

Peter La Tampa was taking medicine for gallstones, and on the eve of the trial, he swallowed his pills as usual. Someone, however, had substituted poison pills of exactly the same size and colour. An autopsy showed that he had swallowed enough strychnine to kill eight horses. So the state lost its only witness against Genovese, who was released.

The Sicily invasion was an opportunity that had never come before, and would never be repeated in the same way. Soon, Sicily was an important centre of the world's drug traffic, a distinction later to be shared with the Bahamas. Oranges exported from Sicily would be injected with heroin, and even slabs of marble, exported to the United States as headstones, were found to be ingeniously hollowed out to carry the same valuable cargo.

Drug-smuggling had already begun in both islands before the war, of course, and in 1945, Basil McKinney, who had been disqualified in a Nassau Yacht Club race on the afternoon before Sir Harry Oakes's death, suffered an infinitely more unfortunate experience. He was charged in New York, along with several other Bahamian residents and a number of Americans, with conspiring to violate the United States Narcotics Act by shipping morphine and opium from the Bahamas to the United States.

It was alleged that, from March, 1940, until wartime conditions made them postpone further trips, the Bahamians had used their own yachts to carry the drugs. The Americans had Italian or Sicilian backgrounds: Ralph Carbone; Steve Armone; Charles Albero, alias "Charlie Bullets"; Charles Salerno, alias "Charlie Four Cents"; Nicholas Felarno, alias "the Gigolo"; Joseph Valucci; Joseph Tocco, alias "the Eye"; Charles and Joseph Tomko; and Richard Roe, alias "Scotty." In the absence of a vital prosecution witness, the case did not proceed.

In those days, drug smuggling through the Bahamas was an amateur business, because smugglers lacked a ready and nation-wide market. Today, all that has changed. The United States Drug Enforcement Administration estimates that the annual turnover from drug smuggling exceeds $79 thousand million — and that 80 per cent of all drugs smuggled into the United States enter by way of the Bahamas.

Profits are proportionally spectacular. The price of a kilo of cocaine in Colombia is around $200,000 and will fetch at least five times as much once it is landed in Florida, and ten times as much if the shipper peddles it himself, suitably diluted.

Despite the use of a task group equipped with special aircraft, helicopter gunships carrying advance warning radar, and a fleet of fast cutters, the trade prospers, for these profits make the takings of the rum-runners in Prohibition days look like small change. Admiral Daniel J. Murphy, a task group director, claims that "billions of dollars" from this traffic are laundered through the Bahamas, where international banking provides a quarter of the gross national product.

Nassau has branches of 318 British, Canadian, American, European, and Far Eastern banks on and around Bay Street. All observe proper secrecy about the financial transactions of their clients. As one realist has observed, "Crooks don't need to rob banks any more. They just buy them."

On May 8,1945, the day the European war ended, and less than a week after the Duke and Duchess of Windsor left Nassau, lawyers acting for Lucky Luciano presented a petition "for executive clemency and freedom" on behalf of their client to Thomas E. Dewey, who, partly through that client's influence, had been elected Governor of New York with a 600,000 majority.

Luciano had waited impatiently for this day, although his time in Great Meadow Prison had been made as pleasant as possible for him. He was frequently allowed out at night to visit a woman friend, and on these social occasions other friends thoughtfully provided black market steaks for their dinners *a deux,* so in no sense could his continued incarceration be described as severe. However, he was still a prisoner, although he had carried out his side of the bargain. Now he believed it was time for Dewey to deliver on his part of the agreement.

All applications for parole were considered by a Parole Board made up of the Governor's nominees. It was now explained to them that Luciano had helped to shorten the war in Sicily and Italy. His lawyers declared: "He has co-operated with high military authorities. He has rendered a definite service to the war effort."

Even so, it was not until the following June — thirteen months later — that Dewey finally announced that Luciano would be paroled — but with one bitter and unexpected proviso. He would not be allowed to remain in the United States. Instead, he was to be deported to Sicily, the land of his birth.

So Luciano returned to Sicily, and thence moved to Italy. In the first few years of his exile there, he frequently attempted to secure permission to return to the United States, but always unsuccessfully. Luciano accepted the situation stoically, married, and moved to a house outside Naples.

During his early years in Italy, he received regular sums of money from underworld investments in the United States. Former friends and colleagues came to see him whenever business or pleasure brought them to Europe, but gradually these visits tailed away. The Italian authorities tapped Luciano's telephone, intercepted his mail, and harassed him in many ways. They stubbornly seemed to believe what he continually denied — that he was involved with the passage of drugs from Sicily through Italy to other European countries and the United States.

On a January afternoon in 1962, Luciano travelled to Rome airport to meet a friend arriving from the States. As they walked back to Luciano's Alfa Romeo, he suddenly suffered a massive heart attack and collapsed on the ground.

He died, as so many others had died on his orders, or by the hand of those he controlled, sadly, without dignity, and in public. In his case, on the concrete of the car park at Fiumicino.

Death also came to Don Calo Vizzini in the open air. In 1955, he had a heart attack while being driven home to Villalba in his car, and asked his companions to lift him out and let him lie down on the grass verge by the roadside.

Within a few minutes he was dead. His driver later reported that Don Calo's last words were, "How beautiful life is."

Four black, plumed horses drew his hearse, and hundreds of mourners, all dressed in black, walked behind the cortege. Don Calo's uncle and cousin were bishops; his brother was a priest. They were also present, with dozens of politicians and other clerical dignitaries. Wreaths, each one tied with black ribbons, on which the donor's name was written in gold letters, had arrived from every part of Sicily.

Meyer Lansky died of cancer in Miami Beach in January, 1983. He was 81. In helping to organize and transfer crime from back streets into company boardrooms, and through "laundering" money from gambling operations into legitimate businesses, Lansky was said to have accumulated a fortune estimated at between $100 and $400 million dollars.

He had a dislike of violence, and although repeatedly prosecuted, was only jailed once (for two months, in 1953, for a gambling conviction in Saratoga Springs, New York).

In the 1970s, Meyer Lansky moved to Israel, and refused to return to the United States to face two Federal indictments. Finally, when the Israeli government persuaded him to leave, he moved on to Switzerland and then to South America, before returning to the States. The FBI arrested Lansky at Miami airport, and he was convicted on a criminal contempt charge and sentenced to one year and one day. An appeals court reversed this decision.

Thomas E. Dewey was the Republican presidential candidate in 1944 and 1948. He was not elected.

General Fulgencio Batista lost the presidential election in Cuba in 1944, as Meyer Lansky had forecast he would. Once more, the Outfit began to consider how best they could offset any permanent loss of their investments in Cuba should Batista not return to power — as he hoped to do — or if his successor proved to be uncb-operative. An expansion into the Bahamas still seemed the most logical move.

Stafford Sands became a member of the Executive Council in Nassau in the following year. He realised the enormous attraction that gambling casinos would have for tourists — and how desperately the Bahamas needed tourists, not only rich visitors, but tens of thousands of the less wealthy whose custom would cushion what otherwise could be yet another slump.

To many, starved of colour and relaxation after a long and weary war, the prospect of sunshine, warm sea, and dazzling beaches on islands where English language and laws obtained — and, of course, the prospect of big winnings in a casino — only eighty miles from the United States, must seem attractive.

Stafford Sands applied for a Certificate of Exemption under the sub-section of the Penal Code which he had drafted in 1939, asking for a monopoly of casino gambling for 25 years.

The Executive Council turned down his request. The Bay Street Boys might not mind a rich man becoming richer through a gambling concession, but they expected to share in his good fortune.

Stafford Sands accepted ExCo's decision, but resigned from the Council to devote his great energies and abilities to building up his law practice. No one could dispute that his ideas for attracting thousands of new tourists were sound, and in 1950 he was appointed Chairman of the Development Board.

Shortly afterwards, Wallace Groves, a wealthy American businessman, who had a home on Little Whale Cay, thirty miles north-west of Nassau, proposed to Stafford Sands that a free port — without any customs dues — should be established on Grand Bahama, the nearest island in the Bahamas group to the United States mainland. This, he believed, would attract tourists, industry and other investment to the islands.

Sands agreed, and drafted a bill granting to Groves's company, the Grand Bahama Port Authority, 50,000 acres of land, with freedom from practically every form of tax until 1990. Firms they licensed would also be free of excise or import duties for the next 99 years.

Despite such generous concessions, and what a Royal Commission of Inquiry would later call "almost feudal powers", Freeport was initially a slow starter, although a harbour was built, and work begun on a bunkering installation.

As Dr. Paul Albury noted in his authoritative book, *The Story of the Bahamas,* "a pall of despondency had descended on the embryonic town ... With something akin to desperation, the promoters turned to tourism and residential land development as a source of hope ..."

The government, attempting a rescue, granted to the authority another 50,000 acres on condition that they built a 200 room hotel. But how could this be filled? What would attract most tourists? In Dr. Albury's words, "Those who pondered the problem became convinced that gambling casinos would more than compensate for whatever other deficiencies there might be."

Others had reached the same conclusion — if from a different viewpoint. Although Batista had by then been re-elected President of Cuba, and gambling there was continuing, Castro was in the ascendant, and on New Year's Day, 1959, Batista resigned the Presidency and fled.

With him went several senior members of the Outfit who realised that, whether Castro would be cooperative or not, their profits from Cuba were unlikely to continue on anything like the same scale. It was now imperative that the Bahamas would allow gambling — and the sooner the better.

In early 1963, Stafford Sands applied for a Certificate of Exemption to allow gambling on Grand Bahama. ExCo approved the Certificate with what the same Royal Commission of Inquiry called "unusual expedition".

Among many modern amenities in the new Lucayan Beach Hotel, constructed after the second grant of land, was a large handball court, set conveniently near the restaurant, the night club and the main entrance. This was quickly transformed into a casino, capable of housing more than 1,000 gamblers and spectators. Croupiers were specially imported from Europe, and it was enthusiastically described as "one of the grandest wagering halls in the western world ...", the "new 'Monte Carlo' of the Bahamas."*(Michael Craton, *The Sun 'n Sixpence).*

In Dr. Albury's words, "this turned out to be the touchstone of success. From that day, Freeport began to move. Its forward march was astonishing to all who saw it or heard of it; it excited the imagination of the business world ..."

Freeport now occupies an area of 211 square miles and is a totally modern, well laid-out city, with wide avenues, new hotels, and attractive houses. Seven British, American, and Canadian airlines and the Bahamas airline, Bahamasair, use the international airport, which handles nearly three hundred landings and departures every day.

Twenty years ago only sixty people and firms were licensed to do business in Freeport. Now, there are fifteen hundred, with huge cement and pharmaceutical factories; electrical concerns; an oil refinery; a liquor distillery, and a bottling plant. Where once the Lucayan Beach Hotel experienced difficulty in filling two hundred rooms, Freeport now has four thousand hotel rooms of the highest standard. The aim is to attract to Grand Bahama as many as possible of the estimated three million Americans who now drive from their cities to Florida every year.

While this transformation was taking place, changes were also in hand for Hog Island, which Huntington Hartford, heir to the Great Atlantic and Pacific Tea Company (the A & P) had bought from Wenner-Gren. He renamed it Paradise Island, and built a hotel and a night club and constructed a golf course, intending to develop an exclusive tourist resort. The island could only be reached from Nassau by ferry, however, and after heavy losses in his first year, Huntington Hartford applied for permission to build a bridge to link Paradise with

Nassau and also to construct a casino. Both proposals were turned down.

He sought the advice of Stafford Sands - now knighted for services to the Bahamas — and a satisfactory conclusion was quickly reached. Huntington Hartford sold a majority holding in the project to an American company; Exco approved plans for the bridge and a casino.

Then, on October 5, 1966, *The Wall Street Journal* published an article which won its authors, Monroe W. Karmin and Stanley Penn, a Pulitzer Prize, and caused consternation in the Bahamas.

"Is There Link to U.S. Crime?" asked the headline, and the article went on to describe the "affable but cold-eyed man in charge" of the casino in Freeport as " 'a runaway New Yorker' wanted by American authorities. He is balding, 61-year-old Frank Ritter, alias 'Red' Reed ..."

They revealed that the visionary Mr. Groves had what they called "a blemish in his background. He's an old Wall Street operator who was convicted of mail fraud in 1941 and sentenced to two years in prison."

They reported that "corporate records indicate Sir Stafford received for his services more than $1,000,000 from a Groves-controlled company. This handsome fee was divided into several payments. Records of the company for 1964 show payments to Sir Stafford of $515,000 for legal services and also legal retainer payments of $10,000 per month."

There was a further "consulting agreement" for the Prime Minister of the Bahamas, Sir Roland Symonette, who had bought de Marigny's properties 23 years earlier, for a Nassau dentist, for Symonette's son, who was Speaker of the House of Assembly, and for the Minister of Maritime Affairs. They claimed that the Prime Minister received $16,800 a year, and his son, $14,000 a year. The Prime Minister denied he had received anything. The Maritime Minister refused to discuss the matter. "That's my private business," he said.

The writers also reported that a public relations firm in New York had paid $50,000 to buy the manuscript of a book entitled *The Ugly Bahamians,* which dealt with matters the Bay Street Boys preferred to keep private.

Mr Ritter had two associates, Max Courtney (real name, Morris Schmertzler) and Charlie Brud (real name, Charles Brudner). "Ritter has been indicted three times in the U.S. for tax evasion and other offenses. Allegedly, the three men operated a nationwide bookmaking business from New York before they skipped town ..."

The writers added, "U.S. authorities are after bigger fish — Meyer Lansky, the notorious Florida mobster who ranks high in the U.S. crime syndicate. The Lansky reputation is so black that the Nevada Gaming Control Board bars him from Las Vegas casinos. U.S. officials suspect that Lansky controls or gets a piece of the profits of the Lucayan Beach casino."

They went on to name those involved, who, they said, were connected with Meyer Lansky, although such suggestions drew what they called "staunch denials" from the Assistant Commissioner of Police in Nassau. Within days, Frank Ritter, Max Courtney, and Charles Brud resigned, "as a result of the unfortunate publicity given them."

The publication of this article had two significant results. First, a Royal Commission of Inquiry was set up to examine gambling in the Bahamas. As a result, stringent safeguards and checks were adopted. Second, an election was called, in which the matter of these "consultants' fees" played a prominent part.

The result was a dead heat between the United Bahamian Party and the Progressive Liberal Party, largely black. Each gained eighteen seats. The Labour Party gained one seat, and one independent member was elected. These two members joined with the P.L.P. so that they could form a government. Its black leader, Lynden O. Pindling — like Stafford Sands, a lawyer and a grocer's son — was now in charge. White rule in the Bahamas was over forever. Soon, the Bay Street Boys would become as much a part of the past as the pirates and the wreckers. Sir Stafford Sands, who had always insisted that money said to have been paid was purely for his professional advice, resigned, sold up, shredded his papers, and moved to Spain.

Within six years, the colony became the Commonwealth of the Bahamas, and the Union Jack was lowered for the last time. The new Bahamian flag raised in its place bears a black triangle against three horizontal stripes: turquoise, gold, turquoise. The triangle represents the Bahamian people's vigour and energy and points to their determination to develop the rich resources of land and sea, symbolised by gold and turquoise. Woodes Roger's homely, laconic motto, "Pirates

Expelled, Commerce Restored," was replaced by words considered more suitable: "Forward, Upward, Onward Together."

One man who resolutely refused to accept any inflated consultancy fees or other commissions whatever in connection with developments on Grand Bahama was Harold Christie. He might be a hard man in a business deal, but he was scrupulously honest. Indeed, Harold Christie felt so strongly about such fees that he warned his younger brother, Frank, that if Frank ever joined these so-called consultants, "you can get out of my office and never come back."

Harold Christie lived to see his dream for the Bahamas come true. They did become home for the very rich, and a tourist resort without parallel. Both these aims he achieved largely through his own immense energy, integrity, and enterprise. His efforts over so many years were recognised by the knighthood conferred on him in 1964.

But although Harold Christie realised his dream, it cannot have been quite as he had originally visualised; but then, no dream ever is. When the Bahamas were, in the Duke of Windsor's opinion, a third-rate colony, wealthy tourists from Europe, the United States and Canada would visit Nassau to enjoy winter sunshine, warm sea, and a relaxed way of life.

Now, cruise liners arrive week in, week out, packed with a different type of tourist, largely from the United States and Canada. Taxis and air-conditioned buses transport them direct from their ships to casinos. Here, in a huge, luxurious, splendidly appointed complex, they can gamble, eat, drink, dance, relax, and gamble again until it is time for them to be deposited back on board ship — and the new arrivals collected.

Night becomes day, and day an endless twilight under the vast candelabra of the casinos. Outside Nassau, the Playboy Casino was constructed on the site of Sir Harry Oakes's house, as part of the Ambassador Beach Hotel. The hotel brochure calls it "the star of Nassau nightlife." For newcomers, what are described as "free casino lessons" are given at four o'clock each afternoon.

Those who remember Westbourne find it strange, almost uncanny, to see how closely the architecture of the casino building resembles that house. Where Sir Harry Oakes died, dark glass windows facing the beach reduce the sunniest days to dusk, roulette wheels turn, and croupiers call *"Rien ne va plus"*. Now a new, more impressive hotel is being built farther along the beach, and to cope with its constantly increasing clientele, the casino may be moved to a larger building as part of this.

Grand Bahama has its splendid El Casino, built in the style of a Moorish palace. The casino on Paradise Island is flanked by two new and magnificent hotels, the Britannia Beach and the Paradise Island Hotel. The brochure issues a beguiling invitation: "Come. The red carpet's waiting, at the resort that's like no other, the resort that's a whole destination in itself," and adds: "Try your luck, naturally, in our Casino."

An early casualty in the Bahamas since independence was the general sense of personal security, first seriously fractured by riots during the Second World War.

In hotels, uniformed guards patrol the corridors and grounds. They walk in pairs and carry night-sticks and walkie-talkies. Hotel bedrooms display large notices about the importance of double-locking bedroom doors, putting on safety chains, and checking the identity of callers before opening the door.

Residents will check by walkie-talkie with each other's homes before retiring for the night, in case a telephone line has been cut, preparatory to a robbery. The great houses along the beach have floodlights on rooftops to light up their grounds and patios. Many are illuminated by day and night, to confuse possible intruders as to whether they are empty or occupied —all this in an island where Sir Harry Oakes, the richest of the rich, never even locked his door.

No one, rich or poor, is advised to walk along any street in Nassau after six o'clock in the evening. Many visitors are reluctant to do so at any time.

The coast road from Nassau to the ultimate outpost of western wealth, Lyford Cay, which could also be called Sir Harold Christie's crowning achievement, runs along the edge of the sea, past Cable Beach. The houses, pink-walled, white-walled, are festooned with TV and radio aerials and complex alarm systems, and have evocative names, such as Nirvana and Eden.

At Lyford.Cay, the really rich, who cannot count their wealth, live on the tip of the island, separated from less wealthy neighbours by distance, a high wire-mesh fence, and other less obvious security measures.

Lyford Cay has a guard house, like a customs post, with a red and white striped pole that is lowered as though at a frontier — which, in a sense, it is. Visitors are allowed past this post only after the uniformed guard has checked by telephone with the people they claim they have come to visit. All this is very necessary and proper, for in this small area are probably congregated more millionaires than any other place of similar size on earth.

At the edge of this enclave stands Lyford Cay City Market, an elegant pink building with a boutique, an art gallery, and other emporia almost too sophisticated to be called shops. Rather, they are beautiful places where merchandise can be exchanged for money.

Lyford Cay has its own police station, a special branch of the Royal Bank of Canada (the first bank to be established in the Bahamas), and, with a name that recalls earlier, rougher days, and the foundation of some people's fortunes, the Rum Keg Bar. On the other side of the road stands the Church of St. Paul the Apostle.

Within this elegant enclave for the super-rich, helicopters deposit guests, telex machines clatter, older men, perhaps accompanied by women younger than their daughters, sun themselves at the edge of the ocean —and keep a close eye on the Dow Index. Whatever money can buy, these residents (or their companies, corporations, and trusts) have already bought. Whatever they want that is for sale must already belong to them.

In the marina nearby, yachts and motor cruisers, the toys of the wealthy, ride at anchor. Each has cost more than most people earn in a lifetime. They are lovingly washed and polished by hired hands — and many are hardly ever used.

At the opposite end of New Providence — and on other islands, from Grand Bahama to Paradise — others cherish a secret dream. One day — no doubt, quite soon — they will also become rich, not through their own efforts or enterprise, but through winning at blackjack, craps, roulette, or on the fruit machines.

Millions of visitors are drawn to the Bahamas every year, not only by sun and sea and white, sandy beaches, but by the wish to make this dream reality.

Was it also shared by whoever killed Sir Harry Oakes?

Acknowledgements

My thanks are due to my wife, Joan Leasor, for her research in Nassau and Portugal; to Mrs. Barbara Pickering, for research in England and Canada; to Mrs. Margaret Wood, for research in the Public Record Office, London; and to Mrs. Susan Wood, for research in the National Archives, Washington, D.C. I should also like to express my indebtedness to the librarians and staff of the London Library and the Nassau, Salisbury, and Wilton Public Libraries.

Bibliography

Albury, Paul. *The Story of the Bahamas.* London: Macmillan Caribbean, 1975.

Allsop, Kenneth. *The Bootleggers.* London: Hutchinson, 1961.

The Bahamas Handbook & Businessman's Handbook, 1976-77, 1979-80,1981-

82. Nassau: Etienne Dupuch, Jr., Publications. Bocca, Geoffrey. *The Life and Death of Sir Harry Oakes.* London: Weidenfeld & Nicolson, 1959.

Bradley, General Omar. *A Soldier's Story.* London: Eyre 8c Spottiswoode, 1951. Brody, lies. *Gone With the Windsors.* Philadelphia: John C. Winston, 1953.

Bryan, J., HI, and Charles J. V. Murphy. *The Windsor Story.* London: Granada, 1979.

Churchill, Winston. *The Second World War,* vols. 4 and 5. London: Cassell, 1952.

Commission of Inquiry into the Organisation of the Business of Casinos in Freeport and in Nassau. London: Her Majesty's Stationery Office, 1967.

Craton, Michael. *The Sun 'n Sixpence: Guide to Nassau and the Bahama Out Islands.*

Ed. by S. P. Dupuch. Nassau: Etienne Dupuch, Jr., Publications, 1964. Dupuch, Sir Etienne. *A Salute to Friend and Foe.* Nassau: *The Tribune,* 1982.

Flower, Desmond, and James Reeves, eds. *The War: 1939-1945.* London: Cassell,

1960. Gage, Nicholas. *The Mafia Is Not an Equal Opportunity Employer.* New York: McGraw-Hill, 1971.

Garrett, Richard. *Mrs. Simpson.* London: Arthur Barker, 1979.

Gosch, Martin, and Richard Hammer. *The Last Testament of Lucky Luciano.* London: Macmillan, 1975.

de Guingand, Major General Sir Francis. *Operation Victory.* London: Hodder & Stoughton.

Hamshere, Cyril. *The British in the Caribbean.* London: Weidenfeld & Nicolson.

Hibbert, Christopher. *The Roots of Evil.* London: Weidenfeld & Nicolson, 1963.

Houtts, Marshall. *King's X.* New York: William Morrow, 1972.

Montgomery Hyde, H. *Crime Has Its Heroes.* London: Constable.
KESSELRING, The Memoirs of Field Marshal. London: William Kimber.

Lewis, Norman. The *Honoured Society.* London: Collins, 1964.

Maine, Basil. *Our Ambassador King.* London: Hutchinson.

de Marigny, Alfred. *More Devil Than Saint.* New York: Beechurst Press, 1946.

Maxwell, Elsa. / *Married the World.* London: Heinemann, 1955.

Messick, Hank. *Lansky.* London: Robert Hale, 1971.

Syndicate Abroad. Toronto: Collier-Macmillan.

The Murder of Sir Harry Oakes Bart. Nassau: *Nassau Daily Tribune.*

Moseley, Mary. *The Bahamas Handbook.* Nassau: *The Guardian.*

Patton, General George S. *The War As I Knew It.* Boston: Houghton Mifflin, 1947.

Pye, Michael. *King Over the Water.* London: Hutchinson, 1981.

Servadio, Gaia. *Mafioso.* London: Seeker & Warburg, 1976.

Shattuck, G. B. *The Bahama Islands.* New York: Macmillan.

Snyder, Louis L. *The War.* New York: Dell, 1964.

Wilmot, Chester. *The Struggle for Europe.* London: Collins, 1952.

Windsor, The Duchess of. *The Heart Has Its Reasons.* London: Michael Joseph,
1956.

Windsor, The Duke of. *Edward VIII: A King's Story.* New York: Putnam, 1951. Wolf, George, with Joseph Di Mona. *Frank Costello: Prime Minister of the*
Underworld. London: Hodder & Stoughton, 1975.

Newspapers, Periodicals, and other References

The Guardian, Nassau;

Maclean's magazine, Canada;

Newsweek, U.S.;

New York Times, New York;

Time magazine, U.S.;

The Times, London;

The Tribune, Nassau;

Wall Street Journal, New York.

Current Biography, 1942.

Transcripts of the trial of Marie Alfred Fouquereaux de Marigny.

Papers from the Public Record Office, London

C023/714

C023/714/1
C023/714/5
C023/714/27
C023/714/43
C023/714/33858
F0371/34231
FO371/37307
FO371/37308
FO371/37309
F0371/37325
F0371/37327
F0371/37328
F0371/37356
F0371/43815
FO371/77310
Papers from the National Archives, Washington, D.C.
740/0011

2A
EW1939/579
1   740/0011
EW
1939/21295
800/20211/
WG/l
800/2021
l/WG/80$^{1\wedge}$
800/2021
l/WG/248
800/2021*V-*
/5V/2
800/20211/2
71
812/516/646
844E 001/55
844E 001/62
Vi   844E
001/63 844E
001/69 844E
001/73

FOLLOW THE DRUM

James Leasor's fictional tale, based on the events surrounding the Indian Mutiny.

India, in the mid-nineteenth century, was virtually run by a British commercial concern, the Honourable East India Company, whose directors would pay tribute to one Indian ruler and then depose another in their efforts to maintain their balance sheet of power and profit. But great changes were already casting shadows across the land, and when a stupid order was given to Indian troops to use cartridges greased with cow fat and pig lard (one animal sacred to the Hindus and the other abhorrent to Moslems) there was mutiny. The lives of millions were changed for ever including Arabella MacDonald, daughter of an English regular officer, and Richard Lang, an idealistic nineteen-year-old who began 1857 as a boy and ended it a man.

Pulling no punches, it shows up the good and the bad on both sides - the appalling stupidity and complacency of the British which caused the mutiny to happen, the chaos and venality of the insurgents, the ruthlessness of the retribution. It has everything, with a story based on the actual events.

MANDARIN-GOLD

The first of James Leasor's epic trilogy based on a Far Eastern trading company:

'Highly absorbing account of the corruption of an individual during a particularly sordid era of British imperial history,' *The Sunday Times*

'James Leasor switches to the China Sea more than a century ago, and with pace and ingenuity tells, in novel form, how the China coast was forced to open up its riches to Englishmen, in face of the Emperor's justified hostility' *Evening Standard*

'In the nasty story of opium - European and American traders made fortunes taking the forbidden dope into nineteenth century China, and this novel tells the story of their deadly arrangements and of the Emperor's vain attempts to stop them. Mr. Leasor has researched the

background carefully and the detail of the Emperor's lavish court but weak administration is fascinating. The white traders are equally interesting characters, especially those two real-life merchants, Jardine and Matheson.'
Manchester Evening News
It was the year of 1833 when Robert Gunn arrived on the China coast. Only the feeblest of defences now protected the vast and proud Chinese Empire from the ravenous greed of Western traders, and their opening wedge for conquest was the sale of forbidden opium to the native masses.

This was the path that Robert Gunn chose to follow... a path that led him through a maze of violence and intrigue, lust and treachery, to a height of power beyond most men's dreams — and to the ultimate depths of personal corruption.

Here is a magnificent novel of an age of plunder—and of a fearless freebooter who raped an empire.

THE CHINESE WIDOW
James Leasor's two preceding books in his chronicle of the Far East a century and half ago - FOLLOW THE DRUM and MANDARIN-GOLD were acclaimed by critics on both sides of the Atlantic. THE CHINESE WIDOW is their equal. It combines the ferocious force of the Dutch mercenaries who seek to destroy Gunn's plan; the pathos of a young woman left alone to rule a fierce and rebellious people; the gawky humour of Gunn's partner, the rough, raw Scot MacPherson; the mysterious yet efficacious practice of Chinese medicine, handed on through thousands of years...

When doctors in England pronounced his death sentence, Robert Gunn-founder of Mandarin-Gold, one of the most prosperous Far Eastern trading companies of the nineteenth century-vowed to spend his final year in creating a lasting memorial to leave behind him... to pay back, somehow, his debt to the lands of the East that had been the making of his vast fortune. He had a plan - a great plan - but to see it through he had to confront a fierce and rebellious people, a force of Dutch mercenaries and the Chinese Widow. Who was the Widow? What was her past-and her power...?

Action, suspense and the mysterious splendour of the Orient are combined in this exciting and moving novel.

BOARDING PARTY
Filmed as The Sea Wolves, this is the story of the undercover exploits of a territorial unit. The Germans had a secret transmitter on one of their ships in the neutral harbour of Goa. Its purpose was to guide the U-boats against Allied shipping in the Indian Ocean. There seemed no way for the British to infringe Goa's Portuguese neutrality by force. But the transmitter had to be silenced. Then it was remembered that 1,400 miles away in Calcutta was a source of possible help. A group of civilian bankers, merchants and solicitors were the remains of an old territorial unit called The Calcutta Light Horse. With a foreword by Earl Mountbatten of Burma.
'One of the most decisive actions in World War II was fought by fourteen out-of-condition middle-aged men sailing in a steam barge...' *Daily Mirror*
'Mr. Leasor's book is truth far more engrossing than fiction... A gem of World War II history' *New York Times*
'If ever there was a ready-made film script...here it is' *Oxford Mail*

GREEN BEACH
In 1942 radar expert Jack Nissenthall volunteered for a suicidal mission to join a combat team who were making a surprise landing at Dieppe in occupied France. His assignment was to penetrate a German radar station on a cliff above 'Green Beach: Because Nissenthall knew the secrets of British and US radar technology, he was awarded a personal bodyguard of sharpshooters. Their orders were to protect him, but in the event of possible capture to kill him. His choice was to succeed or die. The story of what happened to him and his bodyguards in nine hours under fire is one of World War II's most terrifying true stories of personal heroism.
'Green Beach has blown the lid off one of the Second World War's best-kept secrets' *Daily Express*
'If I had been aware of the orders given to the escort to shoot him rather than let him be captured, I would have cancelled them immediately' *Lord Mountbatten*
'Green Beach is a vivid, moving and at times nerve-racking reconstruction of an act of outstanding but horrific heroism' *Sunday Express*

THE RED FORT

James Leasor's gripping historical account of the Indian Mutiny.
'This is a battle piece of the finest kind, detailed, authentic and largely written from original documents. Mr. Leasor has a formidable gift of narrative. Never has this story of hate, violence, courage and cowardice been better told.'
Cecil Woodham-Smith in the *New York Times*

A year after the Crimean War ended, an uprising broke out in India which was to have equal impact on the balance of world power and the British Empire's role in world affairs. The revolt was against the East India Company which, not entirely against its will, had assumed responsibility for administering large parts of India. The ostensible cause of the mutiny sprang from a rumour that cartridges used by the native Sepoy troops were greased with cow's fat and pig's lard — cows being sacred to the Hindus, and pigs abhorred by the Mohammedans. But the roots of the trouble lay far deeper, and a bloody and ineptly handled war ensued.

The Red Fort is a breath-taking account of the struggle, with all its cruelties, blunderings and heroic courage. When peace was finally restored, the India we know today began to emerge.

THE MARINE FROM MANDALAY
This is the true story of a Royal Marine wounded by shrapnel in Mandalay in WW2 who undergoes a long solitary march to the Japanese through the whole of Burma and then finds his way back through India and back to Britain to report for duty in Plymouth. On his way he has many encounters and adventures and helps British and Indian refugees. He also has to overcome complete disbelief that a single man could walk out of Burma with nothing but his orders - to report to HQ - and his initiative.

THE MILLIONTH CHANCE
The R101 airship was thought to be the model for the future, an amazing design that was 'as safe as houses ... except for the millionth chance'. On the night of 4 October 1930 that chance in a million came up, however. James Leasor brilliantly reconstructs the conception and crash of this huge ship of the air with compassion for the forty-seven dead - and only six survivors.

'The sense of fatality grows with every page ... Gripping' *Evening Standard*

THE ONE THAT GOT AWAY

Franz von Werra was a Luftwaffe pilot shot down in the Battle of Britain. The One that Got Away tells the full and exciting story of his two daring escapes in England and his third and successful escape: a leap from the window of a prisoners' train in Canada. Enduring snow and frostbite, he crossed into the then neutral United States. Leasor's book is based on von Werra's own dictated account of his adventures and makes for a compelling read.

'A good story, crisply told' *New York Times*

THE PLAGUE AND THE FIRE

This dramatic story chronicles the horror and human suffering of two terrible years in London's history. 1665 brought the plague and cries of 'Bring Out Your Dead' echoed through the city. A year later, the already decimated capital was reduced to ashes in four days by the fire that began in Pudding Lane. James Leasor weaves in the first-hand accounts of Daniel Defoe and Samuel Pepys, among others.

'An engrossing and vivid impression of those terrible days' *Evening Standard*

'Absorbing ... an excellent account of the two most fantastic years in London's history' *Sunday Express*

WHO KILLED SIR HARRY OAKES?

James Leasor cleverly reconstructs events surrounding a brutal and unusual murder. It is 1943 and Sir Harry Oakes lies horrifically murdered at his Bahamian mansion. Although a self-made multi-millionaire, Sir Harry is an unlikely victim - there are no suggestions of jealousy or passion. Leasor makes the daring suggestion that Sir Harry Oakes' murder, the burning of the liner Normandie in New York Harbour in 1942 and the Allied landings in Sicily are all somehow connected.

'The story has all the right ingredients - rich occupants of a West Indian tax haven, corruption, drugs, the Mafia, and a weak character as governor' *Daily Mail*

PASSPORT TO OBLIVION

Passport to Oblivion is the first case book of Dr. Jason Love . . . country doctor turned secret agent. Multi-million selling, published in 19 languages around the world and filmed as Where the Spies Are starring David Niven.

'As K pushed his way through the glass doors of the Park Hotel, he realized instinctively why the two stumpy men were waiting by the reception desk. They had come to kill him. ...'

Who was K - and why should anyone kill him? Who was the bruised girl in Rome? Why did a refugee strangle his mistress in an hotel on the edge of the Arctic Circle? And why, in a small office above a wholesale fruiterers in Covent Garden, did a red-haired Scot sift through filing cabinets for the name of a man he knew in Burma twenty years ago?

None of these questions might seem to concern Dr Jason Love, a country practitioner of Bishop's Combe, Somerset. But, in the end, they all do. Apart from his patients, Dr Love has apparently only two outside interests: his supercharged Cord roadster, and the occasional Judo lessons he gives to the local branch of the British Legion.

But out of the past, to which all forgotten things should belong, a man comes to see him - and his simple, everyday country-life world is shattered like a mirror by a .38 bullet.

"Heir Apparent to the golden throne of Bond" *The Sunday Times*

PASSPORT TO PERIL

Passport to Peril is Dr Jason Love's second brilliant case history in suspense. An adventure that sweeps from the gentle snows of Switzerland to the freezing peaks of the Himalayas, and ends in a blizzard of violence, hate, and lust on the roof of the world. Guns, girls and gadgets all play there part as the Somerset doctor, old car expert and amateur secret agent uncovers a mystery involving the Chinese intelligence service and a global blackmail ring.

"Second instalment in the exploits of Dr Jason Love... Technicolour backgrounds, considerable expertise about weapons... action, driven along with terrific vigour" *The Sunday Times*

"It whips along at a furious pace" *The Sun*

"A great success" *The Daily Express*

PASSPORT IN SUSPENSE

'A superb example of thriller writing at its best' *Sunday Express*
'Third of Dr Love's supercharged adventures... It starts in the sunshine of the Bahamas, swings rapidly by way of a brunette corpse into Mexico, and winds up in the yacht of a megalomaniac ex-Nazi... Action: non-stop: Tension: nail-biting' *Daily Express*
'His ingenuity and daring are as marked as ever' *Birmingham Post*
When a German submarine mysteriously disappears on a NATO exercise in the North Sea, and a beautiful girl was brutally murdered in the Bahamas, there at first seemed little connection between the two events. But the missing sub was a vital link in a deadly plan to conquer the West, master-minded by a megalomaniac ex-Nazi. And the dead girl was an Israeli agent intent on bringing to trial the ex-Nazis hiding in South America.
Dr Jason Love, the Somerset GP–turned part-time British secret agent, was enjoying a quiet holiday in Nassau, on his way to an old car rally in Mexico, when he witnessed the girl's murder. Before he knew it, he found himself dragged into the affair. He duly travels to Mexico, thinking he has left this behind, but becomes plunged into a violent situation, with his life in danger – and a desperate mission to foil a terrifying plot to destroy Western civilisation as we know it…

THEY DON'T MAKE THEM LIKE THAT ANY MORE
It introduces the randy, earthy and likeable proprietor of Aristo Autos who deals in vintage cars - not forgetting Sara, supercharged with sexual promise, who whets his curiosity and rouses his interest.
In the process of becoming a reluctant hero, he spins across France, Spain and Switzerland, on the track of a rare Mercedes too badly wanted by too many dangerous men. . .
'Devoured at a sitting. . . racy, pungent and swift' *The Sunday Times*
'Number one thriller on my list ...sexy and racy' *Sunday Mirror*
'A racy tale . . . the hero spends most of his time trying to get into beds and out of trouble . . . plenty of action, anecdotes, and inside dope on exotic old cars' *Sunday Express*

NEVER HAD A SPANNER ON HER
In the sequel to "They Don't Make Them Like That Any More" our vintage car dealer gets involved in a scheme to import some vintage cars from Nasser's Egypt. From the run of the mill trades of London our hero finds himself in Cairo and trying to export a Bugatti

Royale, probably the rarest car on the planet. The story has suspense, guns, a beautiful girl and of course masses of old cars. It races from Belgravia, to Belsize Park to the Pyramids and Alexandria. Leasor combines his proven thriller writing skills with an encyclopaedic knowledge of vintage cars to deliver a real page turner.

'Mr. Leasor has a delightful sense of the ridiculous; he also has an educated style which stems from more than 20 very good books.' *Manchester Evening News*

'All good reading, with accurate detail of the cars involved.' *Autocar*

'Vintage adventure for auto-lovers and others alike.' *The Evening News*

HOST OF EXTRAS

The bawdy, wise-cracking owner of Aristo Autos is offered two immaculate vintage Rolls straight out of a collector's dream: one is a tourer, the other an Alpine. The cars, and Aristo, get in on a shady film deal which leads to a trip to Corsica with the imperturbable Dr Jason Love - Somerset GP and part-time secret agent - his supercharged Cord and the infinitely desirable Victoria – and to the cut and thrust of violent international skulduggery.

"An entertaining and fast moving adventure" *Daily Express*

'It's all great fun and games, with plenty of revs.' *Evening Standard*

'. . . a clutch of thrills and sparks of wit.' *The Yorkshire Post*

James Leasor was educated at The City of London School and Oriel College, Oxford. In World War II he was commissioned into the Royal Berkshire Regiment and posted to the 1st Lincolns in Burma and India, where he served for three and a half years. His experiences there stimulated his interest in India, both past and present, and inspired him to write such books as Boarding Party (filmed as The Sea Wolves), The Red Fort, Follow the Drum and NTR. He later became a feature writer and foreign correspondent at the Daily Express. There he wrote The One that Got Away, the story of the sole German POW to escape from Allied hands. As well as non-fiction, Leasor has written novels, including the Dr Jason Love series, which have been published in 19 countries. Passport to Oblivion was filmed as Where the Spies Are with David Niven. He died in September 2007.

James Leasor's books are becoming available as ebooks. Please visit www.jamesleasor.com for details on all these books or contact info@jamesleasor.com for more information on availability. Follow on Twitter: @jamesleasor for details on new releases.

Jason Love novels
Passport to Oblivion (filmed, and republished in paperback, as Where the Spies Are)
Passport to Peril (Published in the U.S. as Spylight)
Passport in Suspense (Published in the U.S. as The Yang Meridian)
Passport for a Pilgrim
A Week of Love
Love-all
Love and the Land Beyond
Frozen Assets
Love Down Under

Jason Love and Aristo Autos novel
Host of Extras

Aristo Autos novels
They Don't Make Them Like That Any More
Never Had A Spanner On Her

Robert Gunn novels
Mandarin-Gold
The Chinese Widow
Jade Gate

Other novels
Not Such a Bad Day
The Strong Delusion
NTR: Nothing to Report
Follow the Drum
Ship of Gold
Tank of Serpents

Non-fiction

The Monday Story
Author by Profession
Wheels to Fortune
The Serjeant-Major; a biography of R.S.M. Ronald Brittain, M.B.E.,
Coldstream Guards
The Red Fort
The One That Got Away
The Millionth Chance: The Story of The R.101
War at the Top (published in the U.S. as The Clock With Four
Hands)
Conspiracy of Silence
The Plague and the Fire
Rudolf Hess: The Uninvited Envoy
Singapore: the Battle that Changed the World
Green Beach
Boarding Party (filmed, and republished in paperback, as The Sea
Wolves)
The Unknown Warrior (republished in paperback as X-Troop)
The Marine from Mandalay
Rhodes & Barnato: the Premier and the Prancer

As Andrew MacAllan (novels)
Succession
Generation
Diamond Hard
Fanfare
Speculator
Traders

As Max Halstock
Rats – The Story of a Dog Soldier

www.jamesleasor.com

Follow on Twitter: @jamesleasor

CPSIA information can be obtained
at www.ICGtesting.com
Printed in the USA
LVHW012350260720
661594LV00017B/2102